*"By the blood of the rose..."*
— Altayon

# ALSO BY THOMAS J. BELLEZZA

## — *The Maven Wars* —

DEATH OF A KING
LEGACY & BLOOD
COMBAT & GLORY
THE CITY OF DAYS
KNIGHT OF BAELIN

## — *Breaking Down Success Series* —

THE FOUNDATION FOR LONGEVITY
FINDING SOLUTIONS WITH TALENT
THE THREE NEEDS OF SUCCESS
TAC: THE ART OF CONVERSATION
TREAT YOUR LIFE LIKE A BUSINESS

## — *How To Write And Outline Series* —

THE 27 PLOT POINT OUTLINE: EPIC FANTASY
THE 27 PLOT POINT OUTLINE: ROMANCE
THE 27 PLOT POINT OUTLINE: MYSTERIES & CRIME

## — *Poetry & Philosophy* —

SHE
PEACE: THE FINAL FRONTIER

Visit the website for a complete list of available titles
Discover more and track upcoming releases at:
www.MakeARightLeftHere.com
For the latest release schedule and new titles

# THE 27 PLOT POINT OUTLINE

## WHEN PLOT MEETS STORY

### THOMAS J. BELLEZZA

All rights reserved.
Copyright © 2026 by Thomas J. Bellezza.

Published by BBR Productions, Inc.
All artwork by Thomas J. Bellezza.

No part of this publication may be reproduced, used for AI training, stored in a retrieval system, or transmitted in any form or by any means, electronic, mechanical, including photocopying, recording, scanning, by any information storage and retrieval system, or otherwise, except as permitted under Section 107 or 108 of the 1976 United States Copyright Act without the written permission of both publisher and author, except in the case of brief excerpts used in critical articles and reviews. Unauthorized reproduction of any part of this work is illegal and is punishable by law—in other words, come on, don't steal what's not yours.

## www.MakeARightLeftHere.com

*"Suit the action to the word, the word to the action."*
— William Shakespeare

ISBN 979-8-9929251-4-2 (Paperback)
ISBN 979-8-9929251-3-5 (Hardcover)
ISBN 979-8-9929251-5-9 (ePub)

*"Write the stories you want to read, the things your voice needs to say, and your audience will find you."*

Because of the dynamic nature of the internet, any web addresses or links contained in this book may have changed since publication and may no longer be valid.

The views expressed in this work are solely those of the author, but that doesn't suggest he means it and doesn't necessarily reflect the views of the publisher, and the publisher hereby disclaims any responsibility for them. As a quick aside, no monkeys were hurt during the making of this book. However, I did take a lot of naps, and there may or may not have been some pizza eaten.

Limit of Liability/Disclaimer of Warranty: While the author has used his best efforts in preparing this book, he makes no representations or warranties with respect to the accuracy or completeness of the contents of this book and specifically disclaims any implied warranties of merchantability or fitness for a particular purpose.

No warranty may be created or extended by sales representatives or written sales materials. The advice and strategies contained herein may not be suitable for your situation. You should consult with a professional where appropriate. Neither the publisher nor the author shall be liable for any loss of profit or any other commercial damages, including but not limited to special, incidental, consequential, or other damages.

Cover Design: BBR Productions, INC.

# CONTENTS

| | |
|---|---|
| **FOREWORD** | VII |
| **INTRODUCTION** | 1 |
|    OUTLINING AND WRITING ARE NOT THE SAME | 2 |
|    WHAT WILL BE EXPLORED IN THIS BOOK? | 2 |
|    WHY THE 27 PLOT POINTS? | 4 |
| **TWO KINDS OF WRITERS** | 7 |
|    PLOTTERS | 8 |
|    PANTSERS | 9 |
|    THE ARGUMENT | 10 |
|    WE ARE ALL DISCOVERY WRITERS | 12 |
| **WHAT IS A NARRATIVE** | 15 |
|    PLOT: WHAT NEEDS TO HAPPEN | 17 |
|    STORY: HOW IT UNFOLDS | 19 |
|    A FULL NARRATIVE NEEDS BOTH | 20 |
| **THE 27 PLOT POINT OUTLINE** | 23 |
| **THE RULE OF THREES** | 27 |
|    THE ACTS OF A NARRATIVE | 28 |

*The 27 Plot Point Outline: When Plot Meets Story*

| | |
|---|---|
| THE SECTIONS OF AN ACT | 28 |
| THE PLOT POINTS OF A SECTION | 30 |
| THE RULE OF THREES IN ACTION \| ACTS | 31 |
| THE RULE OF THREES IN ACTION \| SECTIONS | 32 |
| THE RULE OF THREES IN ACTION \| PLOT POINTS | 33 |
| FROM ACT ONE TO THREE PLOT POINTS | 33 |
| **ACT 1: THE SETUP** | **37** |
| SETTING UP THE NARRATIVE | 39 |
| 1. START WITH CHARACTER, NOT PLOT | 40 |
| 2. CENTRAL CONFLICT (CC) & SUBPLOTS (SUBARCS) | 42 |
| 3. THE RULES OF THE WORLD | 44 |
| 4. THE INCITING INCIDENT | 46 |
| 5. THE PROMISE | 48 |
| **SECTION 1: SETTING UP THE ORDINARY WORLD** | **51** |
| PLOT POINT 1 (INTRODUCTIONS) | 52 |
| PLOT POINT 2 (INCITING INCIDENT) | 54 |
| PLOT POINT 3 (FALLOUT) | 56 |
| **SECTION 2: A PROBLEM DISRUPTS THE PROTAGONIST'S LIFE** | **59** |
| PLOT POINT 4 (REFLECTION/CHOICE) | 60 |
| PLOT POINT 5 (ACTION) | 63 |
| PLOT POINT 6 (CONSEQUENCE) | 65 |
| **SECTION 3: THE PROTAGONIST'S LIFE CHANGES DIRECTION** | **67** |
| PLOT POINT 7 (PRESSURE) | 68 |
| PLOT POINT 8 (PLOT TWIST/PINCH) | 70 |
| PLOT POINT 9 (PUSHED) | 72 |
| **ACT 2: THE CONFLICT** | **75** |
| CHALLENGING THE NARRATIVE | 76 |
| 1. THE CONFLICT | 77 |
| 2. CHALLENGE THE CONTEXT | 78 |
| 3. THE TRUTH OF THE LIE | 82 |
| 4. ONE ACT, TWO PARTS | 85 |
| 5. GENRE PLAYGROUND | 88 |

## Contents

### SECTION 4: THE PROTAGONIST EXPLORES THE NEW WORLD — 91
- PLOT POINT 10 (NEW WORLD) — 93
- PLOT POINT 11 (FUN & GAMES) — 95
- PLOT POINT 12 (JUXTAPOSITION) — 97

### SECTION 5: THE CRISIS OF THE NEW WORLD — 99
- PLOT POINT 13 (BUILDUP) — 101
- PLOT POINT 14 (MIDPOINT) — 104
- PLOT POINT 15 (REVERSAL) — 107

### SECTION 6: FINDING A SOLUTION — 111
- PLOT POINT 16 (CONSEQUENCE) — 113
- PLOT POINT 17 (TRIALS/TESTED) — 115
- PLOT POINT 18 (DEDICATION) — 118

### ACT 3: THE RESOLUTION — 121
- RESOLVING THE NARRATIVE — 125
- 1. RESOLVE THE CENTRAL CONFLICT — 126
- 2. CHARACTER DEVELOPMENT — 127
- 3. TIE UP LOOSE ENDS — 129
- 4. DENOUEMENT — 131
- 5. CLOSURE WITH A PLANNED FUTURE — 132

### SECTION 7: VICTORY SEEMS IMPOSSIBLE — 135
- PLOT POINT 19 (CALM BEFORE THE STORM) — 137
- PLOT POINT 20 (PLOT TWIST/PINCH) — 140
- PLOT POINT 21 (DARKEST MOMENT) — 143

### SECTION 8: THE PROTAGONIST FINDS THE POWER — 147
- PLOT POINT 22 (POWER WITHIN) — 148
- PLOT POINT 23 (ACTION TO RALLY) — 151
- PLOT POINT 24 (CONVERGE) — 153

### SECTION 9: THE PROTAGONIST FIGHTS AND WINS — 157
- PLOT POINT 25 (FINAL BATTLE) — 159
- PLOT POINT 26 (CLIMAX) — 162
- PLOT POINT 27 (RESOLUTION) — 165

### PROLOGUES AND EPILOGUES — 169

## The 27 Plot Point Outline: When Plot Meets Story

| | |
|---|---:|
| PROLOGUES | 170 |
| EPILOGUES | 175 |

### PIRATES OF THE CARIBBEAN: THE CURSE OF THE BLACK PEARL — 179

| | |
|---|---:|
| PROLOGUE | 180 |
| ACT 1, SECTION 1 (SETUP) | 180 |
| ACT 1, SECTION 2 (CONFLICT) | 183 |
| ACT 1, SECTION 3 (RESOLUTION) | 184 |
| THINGS ACT 1 SETS UP | 185 |
| ACT 2, SECTION 4 (SETUP) | 186 |
| ACT 2, SECTION 5 (CONFLICT) | 187 |
| ACT 2, SECTION 6 (RESOLUTION) | 188 |
| THINGS ACT 2 CHALLENGES | 189 |
| ACT 3, SECTION 7 (SETUP) | 190 |
| ACT 3, SECTION 8 (CONFLICT) | 191 |
| ACT 3, SECTION 9 (RESOLUTION) | 192 |
| THINGS ACT 3 RESOLVES | 193 |
| EPILOGUE | 193 |

### START WITH CHARACTER — 195

| | |
|---|---:|
| POSITIONS & MOTIVATIONS | 197 |
| POSITIONS FOR GROWTH | 199 |
| CHALLENGE CHARACTERS | 202 |
| MARY SUE AND GARY STU | 204 |

### OUTLINING A CHARACTER ARC — 209

| | |
|---|---:|
| THE PROTAGONIST'S CENTRAL CHARACTER ARC | 211 |
| SECONDARY CHARACTER ARCS | 213 |
| CHARACTER ARC SUMMARIES | 214 |
| BUILD AS YOU GO, BUILD AS YOU NEED | 216 |
| USE THE 27 PPO FOR ALL ARCS | 217 |
| ADDING SUBARCS (SUBPLOTS) | 218 |

### SHORT-FORM OUTLINE — 221

| | |
|---|---:|
| ACT 1, SECTION 1 (SETUP) | 223 |
| ACT 1, SECTION 2 (CONFLICT) | 224 |
| ACT 1, SECTION 3 (RESOLUTION) | 225 |

## Contents

| | |
|---|---|
| ACT 2, SECTION 4 (SETUP) | 226 |
| ACT 2, SECTION 5 (CONFLICT) | 227 |
| ACT 2, SECTION 6 (RESOLUTION) | 228 |
| ACT 3, SECTION 7 (SETUP) | 229 |
| ACT 3, SECTION 8 (CONFLICT) | 230 |
| ACT 3, SECTION 9 (RESOLUTION) | 231 |
| **EXTENDED OUTLINE** | **233** |
| ACT 1, SECTION 1 (SETUP) | 235 |
| ANALYSIS | 242 |
| **OUTLINING A CHAPTER** | **243** |
| THE BEGINNING: START WHERE? | 244 |
| THE BEGINNING: CONTEXT | 245 |
| THE MIDDLE: CONFLICT AND CHALLENGE | 248 |
| THE MIDDLE: CHALLENGE CHARACTERS TO MAKE CHOICES | 250 |
| THE END: RESOLUTION | 253 |
| THE END: NARRATIVE DRIVE | 255 |
| **OUTLINING A CHAPTER: ZERO DRAFT CHAPTER OUTLINE** | **259** |
| CHAPTER 1: ALIEN INVASION NARRATIVE EXAMPLE | 260 |
| ZERO DRAFT CHAPTER OUTLINE ANALYSIS | 266 |
| CHAPTER 1's OPENING SETUP | 267 |
| CHAPTER 1's MIDDLE CONFLICT | 267 |
| CHAPTER 1's RESOLUTION | 267 |
| SCENE BREAKDOWNS | 268 |
| SCENE 1: BREAK ROOM \| BEGINNING | 268 |
| SCENE 1: BREAK ROOM \| MIDDLE | 268 |
| SCENE 1: BREAK ROOM \| ENDING | 268 |
| SCENE 2: DESK \| BEGINNING | 269 |
| SCENE 2: DESK \| MIDDLE | 269 |
| SCENE 2: DESK \| ENDING | 269 |
| **HOW LONG SHOULD A CHAPTER BE?** | **271** |
| **REVISING YOUR OUTLINE** | **275** |
| ONE FORWARD, ONE BACK METHOD | 276 |
| HOW TO USE THE METHOD | 277 |

*The 27 Plot Point Outline: When Plot Meets Story*

| | |
|---|---:|
| **MY WRITING PROCESS** | **281** |
| THE WRITING PROCESS CHECKLIST | 282 |
| 1. BRAINSTORMING AND BRAIN DUMPS | 283 |
| 2. CHARACTER ARCS AND SUMMARIES | 283 |
| 3. SHORT-FORM OUTLINE | 285 |
| 4. EXTENDED OUTLINE | 285 |
| 5. ZERO DRAFT CHAPTER OUTLINES | 286 |
| 6. TAKE NOTES ON THE ZERO DRAFT CHAPTER OUTLINES | 287 |
| 7. ADJUST THE ZERO DRAFT CHAPTER OUTLINES | 288 |
| 8. ALPHA READERS (FOUNDATIONAL FEEDBACK) | 288 |
| 9. REVISE THE ZERO DRAFT CHAPTER OUTLINES | 289 |
| 10. FIRST DRAFT (PROSE, DIALOGUE, & IMMERSION) | 290 |
| 11. TAKE A BREAK (2 TO 8 WEEKS) | 290 |
| 12. TAKE NOTES ON THE FIRST DRAFT CHAPTERS | 291 |
| 13. SECOND DRAFT (DEEPER IMMERSION & NOTE ADJUSTMENTS) | 291 |
| 14. BETA READERS (READER EXPERIENCE) | 292 |
| 15. THIRD DRAFT (BETA READER NOTE ADJUSTMENTS) | 293 |
| 16. THE BIG READ | 294 |
| 17. FOURTH DRAFT (IF NEEDED: MINOR ADJUSTMENTS) | 294 |
| 18. LINE EDITOR (PROSE & FLOW) | 295 |
| 19. COPY EDITOR & PROOFREADER (GRAMMAR & TYPOS) | 296 |
| 20. FORMAT THE MANUSCRIPT | 297 |
| 21. FINALIZE ARTWORK (COVERS & PROMOTIONAL) | 297 |
| **FINAL THOUGHTS** | **299** |
| **AUTHOR FRIENDS** | **303** |

# FOREWORD

## By Emma Bennet

## FOREWORD

Dear Reader,

In the vast expanse of information available on virtually any topic, including how to plot a compelling book, it can be incredibly challenging to sift through the noise and find those rare individuals who are true natural teachers.

I first encountered Thomas J. Bellezza as a guest on a mutual friend's podcast. He quickly revealed himself as one of those exceptional people who not only grasp the intricate mechanics of storytelling but also profoundly understand why certain techniques resonate so deeply with readers. He doesn't just write well; he knows how to craft narratives that become utterly unputdownable, the kind that hook you from the first page and linger in your mind, drawing you back to reread and rediscover hidden layers time and again.

Naturally, I sought him out, subscribed to his YouTube channel, and insisted on his friendship. What I discovered was that Thomas is one of the most naturally giving people I've ever met, with a genuine passion for uplifting fellow

## The 27 Plot Point Outline: When Plot Meets Story

creatives by freely sharing his hard-earned knowledge. This generosity stems directly from his own insatiable love of learning. When Thomas set out to master the art of writing, he didn't just skim the surface; he dove deeply into the very essence of storytelling, exploring its historical roots, psychological impacts, and timeless principles that have shaped great tales across cultures and eras.

His 27 plot points system distills the chaos of creativity into a structured yet flexible guide. It's not about rigid rules; it's about understanding the underlying architecture that makes stories work on a fundamental level.

Of course, no single method suits every writer. We're often difficult creatures, fiercely independent and prone to rejecting conformity at all costs. There'll be plenty of people for whom the idea of outlining a book sounds like the exact opposite of what sparks their creative fire, perhaps preferring the organic flow of pantsing or discovery writing. But here's the undeniable truth: you cannot write the absolute best story you are capable of without a solid understanding of how stories fundamentally work. This includes mastering the ebbs and flows of the narrative—the deliberate pacing that builds tension, the strategic placement of revelations, the moments when the reader needs a breath to process emotions, and the exhilarating rushes where the pages seem to turn themselves as the plot hurtles toward its climactic peaks.

This is precisely where Thomas' 27 plot points come into their own, serving as a versatile framework, a roadmap that illuminates the path without forcing you onto a single trail. Even if you don't adhere to them rigidly, they provide invaluable insights into balancing character arcs with plot progression, weaving subplots seamlessly, and ensuring emotional resonance throughout.

Use this book in whatever way aligns with your unique process. Whether you're a meticulous outliner, a free-spirited drafter, or somewhere in between, the knowledge contained within these pages will help you understand your plot on a deeper level, flesh out your characters with authenticity and depth, and refine your own writing voice.

Happy outlining—and may your stories soar,

Emma

# CHAPTER 1

## Introduction

**INTRODUCTION**

Outlining is a scary word. A word that keeps authors from using it, pantsers from exploring it, and outliners from fully embracing its strengths. Outlining also has a dark tag of mysticism and concern. It carries with it a collection of restrictions, misconceptions, and the sense of rope wrapped so tight around your potential that it turns your fingers blue, keeping you from writing.

But, Thomas, I'm a discovery writer. I like to see where it goes.

And that's the thing about outlining; it's all discovery. Outlining doesn't start as a completed list of ideas written out in order. No. An outline is blank and without direction until you start and do the work.

I want this book to show you that whether you're a pantser, a gardener, or an intuitive writer, outlining follows the same rules. It's a process of seeing where things go. In essence, it's about discovering the plot one sentence at a time. Or rather, one word at a time.

This book will give you a deeper insight into what outlining offers you as a writer and how outlining is about being malleable. It's meant to be ever-changing, growing, and conforming to best serve the narrative.

*The 27 Plot Point Outline: When Plot Meets Story*

What you'll learn most in this book is how outlining isn't about specific details or filling out an extensive narrative before writing. No. You'll learn how to start with broad general ideas and expand on those ideas with each stage of the outlining process. And it all begins with laying out the 27 Plot Point Outline.

I'll teach you how the 27 PPO guides an outline and what makes it a complete narrative. And if you're worried, know that the 27 PPO isn't designed to tell you every detail on how a story must unfold. But it does show you how the plot sets up, challenges, and resolves a narrative. Most of all, it shows you how to let characters breathe, reflect, and take action.

## OUTLINING AND WRITING ARE NOT THE SAME

As you read this book, you'll notice that I approach outlining as the foundational backend of the writing process. Outlining is much simpler than writing out all the pretty prose. And outlining with the 27 PPO gives you control over each plot point in a rhythmic dance of beats, emotional reflection, and when and where to let your characters take action.

Writing, on the other hand, is when you're going to explore the story of your narrative. I'll get into that later. For now, I want you to understand that the 27 PPO is an outlining process that'll set the stage for you and give you a chance to bring your world to life and allow your characters to evolve naturally as they are challenged, grow, and make choices.

By the end of this book, you should have a better understanding of what an outline truly can be, what it means to create believable character arcs, and how the 27 PPO truly works. Moreover, you'll understand how to shape your outlines with flexibility, avoid outlining traps, and approach narratives with confidence. All of which give you the freedom to jump into later stages of the process: writing the actual drafts with prose.

## WHAT WILL BE EXPLORED IN THIS BOOK?

I'll break down the 27 Plot Point Outline into each of its elements: acts, sections, and plot points. As I explain each part of the outline method, you'll see the ebb and flow of how a narrative naturally takes shape. This breakdown will teach you

*Introduction*

the rules, value, and purpose of each act, section, and plot point. Rules that are meant to be broken once you understand them.

Sure, every narrative needs a beginning, but that doesn't mean you can't start at the end: Pulp Fiction. Every narrative needs a conclusive resolution, but that doesn't mean you have to wrap it all up in a finality: Inception.

But, Thomas, you just used two films. I'm an author who wants to write novels, short stories, novellas, and flash fiction. I'm not interested in scripts.

I'm glad you pointed that out, and plenty more will be used throughout the book. Film examples are great for a few reasons. One, more people have seen a popular movie than read a popular book. Two, you can watch a film or TV show and see the 27 PPO unfold in real time compared to reading a four million-word novel by Brandon Sanderson.

P.S. My epic fantasy novels are long too—it's not a negative.

I'm making a point to explain how I'm going to teach you. It'll be easier to show you what and how each act, section, and individual plot point works by comparing it to a three- to five-minute scene in a film instead of three chapters coming in at about four thousand words.

This'll give you a visual understanding of what's happening and why it's happening. After all, a narrative is a narrative. We're not worried about prose in this book. We're focused on the skeleton, its plot structure, and how a narrative comes together. So, I assure you it's all the same whether you're writing creative long-form fiction or if you're writing out a script for film, television, or stage.

And, as you will also learn, I've had a career in all worlds: film, television, theater, and long-form fiction. This has given me insight into structure, dialogue, character dynamics, word budgets, and other elements to elevate a narrative.

But, Thomas, you keep calling it a narrative instead of a story.

I do. And I'll continue to do so. I'll explain what a narrative is in greater detail within this book. You'll come to learn that a narrative is made up of both plot and story. Plot is what needs to happen, no matter what, and story is how plot unfolds through the emotional experiences and choices of characters.

To be clear, this book focuses on developing a plot within an outline and will only slightly touch on the story of your narrative.

*The 27 Plot Point Outline: When Plot Meets Story*

If you've ever wanted to learn how to outline a narrative, gain a bit more control over its rhythm, or you're a pantser who wishes they had some idea where to lead their plot beats, then this book is for you. And as you've seen, I'll be doing that by exploring the 27 Plot Point Outline instead of other well-known outline techniques. Though, this doesn't mean you can't use what you learn in this book and apply it to other outlining methods.

All narratives have the same plot points, beats, and structure. How you label them, approach it, or organize it all is about you finding what works best for you. For me, I chose the 27 PPO. And therefore I'm going to show you as much as I can about outlining using the 27 Plot Point Outline method.

## WHY THE 27 PLOT POINTS?

But, Thomas, why did you choose the 27 Plot Point Outline?

Growing up around the film and television industry, I naturally learned a lot about Save the Cat, the Hero's Journey, and, of course, the six-act structure. Six-act structure? Yep. Six-act structures are commonly used for television shows. Those pesky commercials.

I haven't always been an outliner, but when I started getting paid and people asked me for an outline, I had to learn the process. They wanted to see the flow of a narrative before investing their money into paying my fingers to write. I can't blame them. Writing for other people does pay great money.

As I discovered outlining, I needed to learn more about it. I was happy with what I learned, what people showed me, and the tricks I discovered to break the rules apart too. The more I got into outlining, the more I saw deeper patterns. I also noticed that there was a lot of "fluff" between major plot points.

The Hero's Journey has 12 distinct steps to it. One being the ordinary world, then a call to action, a refusal of the call, and so on. As you can see, that's much less than 27 plot points. I thought to myself, what do I do between steps 1 and 2? Then steps 2 and 3? Do I just jump right from step 1 into 2? So when the narrative hits step 5, crossing the threshold, I write that, then move onto the next moment, "tests, allies, and enemies"?

Any author knows that the narrative has space between steps, beats, or plot points. Writers know that narratives have wiggle room in general. It wasn't

*Introduction*

until I found a wonderful YouTube channel, Katytastic, that I found a new way of outlining. It's run by Kat O'Keefe; there's amazing information for authors on her channel, but honestly, her stuff can translate to any style of writing.

I was introduced to the 27 Chapter Outline on Kat's channel. Whether she created it or got it from somewhere else, I don't know. In doing my research I've found nothing beyond her channel for its origins. And I've gotten comments and private messages saying other people invented it; I credit her for the discovery.

Either way, I recommend you check out her channel. Plus she has a great personality, is a published author, and knows what she's talking about.

Back to the question: why did you choose the 27 Plot Point Outline?

I loved that she addressed things my mind had already seen in outlines. Those in-between moments that played around major narrative beats. For me, I love seeing outlines in their full glory, and the 27 PPO's plot points had addressed those in-between moments of action, rest, reflection, and character.

She explained it in a way that connected with me on another level. From there I embraced the method and began working on how to assimilate it into my outlining practices. The thing I quickly realized is that not all narrative mediums (film, television, theater, and novels) have twenty-seven chapters. A film doesn't have chapters; it has scenes. So I had to adjust it to fit my approach and career.

My changes were for little things. For example, I found that a scene in a film might be one full plot point. However, if I'm writing a novel, I'll play within a plot point for several chapters. I like to explore the purpose of a plot point, to introduce ideas, play in them, and develop characters throughout.

What you'll notice is that I dissect each plot point into specific needs, ideas, and concepts (you know, rules to be broken). So I'll show you those rules and how to approach a narrative outline. From there I'll break things apart and put them back together for you in a nice structure. Because to truly understand how to use the tools, you need to know why they're used.

And that's what I did with the 27 Chapter Outline and why I adjusted it to focus on the 27 Plot Points of an outline. I found this method easiest to use, understand, and adjust as needed compared to other outlining methods. Though I still use some ideas from my older methods: scene summaries and character arcs, it's this outline method that gave me the most structure and room to play with.

# CHAPTER 2

## Two Kinds of Writers

**TWO KINDS OF WRITERS**

There are two kinds of writers, plotters and pantsers. Even if you're starting your writing journey now, you've probably heard both those terms. Or, maybe you've heard it as architect and gardener? How about an outliner or intuitive writer?

But, Thomas, which am I? And let's be honest, does it even matter?

Honestly? Whatever you've heard, or not heard, the title doesn't matter. It's about the approach you choose, because some writers swear by their detailed outlines (Brandon Sanderson), structuring every scene, chapter, section, and act before writing a single word. Others throw caution to the wind (Stephen King), writing from the seat of their pants and occasionally tossing a monster into the corner.

Truth is, most writers fall somewhere in the middle, myself included. I love a detailed outline, but I also love to see where things go. And still, does that mean anything? Yep, it means that it's all discovery.

But, Thomas, are there major differences between the two approaches?

Yes and no. But whatever you learn in this chapter, it's about what feels most comfortable for you as a writer. And remember: you're allowed to change your method as you grow and develop as an author and learn more techniques.

*The 27 Plot Point Outline: When Plot Meets Story*

# PLOTTERS

Plotters prefer to build a strong framework before they start writing. They create detailed plot outlines, multiple character arcs, worldbuilding notes, and chapter breakdowns before drafting. Some have even been known to develop brand-new languages (not me; nope, I've never spent months working on conlangs).

But, Thomas, that feels like a lot of work!

It is. It can be for sure. Or the outline is what it needs to be for the writer to start. In reality, the goal of an outline is to have a clear roadmap on the backend that minimizes major structural rewrites later. Rewrites where full chapters and scenes are tossed aside because they didn't make sense in your narrative. And I've been there. I wasn't always a plotter.

Plotting helps keep track of things before it all gets out of hand. It keeps an eye on pacing between chapters or scenes. Chapter summaries can show where and when things need to happen no matter what. Often a narrative might get cluttered as too many internal character chapters are in a row, meaning an action chapter is needed. Speaking of, too many action chapters in a row is an issue too.

Oh, as an aside, if you have multiple point of view (POV) chapters, you can see how many chapters are dedicated to one character in a row. Too many in a row might slow down the pacing, while too many POV switches might jar the reader with a faster pace. As a helpful rule, when you can, try using POV chapters to break up the pacing.

Other plotting strengths: when you get stuck, it helps you get unstuck, helping with plot cohesion and a clear cause-and-effect in the narrative's flow. It's easier to adjust the smaller general details in a summary before everything gets bogged down in the greater depth of long-form chapter prose.

But, Thomas, are there challenges to outlining?

Some writers feel it's restrictive or overwhelming to the writing process, especially if overplanning is taken to another level. Honestly, it'll come down to your plotting approach. I get away with using broad, general notes, summaries, and enough information to get me started. Other times I've been known to create full-on languages (wait, I wasn't supposed to say that).

But, Thomas, what is too much information to write out before I start, and what's the right amount?

The truth is, there's a trial-by-fire learning curve, one you'll have to deal with. If it's something you want to try, I recommend playing with it, seeing what you like or don't like about plotting. As you learn what works and doesn't, adjust as needed to make sure you're in control of the outline and it isn't controlling you.

## PANTSERS

Pantsers are commonly known as writers who fly by the seat of their pants. Thus, pantsers. They usually, though not always, write without a detailed outline or any notes guiding them. Pantsers sit at their typewriter, look at the blank white page, and write, letting the narrative unfold. This is how they discover as they go, finding the narrative's plot and story.

Which is another reason pantsers are referred to as discovery writers. Though, as you'll see, I stand by the idea that pantsers and plotters are discovery writers—but we'll get to that soon.

Though pantsers write without detailed outlines, this doesn't mean that they go in blind. Not all go in untethered to an idea, concept, or direction. Some pantsers might have a vague idea of a plot or character arcs without planning too far ahead. This vagueness might be as simple as, "Melissa works as an accountant with the aspiration to one day become a police officer."

Sure, it might be a bit more detailed than that example, but for a pantser, they tend to rely on spontaneity, gut instinct, and letting characters dictate where the story goes based on their experiences and choices in the narrative itself.

The main thing my pantser friends love about this method is a lack of a map, feeling that they must follow an outline to the T. No outline means creative freedom to them, getting to explore the unexpected twists and turns of watching everything unfold before their eyes.

Pantsers rely on the unraveling nature of their instinctual imagination.

However, in reality, pantsing can lead to inconsistencies, plot holes, and getting lost in the complexity of passage after passage, page after page of rereads and note-taking. This process specifically made me realize that I was putting in more effort after the fact than during the outlining process itself.

*The 27 Plot Point Outline: When Plot Meets Story*

But, keep in mind, this book isn't meant to dissuade authors who are on the fence or prefer one way over the other.

When it comes to pantsers, if the argument is that outlining is too much backend work, just know, without an outline, the heavy lifting is now at the end.

So ask yourself, would you rather put the time into organizing an outline first or writing a book and then reverse engineering the full, written-out chapters to see if the plot and story make sense in the end?

## THE ARGUMENT

First off, before I get into the argument, know this: choose what works best for you. If you want to somewhat or fully outline, do it. If you like to sit down and write, do it. However, the argument itself is moot at the end of the day, because it's your responsibility as a writer to find what works for you and hone that, mold that, and adjust it as needed.

If someone tells you to outline because it's the best way, they are wrong. Additionally, if anyone tells you that discovery writing is the best way, they, too, are wrong. Not for any other reason besides their way might not be the right way for everyone, including you.

The truth is, you'll find a path that works for you. And you know what? It might not even be plotting or pantsing; it might end up being an entirely new way, using a weird coloring system, pasting ideas to the wall. Who knows?

The point is, this is an argument people stand their ground with, and my position is that both methods are ultimately discovery writing.

But, Thomas, how are they both discovery writing?

When outlining, you don't know the full, complete narrative. You can't know it; you're making it up as you outline the plot itself. When you're pantsing, you don't know the full, complete narrative. You can't know it; you're making it up as you write and work out the plot itself. In both cases, you have an idea, sure, but you don't instantly have every detail worked out.

Which finally brings us to the great debate: plotter or pantser?

The latter position usually states that outlining takes away the discovery of the narrative, that it doesn't allow for room to play in the sandbox, stifling the

## Two Kinds of Writers

creative process. Pantsers usually add, taking the stance that outlining reduces the excitement of seeing what'll happen and how it'll unfold.

George R.R. Martin has gone on to say this about outlining:

*"As you know, I don't outline my novels. I find that if I know exactly where a book is going, I lose all interest in writing it."*

And this is a valid point. If you feel this way, you are correct. However, some have stated that not knowing where or how the narrative will unfold when pantsing makes a writer lose interest. The feeling of being overwhelmed by the potential of details that are seemingly nowhere to be found yet.

To be fair, Martin also said this about pantsing, or rather, gardening:

*"I have a broad sense of where the story is going; I know the end, I know the end of the principal characters, and I know the major turning points and events from the books, the climaxes for each book, but I don't necessarily know each twist and turn along the way."*

This means that even George has a sense of an outline as a gardener. He knows what the climax will be, what events need to happen, where things should unfold, and how character arcs will end. The difference is that he doesn't know how he'll reach those points; he allows the "discovery" process to get him there.

Stephen King was harsher when it came to plotters, saying:

*"Outlines are the last resource of bad fiction writers who wish to God they were writing master's theses. There's no outline, nothing like that. That freezes it; it takes what should be a liquid, plastic, malleable thing to me and turns it into something else."*

I don't agree with his stance, but that doesn't mean he's wrong. I know, how can I disagree and he's still correct? Everyone's method is valid. So he doesn't like outlining. So what? Does that mean outlining is bad? I don't like the color of puke green; that doesn't mean it's not someone else's favorite color. Two things can be true at the same time; King liking to pants his books is as valid as James Patterson plotting. You know, the guy who's written over 200 novels since 1976.

In reality? Whether you're an architect or gardener, plotter or pantser, you can't know all the details before you sit down and start. Plotters don't have perfectly detailed outlines until they sit down and do the work. I say that loosely too, as it's a work in progress, and well, it should be. No first draft is perfect and is always evolving, as much as no first outline is perfect.

That goes the same for pantsers. Pantsers don't know every single detail of what will befall a first draft. They can't know everything; they're not mystical, magical people. If they were, I'd want to drink what they're drinking.

Pantsers, as plotters do, must work out the details of what will eventually become their narrative. Either process will lead a writer to an unworked draft that will need rewrites and work even after an outline or chapter is written.

Honestly, look at it this way: both might (and should) have some idea of what's going to happen before they start writing at all. Occasionally, a plotter and a pantser will have zero ideas before they start working out their outline or novel. And it's with that truth that you need to realize this very point: it's through the process of discovery that the plot and story of a narrative unfold.

## WE ARE ALL DISCOVERY WRITERS

Believe it or not, most writers blend these two approaches to some degree, either by choice or simply because the process of writing a narrative naturally allows for some form of discovery and planning.

Have you ever had ideas about how you want the story to end or begin, or maybe a scene lives rent-free inside your head? I'm talking about those scenes you set to the side; you know, that one really awesome scene where XYZ happens when Character ABC does that thing. And you have that scene in your head and think, "Where can I place this scene in my narrative?" Or better yet, you write a narrative around that one scene (or all the single scenes you've created).

That's a form of outlining: those scenes give you direction to write your narrative in a way that leads it to those moments. Now you have to discover how

## Two Kinds of Writers

to get to those scenes and make these key moments pay off. This is you outlining, but you're also leaving yourself some room for flexibility.

This is the process of getting a narrative written. It's about taking those broad, general ideas and discovering what you can as you write up to those scenes within them and away from them.

But, Thomas, that sounds like pantsing because nothing is concrete.

Correct. It's not concrete. It's not planned to the T, but it's still an idea. This is the reality: even when you're outlining, you're discovering your plot. And as you're writing out the chapters, you're discovering how they unfold through the story, or rather, the characters' emotional experiences and choices.

Just because Character A has to meet Character B doesn't mean in the outline it'll say how they meet. That's the discovery part—the moments you can explore, the tension of their first meeting, whether they get along, and yeah, sure, they have to work together, but how they work together is the story.

But, Thomas, I don't have any ideas when I start.

And that's okay; some writers start on a blank page and love to see where it goes. This method is the writer's path to pure discovery writing. But what do you do when you're finished? You need to reverse engineer everything by going back, reading the chapters, taking notes, and ultimately having to adjust things.

Those notes help you lay out an outline after the fact: the "what needed to happen no matter what" and "how do I make this all work and connect?"

Either way is a fine choice, but in reality, I assure you, there's always a bit of planning, a lot of discovery, and occasionally things change as you're working on your narrative. As you'll learn, outlining is all about discovery writing to make sure any ideas you have make sense, logically connect to one another, and have a natural flow of cause and effect.

# CHAPTER 3

## What is a Narrative?

**WHAT IS A NARRATIVE**

There are a few ways narrative is taught in school or by writing mentors, and even you, the reader, might have a specific way you look at it. Honestly, those narrative definitions aren't wrong or right. Whatever helps you understand the process of writing and outlining is great.

However, to give you a more comprehensive learning experience while I teach you how to outline in this book, I'm going to streamline the definition. It's important that I define what a narrative is for clarity. My vernacular is based on how I teach students to outline and write. For me, I define a narrative as follows:

> A narrative is made up of both plot and story. Plot is what needs to happen, no matter what, and story is how plot unfolds through the emotional experiences and choices of characters.

So whenever I mention narrative, I specifically mean both plot and story together. When I talk about plot, it's the narrative's foundation—what needs to

## The 27 Plot Point Outline: When Plot Meets Story

happen no matter what. Story, on the other hand, unfolds through the character's emotional experiences and choices and will influence the movement of the plot.

Basically, plot is "Sarah met Chris." Story is how they interact and react to their meetup and choices. And outlines rarely have much story in their first steps of short-form and extended outlines. It doesn't mean there's no story, but usually broad, general ideas are stronger in those first outlines.

However, as you get better at outlining and refining your understanding of the 27 Plot Point Outline, you'll naturally layer in story beats, sprinkling them all throughout each step.

But, Thomas, what do plot and story look like?

"Sarah met Chris" is a broad, general statement of plot.

"Sarah entered a deli, noticing an attractive man, Chris. Becoming shy, she avoided his eyes by reading a magazine near the end of the line." That's story in outline form.

Sarah had an emotional experience and made choices in this scene. Sure, these are still written in broad, general statements, but they work for an outline and leave room for writers to explore and discover who characters are in both their interactions and within prose.

But for this book, I'll focus on plot. I say this because story truly comes alive in the prose as you write your drafts out. You'll see this a lot more with direct character experiences and choices written out in your zero draft chapter outlines and definitely in your first draft.

When I teach, I break a narrative down into plot and story for students so they can better understand the difference between their purposes. This'll give authors a chance to hone in on either plot or story. Because when outlining, a plot must be clear, focused, and have cause and effect to move the narrative forward.

Story is where you can play. It's where you can let characters make their choices, challenge the characters, and see how they react to plot beats. That's the fun stuff, the "did my characters just do that when they know that I needed them to go into a different room?" stuff.

Ultimately, plot keeps things moving, and story shows a reader who the characters are and how they're changing as they interact within the plot.

*What is a Narrative?*

## PLOT: WHAT NEEDS TO HAPPEN

I love plot. Plot is important in a narrative. It's the thing that grounds a narrative, guides it, and keeps it moving. Most importantly, plot is what needs to happen no matter what. Without plot, the narrative doesn't happen.

Without plot, narratives will meander, get lost in "things are happening, but nothing is happening," and be missing half of what makes them whole.

Plot leads characters to a scene, gives that scene much-needed context to what's happening, and shows where the plot will go after the scene ends. In other words, plot is what needs to happen—action, events, character movement, etc.

Simply put, plot is "Sarah met Chris." That's a full plot. We know there are two characters, and we know they meet. Boom. Done. It's not story, nor a full narrative, but we know what needs to happen. On the page, in prose, we'll learn how they meet, why they meet, and what happens after they meet.

And plot alone doesn't carry weight—it's just things happening. Yes, the plot needs Sarah to meet Chris at some point in the narrative. If she doesn't, then the narrative doesn't happen. But plot without story is just things happening.

However, too much plot without context or direction can turn into this happens, and then this happens, and so on. This is why story is so important. It helps to avoid plot becoming a series of bland events where things are happening, but nothing is happening.

But, Thomas, "things are happening, but nothing is happening"?

Yes. Things are happening, but nothing is happening. It means nothing is being earned, explored, or processed, nor are there consequences for characters and their choices. You know, a lack of story.

This happens when characters feel more like chess pieces, placed around the board in a prewritten game, than living, breathing people.

And any time a narrative lacks story, it becomes plot being plot plotting, as plot must plot. That's a lot of plot.

If plot is just plotting, readers aren't seeing it move through emotional experiences and choices of your characters, nor are they experiencing plot from a POV. And yes, an omniscient POV still counts as experiencing it through a POV. Since even an omniscient POV is a present character.

## The 27 Plot Point Outline: When Plot Meets Story

A narrative can fall apart before it ever begins if it's only plot playing out. Sarah meets Chris because they must, or how else will they fall in love? And, you know, it's a love story and needs a happily ever after in the end.

Who wants to watch that? Me? No. You? Would you sit through 80,000 words of "Sarah entered the deli, saw a man, Chris, and fell in love. She asked him out, and he said yes without a single step of hesitation."

There are hundreds, if not thousands, of romance stories, a ton of action adventures, and endless dramas, thrillers, and fantasies waiting to be read. Oddly enough, Sarah meeting Chris can be any one of those genres. But, when it turns into things happening, and nothing is happening... plot is plotting in a collection of empty things that happen simply because they needed to happen.

But, Thomas, what is plot?

Plot is... well, plot is what needs to happen to a character; it's where they have to go and what they do when they get there. It's how they get to and from a scene. Plot is what needs to happen once in a scene, what gets them out of it, and the stuff that needs to happen no matter what.

Plot is what happens on the surface. Plot is "things happening" because they need to happen; plot is "Sarah met Chris."

And in an outline, plot is simple, broad general ideas.

- Sarah met Chris.
- They fell in love.
- They end up married.

From there, build on the simple, broad general ideas as you're outlining, adding more complex ideas to the plot while still remaining general and broad.

- Sarah met Chris at a nice deli in New York.
- They fell in love over the next year.
- They end up married on their second anniversary in the same deli.

These simple, broad general ideas (plot beats) allow you freedom to play in the unknown of the plot points, giving you room to develop narratives, adding more and more details until you write your first draft. It's there, in the first draft, when you can add specific details for story to unfold in prose.

However, if you want, you can write out specific details in an outline to fill in plot details. Just don't waste hours, days, weeks, months, or years figuring out the best friend's name or the car he drives. It's not important in the outlining process, at least not at this stage.

## STORY: HOW IT UNFOLDS

Story comes when you ask yourself the right questions about plot, questions that challenge it, push back on it, and, in some cases, throw it out the window. These challenges lead to tension, conflict, and hopefully character resolution, moving plot forward. However, story is strongest when discovered in character agency.

Plain and simple, story is character development that adds character to a narrative and builds on character arcs. Without story, it's a collection of things happening because they need to. Story gives life to things happening through truthful character movement, reactions, behavior, or complex human emotions (even if they're aliens from Mars).

And story should unfold in two stages: first during the outlining process with broad, general ideas as characters make choices that lead to consequences (good or bad). The second is in writing your pretty prose.

Outlining is where the external journey is explored. Prose is where the internal journey of characters is experienced. These two areas create meaning in narratives, showing character development and earning things happening.

Story is from a character's lived experiences within plot. Meaning, Sarah met Chris is plot. Once you know how the plot plays out, it's your job as a writer to figure out certain questions to develop the plot and let story live out within it. Search for questions that'll create a cause and effect, an ebb and flow, for plot and story to play together: rinse and repeat.

But, Thomas, what does that even mean?

In every narrative, something needs to happen; characters make choices, they experience consequences of those choices, make choices based on the results, and then repeat until there is a resolution.

*The 27 Plot Point Outline: When Plot Meets Story*

That process is what story looks like. And this is why every scene needs a setup for context, a conflict to challenge the context, and a resolution for forward momentum. Without character involvement, there's no story, just a narrative and things happening... then this happens, then this happens, and then this happens.

Basically, if Sarah met Chris is plot, then how they met, their meeting, what happens after the meeting, and their emotional experiences and choices are story. Without story, it'll just be a woman met a man, they fell in love, and lived happily ever after.

Our job as writers is to look deeper into each beat and ask questions that lead to answers that best fit each character. Sarah enters a deli—okay, how, why, when, where, and what's going on? These answers will be reflected in the choices Sarah makes when entering the deli, inside the deli, and after she leaves the deli.

So now you know that story is where characters are developed, emotions are explored, and readers experience plot through the characters themselves. And that's the reality of story. It must unfold through the emotional experiences and choices (big or small) of your characters, showing how they react and experience the consequences of those choices.

## A FULL NARRATIVE NEEDS BOTH

A narrative is what an audience receives. It's the woven combination of plot and story working together to make a full and complete reading experience. And now things are happening and also earned and experienced through the characters.

And more often than not, narrative is shaped by intention. That's right; you, the writer, choose what gets shown, felt, and the order it all plays out. This is what makes outlining a craft. Being a writer is about making choices, believing in those choices, and moving the plot around those choices.

Understand this: plot without story is hollow. As much as story without plot becomes directionless. Narrative is where both play together with a purpose. To make a complete narrative, there needs to be direction and emotional truth to how the characters experience things and make choices. Simple... ish.

I promise I won't repeat the same thing over and over as you get into the heart of this book. I'm repeating myself so the definition of a narrative sticks with

*What is a Narrative?*

you. So the idea that it's made up of plot and story guides the approach. Once we get into the outlining process, I'll focus on plot (and some story).

Though, keep in mind, story appears more and more as you close in on a first draft. You'll see it develop in the finer details of how characters make choices. Short-form and extended outlines will mostly have plot. The zero draft chapter outlines are when character voices show up—adding story into the process.

The truth is, an audience needs to feel something, anything, to connect to characters to have the slightest bit of interest in the plot. No one's interested in something they can't feel, see, or experience. Oh, sure, six characters break into a bank at the start of a narrative, hold it up, and have big guns. The cops show up, lights and sirens blasting. But so far that's spectacle, and spectacle can only last so long before audiences seek something deeper.

That's why even popcorn movies like Transformers have story. Story is there for people to connect to something. Thus, it's a blockbuster summer movie with a love story as much as it's a kid getting his first car story. But they also have a Megatron plot in the background.

Don't get me wrong, plot is the draw that pulls an audience in. I mean, transforming robots in disguise from outer space? Autobots waging their battle to destroy the evil forces of the Decepticons!? That's awesome, period. No notes. But the truth is, without those emotional beats, audiences get plot fatigue.

So remember: Plot = Direction. Story = Character. Both = Narrative.

# CHAPTER 4

## The 27 Plot Point Outline

**THE 27 PLOT POINT OUTLINE**

The 27 Plot Point Outline is used to give you control over the narrative's plot, its rhythm, and emotional movement therewithin. It guides you to develop plot and story through the natural order and flow of each plot point. And all narratives do this, whether it's a film, television show, or a book. Some might even argue that a well-crafted speech or stand-up comedy bit does the same. You may or may not notice it when reading or watching (which is good as the audience), or as a writer you may see it everywhere.

But, Thomas, what can "it" be?

The "it" is in how every narrative is the same: a beginning, middle, and end that unfolds through emotional experiences and choices of characters. These components do very specific things, even if you change up the specific details that come from your mind as a writer. For example...

All narrative beginnings have one thing in common: context. Context is king. Without context, narratives can't challenge or reframe what's to come in its middle. Whether it's the mundane start to a protagonist's life or a super spy in an action scene finishing a mission, beginnings give us context.

## The 27 Plot Point Outline: When Plot Meets Story

At some point that context must be challenged or reframed. This creates stakes, tension, pushback, growth for characters, and engagement. The more you set up context, the more you can play with it in the second act, giving characters a chance to experience story in your narrative.

These challenges or reframings place a protagonist into a position where things must resolve. This resolution helps relieve the growing tension. And too much tension will be hard to handle for any reader. Which means narratives need resting points and regrouping beats, not just for characters but readers too.

So, to recap, if you're an outliner or not, all narratives have a beginning, middle, and end. That sequence will repeat throughout every part of a narrative: acts, sections, chapters, scenes, and character arcs. And beginnings, middles, and ends all have specific jobs, jobs that'll keep the narrative moving forward.

Whether you're a pantser or an outliner, a gardener or an architect, the 27 PPO isn't here to control you; it's here to gently guide you. So use it however you need to, and let it help you figure out where your plot should go.

The thing that makes the 27 PPO effective is that it's not about specific things; it's about broad, general ideas being placed into rule-based plot points. It is this freedom that makes the 27 PPO versatile for genres in many ways.

For example, I personally love writing adult epic fantasy. Does that mean I have to write out and explain the entire world and its rules in one chapter? No. In an epic fantasy novel, you have room to play with.

See, in romance, Plot Point 1: The Ordinary World can be established in one tight chapter. In epic fantasy, it's not an issue to play it out over three, or even five or more, chapters before the inciting incident of Plot Point 2 happens.

The 27 PPO isn't about chapter counts; it's about plot points and what context must be established within said plot point. For example, PP1 must set up the context of the ordinary world before PP2's disruption.

So yes, even PP2 can be one or more chapters to establish the disruption, but it still must disrupt the ordinary world. While in romance, this disruption might happen in one chapter, establishing the lovebirds' meet-cute.

But, Thomas, I like writing shorter books.

## The 27 Plot Point Outline

That's the other side of the 27 PPO. The 27 PPO has 3 Acts, 9 Sections, and 27 Plot Points. Each act has its own three sections, and each section has its own three plot points. Thus, 27 Plot Points.

But, Thomas, what does that mean for me and my shorter books?

27 chapters x 3,000 words per chapter equals 81,000 words (a nice tight book for any genre). Does that mean you can't write more than 27 chapters? Not at all. Chapters don't really have a one-size-fits-all approach. We'll talk about that in another chapter.

For now, let me conclude with this: the 27 Plot Point Outline gives you range, options, and a chance to see how to move a narrative around. The rules of this method give insight into when and where the pace must slow down or speed up, when characters can play a bit, and even when narrative beats must be set up, challenged, and resolved.

Even with its rules and direction as a helpful guide, writers can use the 27 PPO to adjust and break those rules as they learn more about them. I'll say this much: you'll figure out where to lean in on plot points, pull back, and kick aside certain ones as narrative beats start making more sense to you.

So with that, get ready to take some notes, have a little bit of fun, and let the lessons begin in the next chapter, The Rule of Threes.

# CHAPTER 5

## The Rule of Threes

**THE RULE OF THREES**

The 27 Plot Point Outline is built on micro narratives. The macro narrative of an outline focuses on a central conflict. Traditionally, the CC is a protagonist's main character arc, or rather, their central character arc. Additional character arcs and subarcs are then built around the protagonist's central character arc.

However, I'm going to focus on the protagonist's central character arc, or rather, the central conflict, showing how the Rule of Threes breaks it up into smaller, focused micro narratives.

The Rule of Threes creates a natural rhythmic ebb and flow, guiding a narrative as needed. It'll allow for the escalation of tension, give your characters a chance to reflect or take a breather, and earn resolutions, among other things.

If you read books, watch movies, or binge television shows, you'll notice how every narrative follows the Rule of Threes. The rule creates a natural pattern for a narrative's acts, sections, plot points, chapters, and scenes.

Yep, that's right. The Rule of Threes shows that a narrative is constantly creating new beginnings, middles, and ends at every level of a narrative and cycles back to the start of it all. Acts, sections, plot points, chapters, and scenes need to establish context, challenge it, and finally resolve it forward. Repeat.

## THE ACTS OF A NARRATIVE – DIAGRAM 1A

Let's take a gander at Diagram 1A. At its core, a central conflict has three acts that set up a beginning, middle, and end. Over the course of its first act, it'll develop the needed context for the central conflict (among other things).

The second act challenges and reframes the context presented in the first act. The second act is when characters are pushed to their limits, presented with a new problem/conflict, and given a chance to prove who they are. All this happens before they rush into the resolution of Act 3.

It's in the third act when characters take a potential solution they found in Act 2 and try to resolve the problem created by the midpoint conflict. This will lead characters headfirst into the climax of Act 3.

Great, now we know what the macro narrative of a central conflict looks like. So, knowing this lets us go deeper into the micro narratives to explore the 27 Plot Point Outline and why the Rule of Threes is so important.

The Rule of Threes pattern, having a beginning, middle, and end, gives writers a chance to zoom in on the narrative. Now each act in the central conflict can be broken down into its own beginning, middle, and end. This splits the acts into their own, smaller micro narratives.

## THE SECTIONS OF AN ACT – DIAGRAM 1B

Diagram 1B shows us how each act gets three sections all to itself. I love how the Rule of Threes gets us writers to ask what the purpose of each act is.

*The Rule of Threes*

Act 1 sets up the central conflict: a farm boy living on Tatooine, soldiers storming Normandy, or a party of hobbits at a Shire. Act 2 challenges the context of Act 1: finding a planet destroyed, traveling in a war-torn country in search of a private named Ryan, and the fellowship uniting. Act 3 brings the central conflict to a resolution, wrapping it all up: destroying the Death Star, getting Ryan home, and Sam won't let Frodo go alone.

This means that Act 1 must set up a central conflict's context. If we look at Star Wars EP4, A New Hope, each section of Act 1 sets up, challenges, and resolves the central conflict, pushing the narrative into Act 2.

But, Thomas, what does that look like?

Section 1 shows us Luke Skywalker in his ordinary world. He works on a moisture farm with Uncle Owen and Aunt Beru. He has dreams to see the galaxy. They buy droids, which leads to a message about Old Ben Kenobi. R2-D2 leaves in the middle of the night to find Kenobi. "Beep Boop Beep Boop."

Section 2 challenges Luke's understanding about his ordinary world. He is attacked and saved by Ben, brought to a small little hut, and Luke learns about the princess. Luke is given a lightsaber and a mentor all in one afternoon.

Section 3 resolves Act 1 by killing Luke's aunt and uncle. Luke has lost it all and decides to help Kenobi fight back against the Empire. Stormtroopers and the death of his family push Luke into Act 2's new world. Luke cannot go back to his old life.

This will continue for each act. As you can see, the first act of Star Wars: A New Hope had its own micro narrative. We meet Luke; he has a disruption in his life, and it leads to Ben, which in turn leads to Luke losing his family.

Yes, it's a narrative all its own and sets up the context needed for when the central conflict "imperial marches" into Act 2 and so on. See what I did?

| ACT 1 | ACT 2 | ACT 3 |
|---|---|---|
| **B** SECTION 1 | SECTION 4 | SECTION 7 |
| **M** SECTION 2 | SECTION 5 | SECTION 8 |
| **E** SECTION 3 | SECTION 6 | SECTION 9 |

*The 27 Plot Point Outline: When Plot Meets Story*

## THE PLOT POINTS OF A SECTION — DIAGRAM 1C

| ACT 1 | ACT 2 | ACT 3 |
|---|---|---|
| SECTION 1 | SECTION 4 | SECTION 7 |
| (B) PP1 | PP10 | PP19 |
| (M) PP2 | PP11 | PP20 |
| (E) PP3 | PP12 | PP21 |
| SECTION 2 | SECTION 5 | SECTION 8 |
| (B) PP4 | PP13 | PP22 |
| (M) PP5 | PP14 | PP23 |
| (E) PP6 | PP15 | PP24 |
| SECTION 3 | SECTION 6 | SECTION 9 |
| (B) PP7 | PP16 | PP25 |
| (M) PP8 | PP17 | PP26 |
| (E) PP9 | PP18 | PP27 |

Each section has three plot points; each beginning plot point sets up the section, followed by a middle plot point to challenge and reframe it, and resolving it in a third and final plot point.

Sections have their own micro narratives to zoom in closer on the central conflict. This doesn't create a new, completely separate narrative from the central conflict, but it does zoom in on the central conflict and explores the purpose of what a section should do for the narrative.

As you get deeper into this book, Chapters 6-17 will explore each act, its sections, and the plot points in greater detail. As for this chapter, it's here to give you a look at how a narrative structure breathes, keeping it from rushing from one moment to the next.

The Rule of Threes opens the door to writing multiple micro narratives to the macro of it all, looking at the acts as opportunities to ask yourself, what is the ordinary world setting up? What does the new world challenge? How does the resolution bring it all together?

Take that mentality and apply it to acts, sections, and plot points, asking yourself how to set up context within it, challenge the context, and resolve it.

For example, Section 1: Setting up the Ordinary World does just that. It takes three plot points to establish the ordinary world of a central conflict, then it disrupts it and resolves it all in one section, leading a narrative to the next section.

*The Rule of Threes*

Section 2: A Problem Disrupts the Protagonist's Life. Now the next plot points, 4-6, explore what a protagonist does with their new situation, how they'll take action to fix the disruption, and what leads their actions to the consequence.

My point is each section has its own micro narrative. One that can now explore the deeper dive of acts. This lets narrative beats breathe and adds depth to what's going on in the narrative, to the characters within it, and to how it all plays together. So use each of the three plot points in sections to do the same thing, and give the narrative some breathing room.

## THE RULE OF THREES IN ACTION | ACTS

It's always best to start with the macro of a narrative and then go deeper. Like all narratives, you start by asking yourself, "Self, what's the purpose of Acts 1, 2, and 3?" You have to put time into that; it's important (it can always be adjusted later).

Let's assume I did the work already, and I'll break down Act 1 into three parts: beginning, middle, and end, with a summary for each part of that act.

The central conflict is about a protagonist who doesn't feel like their life is going anywhere, as if they're wasting their potential at a dead-end job and want to do more, until they are pushed to do more against an alien invasion that tests and challenges them to be all they were always meant to be.

Act 1 (Setup)

A bored accountant despises his mundane job and gets unwanted excitement when aliens invade his building. He leads his best friend and love interest in the chaos. They encounter his wounded boss, who reveals himself to be an alien.

Act 2 (Conflict)

The protagonist gets temporary superhuman abilities from a device the boss has. They're ambushed by an alien commander as they try to contact a group of sympathetic aliens. The boss sacrifices himself so they can escape. The protagonist joins a human resistance.

Act 3 (Resolution)

They try to stop the alien commander, and the protagonist's best friend gets captured. He's captured trying to rescue his friend and brought to the alien commander. There's a battle, a nuclear weapon is activated, and a massive fight leads to the protagonist "dying."

## THE RULE OF THREES IN ACTION | SECTIONS

Now that the central conflict is set through the three acts, let's go a bit deeper and zoom into the first micro narrative: the three sections of Act 1.

Act 1: Section 1, The Beginning (Setup)

Introduce the protagonist, their best friend, the love interest, his hate for his mundane job, and the status quo. It all goes to hell when normalcy shatters at the arrival of aliens. The protagonist finds his best friend and love interest, and they must escape.

Act 1: Section 2, The Middle (Conflict)

The protagonist goes from a panic of being thrust into an invasion to taking action, shifting out of hiding, and trying to find safety. He realizes the alien invasion is citywide and humans are captured. This failed escape teaches him that survival requires more than running.

Act 1: Section 3, The End (Resolution)

The protagonist's world he knew shattered in a new revelation: the boss he hated is actually a sympathetic alien, who's willing to help. The protagonist accepts a new path ahead of him, requiring him to become more than a survivor but to become a fighter.

*The Rule of Threes*

## THE RULE OF THREES IN ACTION | PLOT POINTS

Now it's time for another zoom to go deeper into Act 1, Section 1, the beginning, and explore the first three plot points.

> Act 1: Section 1, PP1, The Beginning (Setup)

Stuck working a crap job, the protagonist is surrounded by people who are incompetent, yearning for more. Everyone relies on him at the expense of his own responsibilities, and only his best friend and romantic interest keep him going, despite his dissatisfaction.

> Act 1: Section 1, PP2, The Middle (Conflict)

The inciting incident brings external danger—the aliens arrive! This revelation reveals that the protagonist's life was compromised (some coworkers were disguised aliens). The aliens take action, creating an immediate need for them to survive as aliens round up employees.

> Act 1: Section 1, PP3, The End (Resolution)

The protagonist immediately steps up as the leader, demonstrating the capability that was wasted in his crappy job. He learns quickly that panic leads to the death of other employees, teaching him that survival will require not just hiding but strategic isolation.

## FROM ACT ONE TO THREE PLOT POINTS

As you can see, starting with broad, general ideas allows us room to add a little more information with each additional micro narrative. We took broad, general ideas in Act 1's beginning, expanded on them in the sections, and dove deeper into the three smaller plot points of that first section.

## The 27 Plot Point Outline: When Plot Meets Story

This continues for the central conflict into Acts 2 & 3, their associated sections, and plot points. This expands on the nuance of a growing narrative.

As you'll learn, the process is to map out information, starting small and adding detail with each step: brainstorming, character arcs, a short-form outline, the extended outline, zero draft chapter outlines, and the drafts.

For now, there are no chapters or scenes. The purpose of this method is to find a rhythm and beat to the narrative, making sure it sets up enough context to challenge it and resolve it forward. In other words, the narrative momentum. Ultimately, give yourself room to say, "What needs to happen in this plot point?"

The short of it: even chapters and scenes need a beginning, middle, and end. Chapters are another micro narrative that goes deeper into the plot points of a central conflict, as scenes are a micro narrative to chapters.

But, Thomas, chapters and scenes aren't micro narratives.

Well, let me tell you. Every chapter and scene needs a beginning, middle, and end. A chapter on its own still needs to set up context, challenge it within the chapter itself, and resolve the chapter, moving the narrative forward. It's the same with scenes within a chapter as well.

In closing, I hope this book guides you to think about the what, where, why, and when of a narrative. Even if you're still on the fence about outlining or not, this book will teach you a great deal about narratives. So yes, the purpose of this book is to teach you how to use the 27 PPO to outline, but regardless, I want you to learn how a narrative works. Ultimately, this'll give you choices so you can take advantage of your narratives.

So, with that said, enjoy as you turn the page to learn about Act 1!

*The Rule of Threes*

# ACT 1

### SECTION 1
PP1: Introductions
PP2: Inciting Incident
PP3: Fallout

### SECTION 2
PP4: Reflection/Choice
PP5: Action
PP6: Consequence

### SECTION 3
PP7: Pressure
PP8: Plot Twist/Pinch
PP9: Pushed

# ACT 2

### SECTION 4
PP10: New World
PP11: Fun & Games
PP12: Juxtaposition

### SECTION 5
PP13: Buildup
PP14: Midpoint
PP15: Reversal

### SECTION 6
PP16: Consequence
PP17: Trials/Tested
PP18: Dedication

# ACT 3

### SECTION 7
PP19: Calm Before The Storm
PP20: Plot Twist/Pinch
PP21: Darkest Moment

### SECTION 8
PP22: Power Within
PP23: Action to Rally
PP24: Converge

### SECTION 9
PP25: Final Battle
PP26: Climax
PP27: Resolution

# CHAPTER 6

## Act 1: The Setup

## ACT 1: THE SETUP

I've said it enough times so far, but it never hurts to say it again: Act 1 sets up the central conflict of a narrative. This includes, but isn't limited to, the world and its rules, who characters are (motivations and positions), and a central conflict itself. And, of course, sprinkle some subarcs in there for good measure.

Things can't be challenged/reframed in the second act if they're not set up properly in Act 1. Thus, context is king, even more so in the first act. Without context, readers can get lost. And remember, readers enter narratives way before they know who characters are and well after you, the author, have sat with these characters for days, months, and years.

Yep, no matter how you look at it, you have a beautiful relationship with your characters, their world, and where the narrative is going. Readers don't. So use Act 1 to set up enough context for the readers to understand what's going on and to know your characters enough to want to follow them.

And this is the thing: you can't just spring it all on the reader either. You have to, well, kind of ease them into it. Sort of how I did with this book. I gave you some pieces of information on outlining, explained a little more each time,

## The 27 Plot Point Outline: When Plot Meets Story

and continued to build on the elements in new chapters. That's the thing. You're in control of how the information (pace) unfolds.

A quick tip: vague but informative. Give readers enough information to know what's going on while leaving them with enough unanswered questions to stay engaged, feeling like they're discovering the answers as they read. And that's Act 1 in a nutshell.

You never want readers popping in and saying, "What's going on? I just got here. I'm still trying to catch up on strangers doing things... on a farm... and something about dragons and The Sword of Bloop Bloop."

Now, as you outline, yes, keep things general and broad. However, the better you set up the context of what this world is about, the more you can play with it, mold it, and dive deeper into it in Act 2. The key is to allow the reader to understand what a character's potential is without giving it all away. The more a reader understands their potential, the greater you can challenge it in Act 2.

For example, a really smart character, great at figuring things out, is also, well, kind of naive. Thus, in Act 1, show them solving puzzles at a university or living in a desert, where they built a C-3PO unit from a box of scraps.

Setting this all up gives the context to challenge and reframe it in Act 2. Readers see how smart they are. In Act 2, their limits are exposed. Meaning, their intelligence shouldn't always get them out of situations in Act 2. Have them use other resources and rely on people so their area of expertise doesn't help them survive in space. Because in space, no one can hear you scream.

This is the best part: the better you set up the central conflict, characters, and world, the better it'll earn the midpoint conflict when the truth of the lie is revealed in Act 2.

But, Thomas, do I have to set everything up in Act 1? What if I want to bring magic in during Act 2?

You can do anything you want. However, it'll feel earned if magic is at least mentioned in Act 1. You don't have to show it being used, but you'll need to set it up. Because anything you set up in Act 1 can now be played with in Act 2.

But, Thomas, won't I give away too much if I bring up magic in Act 1?

You have magic? Great, I love magic! And no. Learn to explore, expand, and qualify what readers understand in steps and stages. Mention magic in Act 1,

*Act 1: The Setup*

saying it's a lost art or that someone doesn't believe in it. Or show it being used, even poorly, or maybe not useful at all, setting limitations.

Ah yes, limitations. Characters need limitations so those limitations can be broken as a narrative moves forward. Luke used the Force at the end of Star Wars: A New Hope. It works because he struggled to use the Force earlier in the narrative. That, and it was mentioned in Act 1, he trained with Ben in Act 2, and the final act shows him using it in a small way. "Luke, use the Force."

It's not until in Empire when he grows with the Force and is challenged even more. Of course, in Return of the Jedi... well, spoiler alert, he wins.

Maybe you have sea monsters. Wonderful! I love sea monsters. If so, set up the sea monsters in Act 1. Talk about them, what they're known for, stories, or the potential for their greatness, and then challenge it in Act 2.

"Oh, Davey lost his ship to sea monsters; those evil, soulless creatures..."

In Act 2, characters meet a sea monster, and you know what? It's really nice and compassionate. Act 2 reveals the truth of the lie: they thought they were evil creatures, and it turns out they aren't (the reader thought that too). But now this stigma challenges and reframes what was set up in Act 1.

However, whatever you choose to set up with context, make sure you do a great job of showing your characters, who they are, and their relationships, and the world itself.

Don't worry about not having enough time to do this in the first act. I assure you, you literally have the first three sections and nine plot points of Act 1 to let it breathe out, giving readers a chance to discover your narrative, characters, and the world. That's a minimum of nine chapters to give context for Act 2.

Before you ask about chapters, there's a full chapter on that: how many you should have, lengths, and using them for effect, but, as I was saying, don't front-load Act 1 to get in all the information (or more than you think you need). Exposition dumps kill engagement and overwhelm readers. When in doubt, seed and spread it out. It's okay to seed exposition over the first act, expand on it in the second act, and allow it to pay off in the third act.

## SETTING UP THE NARRATIVE

The following list of information will help you understand the purpose of Act 1

*The 27 Plot Point Outline: When Plot Meets Story*

and how to get the most out of it. And, like all rules, learn them before you break them. Use this list as a guide to set up the first act, add enough context, and learn how to push the narrative into Act 2.

## 1. START WITH CHARACTER, NOT PLOT

But, Thomas, why would I start with character if I want a plot-driven narrative?

Because starting with character ensures that their choices make sense in a narrative's movement even if it's plot-driven. You must know who the characters are before placing them into situations. Otherwise, a lot of things are happening, but nothing is happening as you move them around the board.

I say board because you never want a character to feel like another game piece being used instead of the characters themselves choosing. That's the thing: plot-driven narratives must feel earned, emotionally connected to the characters, and have movement beyond this happens, and then this happens, and so on.

Besides, are characters interesting because they're a strong female who's amazingly good at hand-to-hand combat, doesn't take crap from anyone, and graduated at the top of her science class?

These are things. Things aren't interesting on the surface. Substance. You need substance, depth, and dimension that all go deeper than their accolades. No real person is a list of skills on their resume. People are a collection of nuance, complications, and things that drive their behavior to do or not do, say, and not say. And you get there with what matters: motivations, positions (beliefs), flaws, relationship dynamics, and their strengths and weaknesses.

Who a person is isn't what they are.

But a character isn't likeable because they can fight. Sure, how they fight might get you into the battle, but it's the "why" behind their desire to fight that keeps you coming back to see if they win. For example, do you root for Rambo or the soon-to-be-dead Guy #3 running across the field to kill Rambo?

You root for Rambo. I said, you root for Rambo... Right? I mean, if you don't, don't let him hear that you didn't. He's a scary guy.

But it's true, we root for the person we've spent the most time with. The person we learned about and developed a relationship with. And here's the crazy part: in First Blood he barely speaks at all. And yet, we understand him. We feel

*Act 1: The Setup*

for him. We're right there with him as he cries on the office floor in Act 3, talking about war, PTSD, and his displacement in the civilian world.

That doesn't come from a list: good with the knife, muscles, he shoots a gun, more muscles, can build tunnels, muscles on muscles, and he hides in the mud, killing people with his muscles using a knife.

Which brings me to my point: a strong narrative begins with characters so its plot can logically unfold, giving characters agency, purpose, and their why. Knowing who a character is will give you choices in scenes to see how it plays out.

Rambo wouldn't stand out in the open when fighting people (unless it's Rambo III; I'm talking about First Blood). What we do believe is that Rambo is a hide-and-stab kind of person. We learn this by his behavior, and it's later in Act 2 when we learn why he has all those specific skills. The reveal is earned because of his behavior and choices.

Plot dictates that he must still hide and go kill people, but how he did it connected back to who he is as a character. If he just killed people, the narrative would've lost steam, and Gary Stu would've been on the screen.

Starting with character will help readers discover who they are in Act 1, establishing how capable they are, their positions, motivations, flaws, and other aspects of who they are. This creates a foundation, context, for where they are at the beginning and establishes their baseline, which can now be challenged in Act 2 and pushed to its limits in Act 3.

Challenging characters leads to their growth; using them to simply move the plot forward leads to inauthentic arcs. Knowing their positions, motivations, skills, etc., allows characters to get challenged, fundamentally changing who they are completely, somewhat, or not at all. Without context setting the bar in Act 1, you won't earn the push for change in Acts 2 & 3.

That bar should also establish key relationships and their dynamics. You must show all relationships playing out, including the main cast, the protagonist, and the antagonist force, to showcase their relationships truthfully.

Relationships provide emotional context, create stakes and tension, and add meaning to conflict. It's these truths that draw readers in to pay attention to the development of these relationships. And readers are more likely to care about and like characters when other characters like those characters too.

*The 27 Plot Point Outline: When Plot Meets Story*

Oh, sure, we all like Darth Vader; he's a big, evil, strong, scary villain, but it still comes down to his behavior on screen. We don't like him just because he's scary, but because of how he commands the room and how people react to him, and as we learn more about him in other films—well, he's not the number one villain of all time for nothing.

It's hard to get invested in a floating eye that we see once in a while. It's why we need different characters to fight, save, and become brothers while trying to toss the one ring into a volcano.

When readers care about the connections between characters, threats to those relationships generate authentic tension. Tension that is built on who these characters are as people and what they mean to the people around them.

"Come on, Mr. Frodo. I can't carry it for you, but I can carry you."

That line hits because Sam's relationship with Frodo is established. It's clear. We know the stakes, who they are, why they're doing what they're doing, the loyalty, and, most of all, we understand the love they have for each other.

So use the full length of Act 1, its three sections, and nine plot points to develop the context of the characters, their motivations, relationships, any flaws they have, positions, and strengths before Act 2 begins. In doing so, you'll be able to truly see the character's behavior on the page, but more than that, readers will have enough context to be in your character's corner.

## 2. CENTRAL CONFLICT (CC) & SUBPLOTS (SUBARCS)

Central conflicts are as important as your characters. The CC drives your narrative forward and moves with character agency. Together they keep the momentum going. And no matter what happens in your narrative, its side quests, or a random encounter, everything leads back to the central conflict. Most often, if not always, that central conflict comes from the protagonist's central character arc.

But, Thomas, is this always the case?

No. However, if we look at Game of Thrones, Eddard Stark is the central protagonist and drives the narrative forward. Yes, he... Well, spoiler alert, takes a nap at the end of the narrative (before the book ends), but without him making specific choices (agency), the narrative itself wouldn't unfold.

*Act 1: The Setup*

Eddard Stark has a duty to the North, establishing his ordinary world. And he'd go on doing what he does in Winterfell if the king never arrived. This arrival activated the narrative's inciting incident when the king told him, "I want you to be the Hand of the King."

Now, here's the thing. If Ned had said no, the king would've gone home grumpy, and Ned would've continued on as he always has. Sure, he would have another story, but his ordinary world wouldn't have changed, and the narrative as we know it wouldn't happen.

His ordinary world changes because he... spoiler alert, takes the gig. And thus begins the central conflict, centered around Eddard's central character arc. Therefore, Act 1 must set up this central character arc.

Within a first act, there are secondary characters and potential tertiary, or quaternary, characters. These characters also have their own character arcs, thus plots that move in and around the central conflict. These are known as subplots.

Personally, I consider every plot a character arc. It keeps it simple and lets me break character needs into narrative threads. A character could have multiple character arcs, some you could build on, others you'll discover. A friendship, for example, between two people creates a character arc for both those characters.

But, Thomas, what if the characters are friends or father/son, and there is no adjustment or transformation of the characters through that relationship?

Great question! That's a flat arc. Therefore, they'll make choices based on that relationship. Perhaps their friend gets hurt, and the other friend fights for their honor. The relationship arc stays flat, but it influences their behavior.

Another example of a protagonist's central character arc is Frodo going off to toss a ring into a large volcano (without the assistance of eagles). Yes, that's the central conflict, but other arcs move in and around his central conflict. Frodo and Sam's relationship. Frodo and Gollum's relationship.

These aren't central arcs, but they are character arcs that'll influence the behavior of the characters. Because of these arcs, characters will make choices and influence events as they unfold. Thus, subplots. Or subarcs.

Another example might include characters that deal with an internal or external conflict. A character might need to be the best warrior, and another one is deeply in love with their best friend's girl.

*The 27 Plot Point Outline: When Plot Meets Story*

With all of that said, you must set up the central character arc in Act 1, along with any subarcs. And remember, you have the first three sections and all nine plot points of Act 1 to accomplish this.

Remember, you can continue to introduce subarcs in Act 2, all the way up to the midpoint conflict. I'd recommend not adding new information that'll need to be explored after the midpoint conflict.

You can add new information here because the New World elements of Act 2 are still unfolding: a new character might be introduced, mentors, and an old friend shows up. These relationships (or new characters) create new subarcs. Even entering a new city creates a new subarc: exploring the new city.

And yes, rules are made to be broken, but remember, every new insert of information will need to be earned. And the second half of a narrative has its own job. After a midpoint conflict, characters are trying to find a solution to the problem created by the midpoint itself.

So, if you add new information after the midpoint, you'll have to spend time setting it up, or it could turn into a deus ex machina. Oh, sure, just saying "deus ex machina" sounds cool, but it's not a good solution.

## 3. THE RULES OF THE WORLD

You might be highly familiar with your narrative world (or just learning about it), but the point stands: your readers know zero, squat, nothing, nada about your world and its rules. Act 1 needs to define the rules of the world.

Since this world is new to your readers, you have to explain the general foundation of that world's rules. You don't have to go into specifics, but do you have magic? Are there laws or things that we might relate to based on Earth? You might not have to explain what a horse is, but if they talk, that's a rule.

See, here's the thing: science is real, even if in your world the characters don't know about it. When a human from Earth reads about Mars or the planet of Blardar, they're starting out with what they know as a baseline. The reader has a limited, but fundamental, understanding of how gravity and matter work and that (A) people can't fly without a plane, (B) people can't walk through walls, and (C) people need to sleep, eat, love, and have the sex to make children.

*Act 1: The Setup*

If any of that is different in your world, you need to explain it, and by it, I mean your laws of nature, magic systems, social structures, any technology and its level, and the historical context of that world.

But, Thomas, that's a lot of exposition I need to explain.

Eh, I'd say two things: first, exposition is a bad word. Please put $2 in the swear jar. Second, you don't have to explain anything if you don't want to, but you do need to show it. Are people flying around in Act 1? Great, that's showing that people can fly in your world. But if you don't and they randomly fly around after the midpoint conflict, or going into Act 3, it's not so good.

What about the way people say hi to each other? Must people eat to live? Are you writing epic fantasy? Well, do they sleep, camp, and stay warm by a fire? Or is there a ball of bleemum cast from a flower of Zar keeping them warm?

By the way, you don't have to explain these things. Show the world and its rules breathing, living. When people sleep, rest, and stay toasty by a warm fire, it tells the reader (without telling them) that characters need rest and to be warm.

What about the environment? Do they ride horses or fly dragons (I want a dragon), or do they drive cars? Do they live in brick or wooden houses? These things explore the world's reality and the rules of your world in Act 1. Show things happening, describe them, and build an immersive experience with your readers through the emotional experiences and choices of your characters.

All I'm saying is, if you have unique physical phenomena going on, show it, mention it, or seed it. Magic systems? Well, do you have magic, and if so, does it have limitations, sources, and consequences? Fireball solves everything, but what are the rules? You don't want readers to get upset when the protagonist randomly beats the villain by shooting lightning out from their nose holes.

These elements are as important as understanding the social structures that show the readers about your world's culture, power dynamics, and different societies. Not everyone should be wearing fancy hats in every city, town, or cave. I mean, they could; who wouldn't want a fancy hat, but it must make logical sense.

And it's that hat, or the other levels of technology, that say to the reader: this place is highly advanced compared to our own, but why don't they wipe their butts? Then again, maybe it's the historical reality for people in that world.

*The 27 Plot Point Outline: When Plot Meets Story*

Just because you know the world you wrote doesn't mean readers will or do. If you're writing a fantasy with magic systems, science fiction with advanced technology, or contemporary fiction with specific social dynamics, you need to establish these within Act 1.

By defining the rules of your world in Act 1, you create a coherent world readers can understand and navigate. This gives a narrative room to challenge and reframe any rules in Act 2. In reality, when the world's rules are established early, it prevents the appearance of arbitrary developments. Arbitrary developments become issues when they break a reader's suspension of disbelief. And you don't want to do that. It'll cost you another $2 for the swear jar.

## 4. THE INCITING INCIDENT

Each act, section, and plot point all have a very specific purpose, but they also all affect the central conflict of the narrative itself: Act 1 is no different. Act 1 needs to set up the world, but it also needs an inciting incident. Without it, a narrative would never happen. The ordinary world would just continue on as is.

But, Thomas, what makes it an inciting incident?

Let's use a normal, everyday life of a random person as an example. One might even call this person's normal life their ordinary world. And that ordinary world is their life in the military—the Air Force specifically. Or as the Marines call 'em: the Chair Force. Moving right along.

We need to show, not tell, what that ordinary life looks like. This person flies a jet! And every day they scan over a war zone area in the Middle East. Their job isn't to engage with the enemy; it's to fly over them, take photos, and get back to the aircraft carrier.

So, what we just did is set up their life. Their work life. Every day, except for weekends, they fly a jet, do a loop-de-loop, and come back to the ship. Done.

See, you, me, we can't help it; we have lives. We get up, do what we do, and if someone watched us every day, they'd predict our behavior. They'd study our schedules, us going to work, or going out to run errands. It's the same for this Air Force character. Their life is basically predictable.

Which means it's time to disrupt that life. And there are many inciting incidents available: they could be shot down and have to survive, they could get a call about a parent dying, maybe they get hurt using the bathroom, or they could get a promotion.

Alright, since there are way more ideas than that, let's keep it simple and use one. First, an inciting incident must change things up; no one wants to read a narrative where the same thing happens every single day. Okay, sure, you changed what they ate, and they go to sleep at different times.

But, in narrative, that doesn't change their ordinary world. The death of a parent, them getting hurt, etc., moves the character into a new direction. One they must solve in order to get back to their ordinary world.

However, this is the thing: eventually, they'll realize they can't go back to their ordinary world. Because by Act 2, they're in a new world, and by the end of Act 3, they've changed as a person.

But, Thomas, what about those with a flat arc?

Their situation still changes. Okay, sure, maybe their parent dies and the character wasn't close to them. Does that mean their ordinary world stays the same? Nope. They're now in a world with no parent—even if they're okay with the death of said parent. If it helps, think of it as the circumstances have changed, and it can never go back to what it was.

And an inciting incident is needed in every first act: its disruption creates the central problem that drives the narrative forward. The air force pilot needs to go home to see their sick parent. Or, their plane is shot down. Now they need to survive. This fundamentally changes their ordinary world, and they must try and fix it, or at least deal with the shift.

They can't ignore it; otherwise, the narrative remains in their ordinary world, and nothing exciting will happen. It's another reason the rule: start in the middle exists—or more accurately, start with movement: emotional, physical, etc.

What's interesting is that everyone has an inciting incident in real life too. As kids, we go to school, come home, do homework, eat, watch TV, and go to bed: repeat. But if you move, that changes your world. You now have to find your place in the new location (fix the problem). This is why stories where a kid is uprooted from one location to the next end once they find their footing or lean into their new world as a changed person, becoming their new ordinary world.

But, Thomas, do inciting incidents have to be big events?

No, they don't. In fact, keep in mind that inciting incidents don't have to be overtly dramatic, as in the aliens arrive or a person loses their leg. Like one of the above examples, it can be a job promotion. This subtle but effective change in a protagonist's life shifts their ordinary world, creating new circumstances, new responsibilities, and new rules.

Take Little Giants. It's a simple film about two adult brothers, Danny O'Shea and his brother, Kevin. The narrative follows Danny and his relationship with his older brother. The inciting incident is simple: a coaching position opens up, and the younger, smaller brother must train the little, inept players against his brother's bigger, stronger team. This changes everything for Danny.

## 5. THE PROMISE

If you know who Brandon Sanderson is or watched his videos, he talks about the author making a promise to a reader. This promise sets expectations that need to pay off in a narrative itself, or readers will wag their finger at you.

Basically, if you mention something, you must pay it off.

However, a promise is different than a red herring or foreshadowing. In fact, a red herring doesn't have to pay off anything, but a promise tells the reader: "Hey, expect this experience."

For example, a character in a fantasy, let's call him Bob, mentions to his uncle that he saw a dragon in the southern lands and his father died using magic to destroy it. This promise tells readers that they'll see dragons (or something like a dragon) and magic (or something like magic). In fact, readers will see dragons in the southern lands when the narrative takes the protagonist there.

But, Thomas, what if I want to surprise the reader?

You can do that. But you still need to set up the potential for something. For example, I have berserkers. In fact, I mention that there are four levels to their rage and a fifth one people can't come back from. I'm promising readers that at some point in the narrative, (A) berserkers will go berserk, and (B) someone will reach the fifth level.

Alright, maybe you don't have berserkers, you're writing a romance. The promise to readers is simple: you choose this book, so expect adorable meet-cutes, a romantic relationship, and a happily ever after—for the love of God, please have

## Act 1: The Setup

a happily ever after. Why? Readers already know it's a romance (they bought the book), and thus they'll be rewarded with the perfect relationship.

Which brings me to my point: whether it is the genre itself (romance) or a specific feel, tone, idea, theme, etc. in your narrative, you're making promises to readers. And for these promises to pay off, they must be presented, in one form or another, within Act 1 and before the narrative enters Act 2.

Now, you have options in how you present it. You can seed it, or you can outright say, "I saw a damn dragon eating my sheep!" And with that, the promise to an audience has been set, the contract signed, and readers are ready to enjoy a certain kind of narrative experience.

Believe it or not, this is another reason tropes are loved; sometimes we just want to see friends to lovers, the quest, the chosen one, the hidden world, or newfound powers (oh wow, I can make pizza—it's a power, and I stand by it). A promise is a genre, ideas, tones, tropes, magic, and more. It's "Hey, you bought my book, and this is the kind of book you're going to get." So... give it to them!

# CHAPTER 7

## Setting Up The Ordinary World

### SECTION 1: SETTING UP THE ORDINARY WORLD

Just like Act 1 sets up the narrative, each act has introductions: Sections 1, 4, and 7. These sections set up their respective acts to give context to readers about the characters' circumstances at the start of each act. And like all sections, this first section of an act has three plot points to explore setting up an act's beginning.

Now, unlike how Act 1 sets up the narrative, Section 1 only sets up the first act, giving context to it and the protagonist's starting circumstances. Thus, it must set up who the characters are, their arcs, themes, and the central conflict that'll be explored over the first act.

And sure, Section 1 serves as the entrance to a narrative, but that doesn't mean all information needs to be stuffed into the full first section. Like a foyer to a grand house, Section 1 creates an impression, shaping how readers experience everything deeper within a narrative. I'd even argue that the first section of Act 1 simply lays the foundation of a narrative for you to play in as it develops.

By the end of Section 1, readers should have a clear understanding of the protagonist's identity (and other characters), the nature of their normal life, and

*The 27 Plot Point Outline: When Plot Meets Story*

the stakes raised by the disruption of their ordinary world. The beauty of the first section is that now all the context can be explored in Act 1's remaining sections.

That's right, you can explore and expand on everything you set up in the first section within the following two sections of Act 1. This'll give you room to go deeper into any of the introduced plot points, characters, and world.

Honestly, this is so important, because once you get into the craziness of the narrative, you might not get enough time, space, or quiet moments to do any heavy lifting for strengthening plot foundations, character development, and worldbuilding

What makes Section 1's exploration so powerful is the time spent within it to create emotional connections between the characters and readers, showing a protagonist's vulnerability to set the proverbial stage of their upcoming journey. You know, like the old rule to hook the readers on page one, pull them through an engaging first chapter, and make sure readers want to sit with a character for the next 81,000 words.

The 27 Plot Point Outline's Act 1, Section 1 (and its three plot points), is here to give you space to do all of the above, but also to expand on that first chapter rule. Yes, hook readers in chapter one, but let the characters and narrative expand that relationship with your readers through the first section and its three plot points. Let Section 1 hook the readers too.

Section 1 is your narrative baseline for readers, and basically by the end of Act 1, Section 1, readers should have a clear understanding of a protagonist's emotional, physical, mental, and spiritual starting points. Readers need to know who they are, their positions, goals, the world, and its rules, as well as the stakes of the plot before getting into Act 1, Section 2.

## PLOT POINT 1
## THE ORDINARY WORLD BEFORE THE DISRUPTION (INTRODUCTIONS)

As I explained above, Act 1 sets up a central conflict, and Section 1 sets up Act 1's circumstances. Which means PP1 sets up Section 1's circumstances.

Something to understand is that the 27 PPO gives you direction. Yep. A guide, if you will. Each plot point title tells you exactly what to focus the narrative

*Section 1: Setting Up The Ordinary World*

on. This focus is what you must accomplish for a plot point to be complete. They have rules, rules you can break, of course, but simple rules to take note of.

PP1: The Ordinary World Before the Disruption (Introduction).

As per PP1's name, it's the ordinary world before the disruption of PP2. Therefore, the rule is to use this first plot point to set up a normal, ordinary world of a protagonist before disrupting it.

Now, to be clear, don't explain everything in this first plot point. I mean, you can, but that's a lot of information. Instead, explain it over the span of a few chapters. And yes, you can write one chapter per plot point, but depending on the genre or your needs, that'll change.

But, Thomas, why does that change?

Some genres need a bit more setup. Epic fantasy usually has way more rules to set up than a romance novel, though that doesn't mean a romance novel won't or can't have a few chapters to explore its ordinary world.

Crime narratives might put some extra work into who the detective is before the narrative gets into the nit and grit of it all. Though, you could write a solid Chapter 1 and then jump right to Chapter 2—PP2: The Inciting Incident (the case is introduced).

Remember, there are no "you must do this" rules. They're guidelines to learn from, to pick and choose what's right for your narrative. With that said, you still need to set up an ordinary world in PP1, but how you go about it is up to you.

But, Thomas, how long and how much do I have to set up?

Enough to establish the protagonist's status quo and circumstances of their central conflict, other characters, and the world. You know, enough to earn a disruption. But, not so much that you sit in the first plot point for thirteen or more chapters. Honestly, some narratives can get away with one chapter; others need three to seven.

A quick aside: Look at the word count of your narrative. 10-15% of your word count should land at the start of PP2. 10 to 12 for more traditional narratives of about 81,000 words, and 15% for the epic, science fiction, and mysteries/crime.

*The 27 Plot Point Outline: When Plot Meets Story*

A 100,000-word narrative should land PP2 somewhere between a word count of 10,000 and 15,000 words. Again, this isn't a hard and fast rule; it's more of a concerned guideline to pay attention to. Use it to make sure a narrative keeps its momentum.

But, Thomas, it's the opening chapters. How would the momentum slow?

Just like Act 2's saggy middle syndrome, the ordinary world can fall into a slow crawl. Sure, you might get a lot of great information into the opening, and yes, readers absolutely need to know your world has werechickens in it... But... you can absolutely explore ideas in greater detail using all three Section 1 plot points instead of smooshing it all in PP1.

So, yes, Plot Point 1 introduces the ordinary world before the disruption happens: character motivations and positions and the rules of the world, but, to answer your question, the key to knowing how much is too much:

1. Was there enough context about the plot and established stakes?
2. Was there enough context about the protagonist and characters?
3. Was there enough context about the world's rules?
4. Is the narrative bogged down, feeling slow, and front-loaded?
5. Is the word count about 10-15%?
6. Does my essential information feel like an exposition dump?
7. Can I spread information across Act 1 and/or the first half of Act 2?

## PLOT POINT 2
## THE DISRUPTION OF THE ORDINARY WORLD
## (INCITING INCIDENT)

Just as all narratives have a beginning, middle, and end, each act and section must also have them—as explained in Chapter 5, The Rule of Threes. This means each section has a setup, conflict, and resolution. And since PP1 set up Section 1, it's now time to disrupt it in PP2.

PP2 is when the narrative's ordinary world is literally (no pun intended) disrupted, challenging what was set up in PP1. Without an inciting incident, the narrative never happens, and the protagonist's status quo continues on.

## Section 1: Setting Up The Ordinary World

Sure, another narrative might happen without the inciting incident, but who wants to watch a berserker farm for sixty years? At least give us a famine, for God's sake! Cue the Four Horsemen.

My point is this: you need an inciting incident. It serves as the narrative's catalyst, pushing it into motion. Without it, your ordinary world stays ordinary. I implore you to disrupt the status quo of an ordinary world, forcing a protagonist to take action. The protagonist takes action to solve the problem created by the inciting incident.

This can be as simple as a job promotion or a daughter being taken: "If you let my daughter go now, that'll be the end of it..."

Bryan Mills aside, inciting incidents present protagonists with problems or events that can't be ignored, pulling them out of their normal routine and into the central conflict.

PP2's disruption creates the first official introduction of a protagonist's central conflict, driving the narrative forward. Remember, a conflict doesn't have to be negative. Again, getting a job promotion isn't a bad thing, but it does create a problem: learning new skills, maybe having to be a boss, etc.

Strong inciting incidents significantly disrupt the protagonist's ordinary world. Happenstances, or inconveniences that don't pause or move a protagonist out of their ordinary world, aren't inciting incidents.

Stubbing a toe isn't going to change their ordinary world unless it breaks, or they trip, hitting their head. Now if they stubbed that toe on their boss's desk, knocking the coffee onto their lap... Fired!

Alright, it doesn't have to be that dramatic, but keep in mind that mild inconveniences won't change the trajectory of a protagonist's life. A disruption should force them to confront something they can't ignore or dismiss, making it impossible to continue forward with life as before.

But, Thomas, does it matter if it's a big or small event?

Nope. It's your narrative; do what you want. I'd only suggest that what you do choose has a sense of urgency. Put protagonists in situations, internally or externally, that fundamentally change them to keep narrative momentum on them, giving the protagonist agency.

*The 27 Plot Point Outline: When Plot Meets Story*

Whether an inciting incident is a job promotion or Bryan Mills running around looking like Liam Neeson as he tries to find his daughter, it must happen, or a central conflict will never show up to drive the narrative forward.

A quick aside: PP2 must raise the stakes, pushing the protagonist to deal with emotional, physical, mental, or spiritual situations. This should force them to respond, working to fix the problem and grow as a character. Characters can't grow when they're not challenged.

## PLOT POINT 3
## THE PROTAGONIST REACTS TO THE INCITING INCIDENT (FALLOUT)

Let's say it again: every narrative has a beginning, middle, and end, as well as three acts, three sections per act, and three plot points per section. This narrative cycle is a natural movement of introducing things, setting up context to challenge it all, and reframing things before resolving the narrative forward.

This means that every third plot point must wrap up associated sections, specifically to wrap up its circumstances. The third plot point is to resolve things and lead characters (and readers) to the next narrative section.

Which leads us to PP3: The Protagonist Reacts to the Inciting Incident.

This plot point is a direct reaction to the previous one. In this situation, a protagonist reacts, internally or externally, to what unfolded in the second plot point: the inciting incident. Everything that happens in PP3 is a direct fallout of the problems created by what disrupted the protagonist's world, causing them to have to take direct action and react to what's playing out.

Unlike PP4, and how it allows the characters a breather as they reflect on the inciting incident itself, PP3 keeps the urgency up. The narrative is leading to a conclusion and still dealing with what literally just happened in PP2.

Ultimately, PP3 resolves Section 1. Whereas, PP4 sets up Section 2.

Therefore, the third plot point focuses specifically on your protagonist's immediate response to the disruption. This reaction reveals their character—it's how people respond instinctively to disruptions that tells us far more about who they are than when they have time to consider their actions.

## Section 1: Setting Up The Ordinary World

Approach the immediate aftermath of a disruption with a collection of choices for the characters. PP3 is about response and adaptation, showing readers how a protagonist deals with the change and how it impacts their perspective and decisions. This is a protagonist's first real choice in the narrative. One that'll set a tone for the remaining narrative. Therefore, show how a protagonist responds to the event that has disrupted the ordinary world they knew, and let it happen both emotionally and physically to get the most out of their choices.

Here's an alien invasion narrative example:

PP1: An accountant works his mundane job. Sure, their best friend works with him, and the woman of their dreams sits at her desk to his right, but they hate their boring life, job, and boss (who doesn't?).

PP2: Their world is knocked, literally, out of whack with the arrival of aliens. The aliens take over the office building. Run! Aliens!

PP3: The protagonist runs around, trying to find a place for him and his friends to hide as people freak out... you know, from the aliens!

As you can see, they don't have much time to think. They're reacting to the fallout of the inciting incident, and it keeps them moving to find a solution, any solution to what just happened.

Okay, sure, PP2 might have the protagonist trying to avoid newly arrived aliens, but PP3 is about them reacting and taking action (agency) to avoid those aliens. In fact, PP3 had them running, but it's to find a hiding spot in response to their arrival. A narrative beat that would end once they found a hiding spot.

But, Thomas, how does this plot point bring a resolution to Section 1?

Let's break it down. If Section 1's responsibility is to acclimate readers to a protagonist's life (their ordinary world). This might happen in one, two, three, or five chapters. The trick? No oversharing during the section. Oh, remember to explain just enough context to challenge and reframe it in Act 1's middle section so readers know what's going on.

*The 27 Plot Point Outline: When Plot Meets Story*

Now, what does that look like? Well, see, PP1 gave enough context to get in and show us that they work a crap job and don't like their boss. He works with his best friend and, though reluctant on his part, has a romantic interest.

PP2 comes in and challenges his boring, comfortably mundane life with aliens. The attack reframes readers' and the protagonist's understanding of their once ordinary world: aliens exist!? But we learn something else—the protagonist is able to stay alive in the chaos all while helping their friends get to safety.

PP3 shows the protagonist running around to find a hiding spot. They eventually find one. This brings Section 1's ordinary world to a conclusion, and resolves the middle's conflict, pushing the narrative forward into Section 2.

To be clear, the resolution is that they solved the problem created by the inciting incident—they found a place to hide. The narrative momentum moves forward because now they can get their bearings and figure out what's next.

And all of this starts again in the next section, and then the next, and so on. It's a beautiful cycle of beginnings, middles, and ends.

See? It's like poetry. George Lucas and his wisdom. But seriously, the 27 PPO will continue to guide you, showing you the process of when and where things must speed up, slow down, add relevant context, break stuff, fix it, push things forward, etc. Follow the titles and the rules of each act, section, and plot point, and you'll find yourself developing a strong outline with direction.

# CHAPTER 8

## A Problem Disrupts The Protagonist's Life

### SECTION 2: A PROBLEM DISRUPTS THE PROTAGONIST'S LIFE

Section 2 moves the narrative into Act 1's conflict, giving the protagonist time to experience and explore the disruption of their ordinary world. They are forced to confront these changes head-on, challenging and reframing the context that was set up in Section 1.

Of course, each of the three plot points of Section 2 is an opportunity to play in this disruption. In other words, the problem or conflict created by the inciting incident must be solved. So what does this problem look like, how does the protagonist react to it, and what are the consequences of them taking action?

The purpose of Section 2 is for characters to move through their agency, making choices based on established information set up in Section 1. They're not in a "will they, won't they" situation in Section 2; they're in a "we must deal with this, and how will we deal with this" situation. Keep in mind that the protagonist is in a situation outside their ordinary world (or comfort zone).

By this point in the narrative, enough of who a protagonist is should be explained to readers during Section 1. Section 2 is a chance to show a character's abilities, skills, personality, and behaviors that directly relate to their response to Act 1, Section 2's conflict.

But, Thomas, why is their behavior important?

Behavior is fantastic for character growth, specifically for readers. Story gives readers that visual representation of characters, showing their development in how they move through plot and their emotional experiences and choices.

It's where we get to see who characters are and what they're made out of. Besides, who doesn't want to see what drives a protagonist, how they handle their challenges, and what they've learned?

Watching a protagonist deal with situations, making choices, etc., is how readers form an emotional connection with them, watching characters develop, shaped by their journey as the trials and tribulations move their narrative forward and their character arcs.

## PLOT POINT 4
## THE PROTAGONIST REACTS TO AND REFLECTS ON THE LONG-TERM IMPACTS OF THE INCITING INCIDENT (REFLECTION/CHOICE)

PP4 must set up a protagonist's new status quo and circumstances. The ordinary world was officially disrupted, so they (and the plot) must slow down to regroup and take a breather. And the inciting incident is no longer a sudden shock to the protagonist; thus, they now have a chance to react to and reflect on the long-term impacts of the inciting incident.

This breath is important for a few reasons:

1. The protagonist needs to catch up to what just happened to them.
2. The protagonist must understand what's at stake.
3. A protagonist must understand what their potential options are.
4. Readers also get a chance to catch up and take in what just happened.

Without these considerations, things can start feeling like things are just happening to the point where this happens, and then this happens, and then this happens. Readers could end up getting fatigued if things are moving A) too fast

## Section 2: A Problem Disrupts The Protagonist's Life

and B) not given a chance to release tension. But most importantly, pace, rhythm, and movement; this allows presented information to get absorbed. You'll need to do this from time to time throughout the entirety of the narrative.

See, at this point, Act 1, Section 1 ended, and now we're thrown into the beginning of Act 1, Section 2. Characters had dealt with the inciting incident and an immediate reaction to it. Even if it were action (aliens arrive) or emotional (the guy of their dreams asked them out), you must let it all sink in a bit more.

But, Thomas, why is this important? Can't I keep the narrative going?

That's the thing; you are keeping the narrative moving even when you're slowing things down. The readers will benefit from letting information sink in. It also helps control the pace of the narrative.

Context is key and the rule above all. Without context, the readers won't know what's going on, where characters need to go, how characters feel, etc. PP4 slows things down, yes, and readers can catch up on the new circumstances. But, more importantly, it's a chance to show characters dealing with new information and what it means for them and the long term.

Now, this doesn't mean characters sit around a campfire, singing songs, and talking about the long-term impact (though they can). It also doesn't mean it'll become a massive exposition dump, regurgitating what has happened up to this point. This isn't a five-hour Shakespeare play where audiences are coming in and out randomly, and now the narrative must catch them up.

PP4 is a chance to sit with the protagonist and watch them react to and reflect on the long-term impacts of the inciting incident. The narrative needs to show this through emotional, physical, environmental, and overall changes in circumstances.

Use this plot point as an opportunity to show a protagonist's current state after what went down in PP2 & PP3. Showing is always the better choice; telling is still important for context (though, show as often as you can). Showing characters in their new state and circumstances drives narratives forward without slowing or stopping them.

But, Thomas, how do I show that?

Let's go back to our alien invasion narrative as an example. As a recap, I'll show you the first three plot points again.

## The 27 Plot Point Outline: When Plot Meets Story

PP1: An accountant works his mundane job. Sure, their best friend works with him, and the woman of their dreams sits at her desk to his right, but they hate their boring life, job, and boss (who doesn't?).

PP2: Aliens take over the building where the protagonist works, breaking through windows as some employees transform into aliens.

PP3: The protagonist and his friends run around, trying to find a place to hide while others freak out. Employees try to avoid aliens (who wouldn't), and the three of them finally find a place to hide.

Alright, now that we've established Act 1, Section 1, we need to push on it, and according to the PP4 rules, we must set up the new circumstances. But the other rule is to have the protagonist reacting and reflecting.

PP4: The protagonist and his friends hide as they try to make sense of what's happening (you know, aliens) and formulate a plan. Aliens are rounding people up and taking over the building completely.

Now we have context for what just happened, where they are, and what's currently going on in the narrative. And through this, their behavior will develop who they are as characters, showing the readers how scared they are, who's scared of what, who's thinking of a plan, and who's comforting whom.

These questions and more should be answered, but not all of them need to be. The point is to use this opportunity to show who the characters are.

At this point, the protagonist is beyond the immediate reaction of PP3, and now they can have an intimate or emotional reaction to what has happened, what is happening, and what could potentially happen. They're grappling with their emotions, lingering on the future, or sitting in their fear of even trying to do anything about it in the first place (refusal of the call).

At this point, the protagonist should realize the inciting incident wasn't just another passing moment in their life; it changed it. In doing so, it all deepens their understanding of the stakes and how their world is different.

*Section 2: A Problem Disrupts The Protagonist's Life*

Those stakes and their experience of what had happened in PP4 lay the foundation for the decisions and choices the protagonist will make going forward.

It's this potential for new decisions and choices that will determine, or at least have the protagonist reluctantly acknowledge, that action is required. In the case of the alien invasion, the protagonist can't hide forever, and they must find a long-term solution for safety.

For the record, the protagonist doesn't have to commit to the journey ahead. However, their mindset is shifting toward taking immediate action to remedy their current circumstances. In the alien invasion, the protagonist made a choice to not die and to find long-term protection. They're not thinking, "How do we kill all the aliens?" They're thinking, "How do we live beyond today?"

Again, Act 1 has characters trying to find solutions to fix what happened in the inciting incident (unaware that they can't and it won't be fixed).

## PLOT POINT 5
## THE PROTAGONIST TAKES ACTION
## (ACTION)

It's time for the protagonist to take action, understand, or respond to the inciting incident and how it changed their ordinary world. This doesn't mean they can or will change it (because they can't, but they don't know that). This action is about trying to get through their disrupted world and coming out on the other end.

In a romance, it might be them asking the girl out, or a first date, or the first kiss, etc. Of course, what if it's an alien invasion? The protagonist searches for safety, escaping the building, and/or getting far away. In PP5 the protagonist and his group have to run around the building, hiding from the aliens collecting people, and trying to get to the exit.

Basically, it's a chance for the protagonist to go from being reactionary to having agency, taking action to "fix" their situation. Not that all protagonists are passive by nature, but they were reacting to the change the inciting incident brought. PP5 is a chance for them to shift from a passive role to an active one.

This means a protagonist now makes a conscious choice to step into the central conflict that disrupted their world and take action, rather than just letting events happen to them and around them.

## The 27 Plot Point Outline: When Plot Meets Story

And remember, behavior shows who characters are. If characters make choices, they're developing—at least it's an opportunity for them to develop, or at least it's the plot unfolding through their emotional experiences and choices.

A quick aside: narratives need tension and conflict to keep a reader engaged: will they/won't they in all romances, can Dutch defeat the Predator, and Luke didn't finish his training as he heads off to save his friends. These moments raise the stakes and create urgency.

But, Thomas, how is that important for PP5?

PP5 is in the middle of Section 2. And, in turn, it's the midpoint conflict for Act 1. Escalate stakes when moving into narrative conflicts, otherwise known as their middles. This'll happen in every scene, chapter, act, and section.

Listen, stakes rise when narratives go from PP1 to PP2, just as the stakes rise when narratives go from Section 1 to Section 2. As we know, stakes rise again when the first act slides into the second as much as when the second act moves into the third. This is true for the middle of all scenes, chapters, acts, and sections.

But, Thomas, I raise the stakes with each plot point and section?

Yes and no. Occasionally you must pull the pace back and take a break to let things breathe. This allows for context, setting up what is happening and will happen, and getting everyone on the same page enough to keep going.

What this all means is the following: yes, moving from one section to the next should raise the stakes, and moving from one plot point to another should see stakes raised again. However, some plot points give narratives a breather. Such as PP4, where you need to set up the new circumstances of Section 2.

But, Thomas, you just said to raise the stakes when switching from one section to another. And PP4 starts Section 2.

Correct. Stakes should rise for Section 2 as a whole, and yes, narratives must also slow down to establish context, like in PP4. To be clear, raising stakes in a narrative doesn't mean going all in and destroying the sun.

For example, aliens arrived in Act 1, Section 1, PP2. Stakes were raised from PP1 to PP2. In PP3, the protagonist tries to find a place to hide, raising the stakes once again.

## Section 2: A Problem Disrupts The Protagonist's Life

Heading into Section 2, the stakes are raised again; there are aliens trying to kill the protagonist and humans. The protagonist must survive and escape the building, find a place of safety, and protect the girl of their dreams and best friend.

The circumstances themselves have elevated the stakes of Act 1, Section 2, but PP4 still must set up where they are, what needs to happen, etc. And the stakes raised again in PP5 when they took action to get out of the building.

So, even though the stakes are raised from Section 1 into Section 2, there must be room to set up the beginning of each section, conflicts for the middle of that section, and resolutions that push the narrative forward at their ends.

# PLOT POINT 6
# THE IMMEDIATE CONSEQUENCES
# OF THE ACTION TAKEN BY THE PROTAGONIST
# (CONSEQUENCE)

Before I get into PP6, let's talk about consequences. Consequences don't have to always be bad. They're simply the results of something happening, usually after a character takes action—like they do in PP5.

> A good consequence: a girl said yes to a date with the protagonist. On that date it works out great. A bad consequence might be that she said yes, but on the date they find out they're both first cousins.

And since PP6 is where cause meets effect, your protagonist has made a decision, taken a leap, and must face the immediate consequences of that choice. The consequences, whether positive, negative, or mixed, create an essential part of storytelling: choices have repercussions (results/effects).

Additionally, whatever the character did in PP5, you have to think about raising the stakes again in PP6, allowing the most logical consequence to unfold.

But, Thomas, how are the stakes raised if the date goes well?

Oh, that's a great question. And that means you're thinking like a writer. See, positive consequences can lead to raised stakes too. Going into PP6, which is the date, the protagonist doesn't want to look foolish on the date. If they do, they might not get a second date. Therefore, there are raised stakes.

## The 27 Plot Point Outline: When Plot Meets Story

Which leads me to PP6's purpose: the immediate consequences of the action taken by the protagonist. The action taken causes a consequence (good or bad) that plays out in PP6. The protagonist might not fix the problem of those consequences, but they're dealing with the unfolding of them.

Basically, whatever actions the protagonist took in PP5, it wouldn't solve their problems; it does, however, lead to new circumstances that they must work through. I'd suggest those consequences should add a level of complication to the protagonist's journey. Their decision to take action should make their world more challenging, not less.

The dinner date might go well, but maybe someone from work shows up, asking the protagonist about a date from two nights ago. Sure, their actions taken in PP5 led to a positive result of having a date, but who knew a friend from work would show up?

Immediate consequences could also open up new questions, introduce new threats, or create unexpected obstacles (friend showing up). And hopefully these things keep the protagonist from getting comfortable. These new challenges need to add tension, raise the stakes, and make readers feel that your protagonist is in an active, changing, and challenging situation.

Now, before we conclude, as a quick reminder, PP6 is the end of Section 2 and must resolve the section, moving the narrative beyond the disrupted world, and resolve the problem created in PP5. It doesn't have to resolve it completely, but Section 2 must feel like the protagonist can't go back to it.

Additionally, Section 2's ending should give the narrative some room to connect the switch from one section to the next.

> PP6: In the alien invasion, the protagonist gets outside the building, only to find out it's consumed with lots of aliens too. More so than inside, but inside they know that they have a better chance of survival.

The resolution: their plan didn't work out; the protagonist thought they had a chance outside, but nope, so back into the building, using their knowledge of it to stay a step ahead of the aliens. This resolution moves the narrative with a forward momentum: they have a plan, and readers know what's next.

# CHAPTER 9

## The Protagonist's Life Changes Direction

### SECTION 3: THE PROTAGONIST'S LIFE CHANGES DIRECTION

This is when your narrative officially enters Act 1, Section 3. Its purpose is to resolve the first act's conflict (introduced by the inciting incident). The resolution of this conflict/problem will push the protagonist into Act 2's new world.

So, Section 1 established a protagonist's ordinary world, experiencing its disruption in Section 2, and finally, Section 3 becomes their new reality. This new reality forces the protagonist into a new direction. One they must accept.

Oh, and just because the protagonist is forced into a new direction doesn't mean it's a negative change (it could be). The truth is, it can be a positive change.

The protagonist gets a job promotion, a problem caused by PP2. In Section 2, PP4, the protagonist thought about taking it and decided to take the promotion in PP5, leading to the reality that there are a lot more responsibilities in PP6.

In Section 3, they accept their circumstance—new responsibilities; thus, the protagonist feels the pressures of their decisions and must try to find a way to earn the team's respect. This led to an unexpected twist of handling the new position as a new boss, and because of this promotion, people who got passed over hate them for it, pushing them to deal with this "hate."

*The 27 Plot Point Outline: When Plot Meets Story*

As Section 3 states, the protagonist's life changes direction. It's a turning point in the narrative, solidifying a commitment the protagonist makes (agency) to accept that their world has changed, even if they don't accept the changes.

But, Thomas, how can characters also not accept the change?

Let's say the protagonist's refrigerator breaks. A positive acceptance is accepting that the refrigerator is broken, and they replaced it. Now they'll deal with the results of how they fixed it in Section 3. And a negative acceptance is that they know it's broken but refuse to replace it, trying to fix it themselves in Section 3.

Either choice is correct if it's correct for your narrative and your characters.

But, Thomas, how does this reflect the central conflict?

The fridge breaking is the problem caused by PP2. In Section 2, PP4, the protagonist thought about what to do and decided to replace the fridge in PP5, leading to not having enough money to pay their rent in PP6.

Section 3 is when they accept their circumstance—it costs more than their rent; thus, the protagonist feels the pressures of their decisions and must try to find a way to pay for their rent. Their decisions lead them to an unexpected twist that thrusts them across the threshold of Act 1 into Act 2.

Not having enough cash-o-la for rent is the twist. Trying to find a solution leads them to get a job working extra hours with their father's best friend, which pushes them into Act 2 (where we get to see them try and make it all work).

Remember, it's in Section 3 where they step over the point of no return, leaving behind their old life and accepting their new circumstances (the new job).

## PLOT POINT 7
## THE PROTAGONIST'S LIFE CHANGES AS A RESULT OF THE ACTION THEY TOOK, CREATING PRESSURE AND STRESS (PRESSURE)

This is it, the start of Section 3. As per previous sections, every new section must raise the stakes but also set up and articulate the new circumstances. PP7 does just that, setting up context and showing the new circumstances of the protagonist.

As the rules of PP7 point out, the protagonist's life changes as a result of the action they took (in Section 2) and creates pressure and stress. The narrative

## Section 3: The Protagonist's Life Changes Direction

must show the protagonist move through the consequences of those actions as it increases the what? The stakes and urgency.

I know, you're going to ask about positive or negative stakes/urgency. The reality of any narrative is to always put characters in positions where they can make a choice. PP7 is a fantastic opportunity to place protagonists, characters in general, in situations to make choices. How you increase urgency and stakes gives characters agency to react toward it.

Here's a better way of explaining it: The Alien Invasion Narrative.

We last left our protagonist outside the building, learning that it's safer in the building they're familiar with than out in the city. The point of no return has been reached: there are aliens, and they are, without a doubt, in danger.

> PP7: Their new circumstance adds pressure and stress as they head back into the building. Where aliens continue to gather citizens and fellow employees. The protagonist and his group sneak through the building to find another hiding spot.

Narratively, the pressure and stress is that things calmed down and aliens are now clearly in control. Aliens can focus on what's going on, and if anything... or anyone tries to escape or hide... they'll die.

In the outline, PP7 is a chance to figure out where moments of tension and buildup could be added. And, one chapter could be our protagonist getting back into the building, moving upstairs, and taking an elevator. Another chapter has them move along a third floor filled with aliens. Maybe a third chapter reveals more people being held captive on a top floor, and there's nowhere to really hide.

Notice how the protagonist and their group aren't really trying to fix the problem; they're moving around it, and the context of their situation is explored.

Now here's the thing: the group can get spotted, having to run and hide, getting away, even jumping into an elevator to avoid the killer aliens. See, they're moving around their new circumstances, not trying to change them.

You might be saying, "But, Thomas, how are these the circumstances of the actions the character took in Section 2?"

*The 27 Plot Point Outline: When Plot Meets Story*

And you know what? That's a fair question, one I'll answer. The direct action taken in Section 2 was the protagonist and his friends tried to get out of the building. It led them outside, realizing that the city has more aliens. And now their actions drive the narrative into Section 3, placing them back in the building.

As with the alien invasion, PP7 isn't just about adding pressure, but it's an opportunity to show how a protagonist handles the increased pressure. This will come through in the choices they make. So ask yourself if they're struggling internally or externally, showing courage or intelligence, or if they're afraid.

Remember, all characters have positions, things they're capable of, and strengths and weaknesses. Anytime you can have them make choices, it shows the truth of those things through their behavior and explores who they are.

Ultimately, PP7 sets up the new circumstances leading to the resolution of Act 1, places characters in the mindset that there is no going back to their once ordinary world, and gives them agency to make choices and deal with increasing stakes, urgency, and pressure.

## PLOT POINT 8
## THE FIRST MAJOR PLOT TWIST, OR PINCH, HAPPENS (PLOT TWIST/PINCH)

The narrative is about to change and push the protagonist to keep going forward or change their understanding of their world. It all comes down to the first major plot twist, or pinch, happening.

But, Thomas, what's the difference between them, and do I need both?

You could have both, but it's okay to do either or. As for the difference, a plot twist is a significant and unexpected turn of events that drastically changes the audience's and protagonist's understanding and perspective of the narrative, the characters, and/or the previous events.

And before you ask, no, a plot twist doesn't have to be a "dun dun dun" moment (though it could be). I mean, it worked for Scooby-Doo. "And I would have gotten away with it, too, if it weren't for those meddling kids and their dog!"

## Section 3: The Protagonist's Life Changes Direction

Plot twists change how we understand any information presented in the narrative, giving us a new perspective on it. Keep in mind, this isn't an end of the movie plot twist like in The Sixth Sense, Fight Club, or The Usual Suspects.

These plot twists move the narrative, pushing protagonists to rethink what they knew (and readers). And it doesn't have to be bad. Again, it could be a random moment for the protagonist.

The consequences could be a job promotion to spite someone saying they deserve it, and the boss points to the protagonist and says, "This moron can do your job. You know what? You're fired! Bob, you're the new District Manager!"

The Truman Show is a nice plot twist for the protagonist. Truman just realized something is different, off. It's not a dun dun dun moment—it's enough to still get him to question everything he knew up to that point.

Now, a pinch reminds the protagonist (and readers) about the existing conflict, which in turn increases urgency and danger. Pinches show, rather than tell, the power of the opposition.

Again, like with plot twists, it's not about major pinches, as this is Act 1, but you can. It's all relative. Though, I'd remind you that every section elevates the narrative's stakes. So if you elevate the stakes too high at the end of the first act, where can you go from there?

Star Wars: A New Hope has a great pinch. It's not too out of this world (no pun intended), but it reminds the character and the audience that they're in danger. Luke returns home to find his Aunt Beru and Uncle Owen murdered by the Imperial Stormtroopers. Oh, they can kill two helpless old farmers, but when their shots need to matter, they can't hit sh—Where was I? Oh yes. Luke...

This Act 1 pinch reminds us that the Empire's force is searching for the droids, they won't hesitate, and no one's safe. The Empire is terrifying, powerful, and ruthless, as shown in their effort (behavior). It also takes Luke's last reason to stay on Tatooine away (oh, spoiler alert).

But, Thomas, what about the alien invasion narrative?

> PP8: Oh? Well, Bob and his friends find the boss that he hates. He's wounded. While helping him, Bob notices he's bleeding blue blood, not red blood, exposing the truth: his boss is an alien.

*The 27 Plot Point Outline: When Plot Meets Story*

This reveal is a full plot twist, reframing and challenging what the reader and the protagonist believed and understood. Sure aliens exist, but also their boss too? All information up to this point suggested one thing, and now it's different, new, and changes how they understand their world.

A pinch might be where the aliens discover the group and take one or all of them into custody. Or, while hiding, they find people in custody, and as they try to help them, the aliens kill the group of people being held captive.

Ultimately, PP8 is where narratives take a turn, either adding a surprise element or complication into the mix, leading to the realization that the situation is more complex than initially thought—which, as we know, is a chance to show who protagonists are through behavior (agency and choices).

Both plot twists, or pinches, serve a purpose beyond surprise. It propels the narrative's central conflict forward. If PP8 reframes or reminds them of the antagonist force, it's an emotional reaction, pushing protagonists to no longer ignore their new circumstances. This forces them to change their plans, seek new allies, or dig deeper into the central conflict to figure out what to do.

Whatever the twist/pinch does, know that your job as a writer is to ask questions, think about the situations, and give yourself multiple options to pull the plot around in engaging and interesting ways. PP8 is a chance to shake things up, shift things around, and play with your narrative. So have fun; after all, if you don't like the options, you can come up with new ones.

Do you know why? Because it's all made up, nothing ever needs to stay on the page just because you wrote it down. Great writing is rewriting!

## PLOT POINT 9
## BECAUSE OF THE PLOT TWIST OR PINCH, THE PROTAGONIST IS PUSHED INTO A NEW WORLD (PUSHED)

PP9 brings a resolution to both Section 3 and Act 1. And yes, PP9 has the heavy lifting of resolving the full first act, giving closure to it, and pushing the narrative into Act 2. The goal here is to bring closure to the string of events from Act 1 and also Section 3, resolving any problems or conflicts that had arisen.

## Section 3: The Protagonist's Life Changes Direction

But, Thomas, isn't the resolution the same for both?
Not entirely, but here's a good way to look at it.

In the alien invasion, the narrative focuses on Bob's mundane life, an accountant who's tossed from his comfort zone when the aliens arrive. Act 1 sets things up for the central conflict, but the first act's central onflict is different from Section 3's conflict.

Yeah, sure, the narrative begins with the protagonist: he doesn't like his job, hates his boss, and works with his best friend... Oh, and he loves a coworker, but he's just not told her yet. The conflict of Act 1: aliens show up and disrupt the protagonist's ordinary world, and now the protagonist must try to survive.

The central conflict isn't the alien invasion, though the invasion will still play out over three acts. The CC is the protagonist's central character arc, which is less about an alien invasion and more about the evolution from being passive to being proactive as they try to stop the alien invasion. After all, he found out the world is not what he thought it was.

Section 3's conflict is straightforward:

The protagonist moves around a world he once knew, learning a few things on the way, one being that the building is taken over by aliens, as is the city. Oh, plus, his boss is an alien who's been living here for a while and, over time, has learned to appreciate humankind.

This resolution places the protagonist in a new state of mind.
But, Thomas, how do I resolve Section 3 and Act 1?
Well, here's the thing: whatever your protagonist learns from the twist or pinch in PP8, their emotional reaction will unfold over PP9. Having learned it in PP8, they now sit with it in PP9. By the end of Section 3, a protagonist should experience a change in their direction, causing them to reconcile with it.

And yes, protagonists can question, challenge, and resist change, and in turn, explore it in Act 2 (but PP9 is about dealing with what they learned).

## The 27 Plot Point Outline: When Plot Meets Story

A quick aside: when protagonists react to PP9, it doesn't have to be a negative response. I mean, a twist could easily be that a protagonist always loved a woman and learns that she always loved him (only to find out ten years after he fell for her).

At least they can date now. Yay! Where was I? Oh yes, twists. So, sure, the aside is a positive twist, but in PP9, they'd still need to deal with the reality of this information: oh, she always loved me—why didn't I just make a move back then? So much time has passed and been lost because I didn't just ask.

Which brings us to the other major resolve that must happen at the end of Section 3, Plot Point 9: the final resolution of Act 1.

This final resolution of Act 1 will push protagonists into the second act by reframing their understanding. This new framing leads them across Act 1's threshold and into the second act. As stated in the title of PP9, "Because of the twist/pinch, they're pushed into the new world of Act 2."

Think of PP9 as a chance to show the protagonist transitioning, being propelled forward by the consequences of the twist/pinch and circumstances. Remember, after this plot point, protagonists can never return back to their previous circumstances. That door has closed forever, and they've officially passed the point of no return. Goodbye ordinary world, hello new world.

# CHAPTER 10

## Act 2: The Conflict

**ACT 2: THE CONFLICT**

If Act 1 sets up a narrative, Act 2 challenges it, breaks it, and pushes it to another level. Whatever it does, a narrative's stakes are raised, urgency is felt, and character positions are tested, seeing if they'll change completely, somewhat, or not at all in what they hold beliefs in.

That's a lot to think about for an introduction passage. Let's slow down, back it up, and go a little at a time. First, remember that Act 1 sets up the context. In Act 2, you challenge that context (when and where you can).

Act 1's context should be vague but informative: enough to understand, but not enough to give away all the answers. Besides, this allows you a chance to build upon that context in Act 2, tacking on new information when and where you can to reframe it. Basically, adding new context to who a protagonist is, the characters in general, and their new circumstances.

If you did your job correctly in Act 1, you should see some payoff over the course of the second act. That payoff reveals new information, changing how readers and the characters understand things, or maybe it's all about exposing a truth while opening up new questions (my favorite).

*The 27 Plot Point Outline: When Plot Meets Story*

But, Thomas, do I have to do that for everything I set up in Act 1?

Yes and no. Remember I said to not front-load your narrative in Act 1, dumping all the exposition out? Same thing with Act 2. Spread new context over the course of Act 2 (well, the first half of it). This gives new information a chance to breathe and reduces the chance of a saggy middle.

Oh yes, the saggy middle. I still have nightmares about the saggy middle crisis of aught seven. It's best not to talk about it. But, you might be wondering, "Thomas, what is a saggy middle?" Well, let me tell you.

Saggy middle is when Act 2's narrative momentum lags, stops, and feels saggy, drawn out, and like nothing is happening. It's a common occurrence for most newer writers and causes less engagement in a narrative for readers. Usually, if not always, it kills a narrative in its tracks.

Basically, this is where most books are tossed into the DNF pile. And no author wants to hear that their book was just another book a reader didn't finish.

But, Thomas, why does that happen? It happens in my books too.

It's okay that you're experiencing it. It's something that happens even to the greatest of authors writing their first, second, or third drafts. The good news is that it can be fixed with a bit of work. Because great writing is rewriting!

Which brings us back to vague but informative. This concept is great for keeping a second act interesting. All you do is add new context that reframes and challenges established context through a new lens. It's engaging because readers love learning new things and getting a clearer picture of older stuff, but also, it lets them discover the world and not have their hand held as they're pulled along.

What I mean is, don't fall into exposition dumps, revising the same ideas of Act 1, or feeling like you must explain every single thing to your reader. At the end of the day, they want to feel like they're in on the discovery. Plain and simple, Act 2 is a chance to recontextualize what was set up in Act 1.

## CHALLENGING THE NARRATIVE

Repeat after me, "When in doubt, challenge, challenge, challenge!" None of that rhymed, yet it remains true. This following list will guide you to get the most out of Act 2 and character evolution and development, advancing the plot forward.

## Act 2: The Conflict

Oh, you want Sherlock Holmes' flat arcs? It'll help build your world and tension around those arcs too.

My point is this: Act 2 takes what was set up in Act 1, challenges it, plays with it, breaks it, and elevates the stakes, giving the protagonist a chance to make choices (agency).

## 1. THE CONFLICT

Raise the stakes.

That might've been a bit too vague but informative; you probably want me to go into that a bit more. Here, like I've mentioned more than enough times, every narrative has a beginning, middle… well, you know the rest. The second act is, without a doubt, the middle of your narrative, and therefore, it's the conflict of your narrative. Though Act 2 has its own narrative arc (as all acts do), it must also serve as the conflict of the bigger picture of the central conflict too.

And as we all know, stakes must be raised, create urgency, and push back on the protagonist, characters, and the narrative itself.

For example, in the alien invasion, the first act set up the protagonist's central character arc, his love interest, his best friend, and the boss he hates. Act 1 revealed a city overtaken by aliens and that his boss is an alien, who then tells the protagonist that the aliens are here to take over the world, muhahaha.

But, Thomas, what does that mean for Act 2?

> The second act is taken in a new direction as the protagonist deals with an overrun city. Now in the valley of the beast, the protagonist explores their new circumstances, potential abilities (I'll get to that), and how the military can't stop the aliens.

The stakes have been properly, and within reason, raised. It's all relative, remember? And in this situation, Act 2 will have the protagonist deal with their new reality one step at a time while changing their understanding of the world.

For your narrative, take what you set up in Act 1 and place higher stakes on whatever circumstances the characters were in and/or are moving into.

*The 27 Plot Point Outline: When Plot Meets Story*

But, Thomas, I'm not writing an alien invasion narrative. My narrative is much more about the characters, you know, people and everyday circumstances.

Oh, great! I love that. What about this:

A mechanic runs their local shop and learns about a franchise garage coming in, pushing her to go back into trade school to learn about electric hybrid cars. Why? All her regular customers have been going to the new place: you can't pass up those lower prices!

This situation raises the stakes. She could lose her place, so she must take drastic measures to learn a new skill and go outside of her comfort zone, trying to compete with the franchise prices.

Maybe you're writing a noir, and in Act 2 the character learns that the seemingly easy blackmail case they were investigating goes far beyond that. People in power are involved in a greater depth of all crime happening in their city.

Whatever you make your narrative about, take any established context and break it, toss it around, play with it, and give it a conflict that challenges what the protagonist knows about it and their comfort zone.

And again, it doesn't have to be aliens coming to Earth. It can be, but it can also just be two people who found one another at a local deli, started dating, and now it's getting serious. Welcome to the raised stakes of Act 2: will they last, or will Reuben Feffer try to keep up with Polly Prince in Along Came Polly?

## 2. CHALLENGE THE CONTEXT

Yeah, I know, I spoke about this in the chapter introduction, but let's dive deeper into challenging and reframing context, characters, and circumstances. And to be honest, this is one of five elements that'll help you fix saggy middle syndrome, the first being "the conflict" above.

Engaging narratives are formed by building tension, stakes, and urgency. And how and where might you build those things? The secret is to create natural opportunities for characters to experience tension, stakes, and urgency.

But, Thomas, how do I create natural opportunities?

## Act 2: The Conflict

First begin with what context you set up for plot points, characters and their positions, and, of course, any worldbuilding. If Act 1 sets up that Bob needs to find the Sword of Bloop Bloop, Act 2 makes it difficult to find the sword.

But, Thomas, how do I make it difficult to find the sword?

Give characters obstacles. These obstacles can be as small as Bob needing to gather information on how to get the sword or as big as traveling across the Misty Mountains via the Redhorn Pass only to hit a snowstorm and rockfall and now having to go through the Mines of Moria (please keep an eye on Pippin).

It's not only about finding ways to challenge the context of information, goals, or plot points: that, by itself, can become boring and repetitive. Instead, think about the characters and what was set up for them. In Act 1, it should have been explained what each character is capable of, to then challenge their limits.

But, Thomas, should I really challenge everything and anything I bring up about characters, even if I show a character being capable of riding a horse?

Well, yes and no. If a character's great or really bad at riding a horse, then yes. If they're average at riding six white horses when they come, then no. I mean, you could—you can do anything you want. It's your story. But think about what they're truly capable of (or not capable of) and challenge it.

Do they have a specific skill (fencing, dancing, flirting), an ability (mage, superpowers, not ticklish, can travel through a stone rock to find Jamie Fraser), or a collection of traits (leadership, bravery, kindness)?

Act 2 is where you ask yourself, are they not good at said skill, ability, or trait? Maybe they are amazing at each skill, ability, or trait. Whatever it ends up being, you need to challenge these things in the second act. Which is quite easy.

Because, whether they're really good or bad at something, getting to watch them use it in high-stress situations is interesting. I don't know about you, but if I had a particular set of skills, skills I've acquired over a very long career. Skills that make me a nightmare for people like you... I'd want to see them play out as much as I can. Unless it's fifteen cuts in six seconds of screen time to watch Liam Neeson jump over a fence.

If a character is set up in Act 1 as brave, show them being brave; more accurately, challenge their limits of being brave. How brave are they? Maybe put them in situations where their bravery is tested to the point where they break?

## *The 27 Plot Point Outline: When Plot Meets Story*

But, Thomas, what's the secret to challenging what you set up?

Ah, the straightforward part of the conversation. Do this: if you set up a character capable of doing something, now show them using what they can do to solve problems or deal with their new circumstances. Show them failing when and where you can, as well as letting them win enough to tell the audience, "Hey, this is what they're known for, but for that other thing, they have a 50/50 chance of success."

That, my friend, is how you create tension, stakes, and urgency, keeping things interesting and engaging.

Watching characters doing something they're amazing at and then doing it again... and again... and, oh, look, they did it again... Yeah, even that sentence got boring. You're a writer; challenge your characters (they won't be mad at you). Readers want to watch them trying but not always Gary Stuing or Mary Suing their way out of every situation.

In a romance, a character might think they have it all figured out when it comes to dating, but once they're in a real relationship (not casual), they'll realize there's way more to a commitment. Yes, they were capable of casually dating, getting dates with ease, and showing their dates a great time, but now it's more about partnerships, communication, and the future.

Therein lies the magic of challenging context, reframing it, breaking it, and pushing it to another level. You might be curious about how to do this, and I assure you that you'll learn more as you read the next three chapters.

As you learn more about Act 2, its sections, and plot points, challenging context means adjusting it so it influences new behavior from your protagonists and characters, causing them to make choices and potentially change positions.

This doesn't mean to have a father once believed to be dead show up out of nowhere at the start of Act 2 (though you could); it means to give the context of what the protagonist believes about their father a slight adjustment—a reframing.

Instead of a dun dun dun moment, try something a bit subtle and reframe information. For example, the protagonist has a childhood memory of spending time with their dead father. Now adjust what they knew of their father by having them learn from their much older brother that their father loved baseball.

But, Thomas, how does that challenge and reframe the context?

## Act 2: The Conflict

Because it's new information to that character that adjusts what they did know about their father and how they saw them before the revealed information, ultimately reframing their perspective of that relationship and the memory.

And you don't have to go extreme when challenging context, reframing, pushing, or breaking it. Believe it or not, a lot of smaller adjustments to context will be more entertaining than one massive push. However, everything is relative to the reveal. Which means be aware of the impact of the newly adjusted context presented to the characters.

So yes, the once-believed father can show up near the beginning of Act 2 all you want. But the characters better react to it in a way that drives the narrative through their experience... their shocking experience.

Also, reframing context that shifts the protagonist's understanding of it is not like a plot twist or pinch. It's more about them having just learned enough information to say, "This is different... but why and how?"

Breaking context takes the foundation of what is known and tears it up a bit. In fact, here's where you can play with things a bit more:

> A character is really funny, makes jokes all the time, and is known as the life of the friend's group; then out of nowhere it's revealed that they're an assassin!?

Okay, maybe not out of nowhere, like, don't do that in Act 3 or in the second half of Act 2. However, Act 2's first half can be where you start switching things up—or at least seeding it to be revealed later.

But, Thomas, how is that breaking context?

It breaks the context of what protagonists understood before the reveal. In the example, the character known for humor ends up being an assassin; this is something we didn't expect. Never heard of that happening in a narrative? Watch The Long Kiss Goodnight.

How about this movie: The Matrix? A few things are broken; the first is that he's a programmer who ends up being The One. The second thing he and the audience learn is that his world isn't a real world; it's a simulation.

Whoa.

*The 27 Plot Point Outline: When Plot Meets Story*

Maybe you don't really want to challenge context, reframe it, or break it, so you try being subtle. Subtle is where you push context to its limits a few feet at a time, testing the protagonist's and reader's understanding of it.

Example:

A son grew up watching his pacifist father be a leader among their people for over seventeen years. One day, for the first time, the father takes the son to a city. The son learns the father is a highly respected veteran of a great war, and everyone in the city knows him (a city he doesn't visit). The subtle push? The son notices his father changed his behavior from being a leader to keeping his head down.

But, Thomas, isn't that reframing?

Ah, not exactly. To be clear, the reason it's pushing is because it takes what the protagonist and readers already knew about another character and adds a little information at a time. It's not just one moment of new information. It's a bunch of smaller moments of new information that push the context further and further away from what was known or understood.

Basically, Act 2 switches things up, plays around with what is established in Act 1, and allows the protagonist and characters to make choices, fail, succeed, and discover who they really are through a series of trials and errors. If you play your cards right and add a little, shift some, and break things, you, my friend, will turn your saggy middle into a roller coaster of engagement. Whoa.

## 3. THE TRUTH OF THE LIE

"The truth of the lie is revealed." Ah yes, a major turning point for protagonists, specifically at the midpoint conflict of a narrative. This new truth will change the way protagonists perceive the lie they believed was true. Essentially causing the reversal and kicking off the second half of Act 2.

To truly understand what the truth of the lie is, we must start in Act 1.

Context, context, context. That's right, Act 1 sets up the context of the central conflict, a protagonist, the characters, and the world. And the more these

## Act 2: The Conflict

things are set up, the more they can be challenged. In the case of the midpoint, the "lie" a protagonist believes gets challenged.

This means Act 1 must deliberately set up the lie the protagonist believes about themselves and/or the world around them. You know, positions.

But, Thomas, does it have to be stated outright?

Nay. I mean, sure. Dialogue can be used, but behavior and showing are much stronger than telling readers character positions. And yes, protagonists have many positions, but not all of them will be directly linked to a central conflict.

Since the protagonist's central character arc carries a position specific to the narrative. This position is the lie they believe. In midpoint conflicts, the truth of the lie will be revealed and directly challenge the protagonist's lie, driving the narrative's momentum forward.

So yes, a protagonist can have a simple position of kind of liking the Jets, but also the central conflict is about the protagonist investigating a local heinous murder. Murder, murder! In the night air! Murder, murder! It's a nightmare!

Sorry, I'm a fan of Jekyll and Hyde. Call it a musical theater trigger.

Back to the truth of the lie. First, "I kind of like the Jets" is a position that won't be influenced by the midpoint conflict. The truth won't magically reveal the Jets to be awful, so now the protagonist should really stop liking the team.

However, the truth will reveal an important bit of information, which in turn reframes the case itself. Maybe their initial insight on the case was wrong, or the killer ends up being their half-brother. I'm looking at you, Dexter Morgan.

Though, the truth doesn't have to be a major disruption, like someone discovering that the Good Place is actually Hell—oh, spoiler alert. A subtle reveal is just as strong. The lie could be that a protagonist wants to see the world, go beyond their village, and experience the grandness of a city they remembered from their youth. Lo and behold, they make it to the city, and it's clearly not the place they once called home.

In the city example, the truth breaks and reframes their original position and foundation of their lie: the city is crap and nothing like they remember. This changes their central character arc's trajectory, causing the protagonist to want to leave the city and go home. Basically, their position drove them to reach the city. The truth creates a narrative reversal, thus a desire to leave the city.

## The 27 Plot Point Outline: When Plot Meets Story

The position shifted. It's going to happen. And like all positions, every time it's challenged, the protagonist or any character will have a reaction. Leading to them changing their position completely, somewhat, or not at all. including once the truth of the lie is revealed in the midpoint conflict. And if they don't believe it at all, they double down on their position (belief).

So, if they believe the truth of the lie, changing their position completely or somewhat, they then spend the second half of Act 2 trying to find a solution to their new truth (trying to fix, solve, or change it).

However, if they don't believe the truth that was revealed, they'll double down, and the second half of Act 2's solution is them trying to prove to others and themselves that their position is true... even though it's not.

This'll influence Act 3 in a few ways. Something we'll get more into once we reach those chapters. To make it easy, here's the gist:

Traditionally, protagonists will believe the truth of the lie somewhat or completely. Once they do, they try to find a solution for the truth they learned in the midpoint conflict. When they reach Act 3, they enter the act thinking they've found a solution to the problem and learn that it's more than meets the eye.

Now if they don't believe the truth and double down, they go into Act 3 still believing their own lie, only to learn that it's absolutely false (they're wrong). Basically, the third act's tone, behavior, and approach adjust depending on how a protagonist's positions have changed or not changed.

My suggestion to you: Think about the lie a protagonist believes.

A quick aside: You don't have to know the protagonist's lie while mapping out a short-form outline or extended outline. Sometimes, not always, but sometimes it's easier to see the lie a character believes as the narrative's plot comes together. And often the lie becomes quite apparent as you work on the narrative's story through prose and the character's emotional experiences and choices.

*Act 2: The Conflict*

As you can see, my writing process is filled with opportunities to figure things out in hindsight as you work a narrative, which means don't worry about having all the answers on day one or thirty. Worry about connecting things and making sense of it all to do right by and serve the narrative.

Great writing is rewriting, so as you do the work, figure out what the lie is and, of course, what the truth of that lie is going to be. Eventually it'll all click, and when it does click, it'll elevate your narrative tenfold.

P.S. As you develop your outline and then write your drafts, you can go back through chapters and take notes, seed the truth of the lie they believe, and adjust the behavior of a protagonist as you need. This process allows you the freedom to know that it doesn't have to be perfect at the start. You just need to start.

## 4. ONE ACT, TWO PARTS

One act, two parts is a concept that helps to reframe your approach to the second act itself. This concept isn't new; breaking a second act into two parts is common in the writing community, especially if you're doing four or six "acts."

And yes, the 27 Plot Point Outline is designed to move the narrative plot through three acts. Three acts are fine and dandy, but you can easily divide each act into A/B phases: first half and second half. Doing so gives you six acts instead of three.

I know, six acts? The truth is, as you learn about the 27 PPO, you'll start to realize how flexible it can be. With that said, "one act, two parts" specifically is going to split the second act into two phases: Act 2A and Act 2B.

Each phase has its own rules and purposes: one leading to the midpoint conflict, the other away from it.

Part 2A ascends toward the midpoint conflict, giving the protagonist a chance to explore the new world. Sure, you'll push back on the protagonist, but ultimately, the first half of the second act is about information. Information that will and should challenge the plot, characters, and the established world from the first act. In reality, let the narrative have a nice and steady rise through Act 2A.

## The 27 Plot Point Outline: When Plot Meets Story

And yes, the first half has raised stakes, but also you can have a bit of fun with Act 2A, introducing new characters, plot points, challenging positions, etc. Like I mentioned earlier in this chapter, break things, push on them, and reframe the context, but have fun doing it. You have lots of freedom in Act 2A, testing the waters alongside the protagonist.

Once you're in the second half of Act 2, a few restrictions arrive (break rules as you learn to use them). Traditionally, these restrictions are here as a guide to help vastly improve narratives, keeping them moving. Think of Act 2B as what it is: finding a solution to the problem created by the midpoint conflict.

The created problem is the truth of the lie that is revealed. It's here in the second half of the act where the restriction simply states that you shouldn't add any new, unearned information. Instead, let any new information be connected directly to the central conflict and be narratively important.

Keep the protagonist focused on trying to find solutions. Act 2B energy should increase, elevating the urgency. They need to find that solution. Anything else would feel out of place or unearned for the protagonist. Basically, don't give protagonists completely new, unexplored information where it needs more setup and context.

If you do, then the protagonist goes off course, and no one wants to follow them hunting for the perfect ice cream when aliens are filling up the city.

> A quick aside: Any new information that feels like the protagonist is starting anew might not be right for Act 2B. Sure, they could be starting anew in their search, but you shouldn't set anything new up in Act 2B since characters should solely be finding solutions.

But, Thomas, what if I need to introduce a character after the midpoint conflict, or the narrative won't resolve correctly?

Then seed that character within the first half of the narrative. This gives you fourteen plot points to do so. See, here's the thing: you have the entire first act and first half of Act 2 for seeding small things that'll lead to big results.

Seeding doesn't mean, "By the by, Bob is a vital part of the narrative, and we must find him after the midpoint conflict, or we'll lose."

## Act 2: The Conflict

I mean, you could have someone say that in the first half of a narrative, but you could also be subtle (and should be).

Maybe Bob is a scientist in a specific field, so during the narrative's first half, it's mentioned that they need a scientist of a specific field, or Oxford is mentioned in passing, and one of the main characters points out that they dropped out of that school years ago.

But, Thomas, how's that subtle?
Ah, now you're asking writer questions. If you mention, even in passing, anything that indicates a character went to Oxford, you've now earned the right to reveal it as a solution. Especially if the reveal comes after PP14.

"We need a nuclear scientist to figure out how to stop the bomb."
"Great! I know just the person for this…"

Maybe in the next chapter, the protagonist and their companions walk into a lab, and the protagonist introduces Bob:

Entering the room, Derrick hugged a man in a nice white lab coat. "This is Bob," he said. "We went to Oxford ten years ago. He's the best person I know in the field."

I exaggerated the simplicity of it for sure, but my point still remains: this info isn't coming out of nowhere. It's earned and seeded.
Make sure every reveal in a narrative can be linked back to something, anything, that gives it weight. You know, seed it. This earns victories and payoffs without slowing down the narrative's movement.
Keep new information tied to a narrative's first half, introducing new information, building on any context, and playing with that context. It's in Act 2B where the characters (and readers) want answers. Answers that start making sense for the problem created in the midpoint conflict. You know, find solutions. Answers, by the way, that keep the narrative moving toward Act 3.

*The 27 Plot Point Outline: When Plot Meets Story*

A quick aside: Don't add new information into the third act either. New information needs to set up context. New character? Context. New plot element? Context. New rules of the world? Yep, you need context. Things won't make sense or pay off without context.

# 5. GENRE PLAYGROUND

I really love the diversity that comes with Act 2. This act has the power of change, not only with character growth and development, but also you, the author, can have fun. That's right, the second act opens up opportunities to shift the tone, genre, and style of the narrative.

But, Thomas, isn't that going to be confusing to the audience?

Only if you do it in a way that's confusing. Otherwise, have you heard of The Predator? "Get to the chopper!" Well, if you've never seen it, for shame, but still, watch it. And let me tell you why you should watch it. The film begins one way and changes into something completely different in Act 2.

But, Thomas, how?

If you grew up in the 80s, then you've seen an action flick. During this time action stars emerged, like Sylvester Stallone, Bruce Willis, Sigourney Weaver, Jean-Claude Van Damme, and even Harrison Ford. Oh... did I miss anyone? I think I did... Arnold, Seven-Times Mr. Olympia Schwarzenegger.

Which brings me back to The Predator. Arnold was known for all things action flicks. How could he not? Terminator? Commando? The Running Man and Raw Deal? His biggest action flick was Hercules in New York. Well, Arnold Strong... But my point is, if he was in a film, the audience expected a very specific experience: action!

Act 2 can play with these expectations, and John McTiernan used it to his advantage when directing The Predator.

The film starts off just like any other action flick: it sets up the main characters, and they have macho moments and kill people—oh, and puns. Did I mention the puns? Stick around! You would've laughed if you had seen the movie.

## Act 2: The Conflict

This movie has it all, everything you'd expect from a completely cheesy, albeit fantastic, action film, including an impromptu in-the-air hand clasp arm wrestling match of pure manhood between Arnold and Carl Weathers.

Oh, man, it was great.

But, Thomas, what's this have to do with genre shifting?

Oh, yes. The second act shifts from an action flick to something more. It becomes an intense horror monster survival narrative with a serious dramatic presentation. The jokes vanish after the village is taken down, and then the group of action stars go from hunting to becoming the hunted. Another thing, Act 2 is reframed and leans more into the science fiction of it all too.

My point is: Act 2 is a playground for narrative opportunity. It's a new world after you leave Act 1, so have fun with new world rules. The new world is there to add new rules and tone shifts (even if only a little).

Also, you don't even have to stay within one genre shift. You can double up things and play with ideas, making it all your own. A narrative starts off as a romance and shifts into a thriller. Start a high school comedy off and shift it into a vampire flick.

To push my point home, here's a quick list of films to give a look-see.

1. From Dusk Till Dawn: Crime/hostage thriller (Vampire horror)
2. The Cabin in the Woods: Typical slasher (Satirical sci-fi)
3. Hot Fuzz: Buddy cop (Action Thriller)
4. Tusk: Comedy (Body Horror)
5. Grosse Pointe Blank: Black comedy/romance (Action thriller)

There are a lot more examples out there, and you're not restricted to any one thing or one genre. You're allowed to play around and try things, and I assure you, that's how you have fun: experiment when you can with what you can.

Besides, you can always revert back if you don't like the feel of it. There's no harm in creeping around Act 1 in a genre and changing it in Act 2.

However, I do recommend maintaining a connection within the switch from Act 1 to Act 2. Even The Predator kept it grounded in its established Act 1 rules, reframing its genre to shift them from the hunters to the hunted.

## The 27 Plot Point Outline: When Plot Meets Story

So, have fun, and do research to get a sense of how subtle the changes are or how grand they can get. Know that you don't have to change genres, but it's one of many options to think about when entering Act 2.

A quick aside: if you're stuck, having options can bring new life into an otherwise dulling narrative. Especially if it's been frustrating you. Trying and playing with new things can get the brain working.

# CHAPTER 11

## The Protagonist Explores The New World

### SECTION 4: THE PROTAGONIST EXPLORES THE NEW WORLD

Welcome to the beginning of the middle. The doors are officially opened to enter the next stage of events, starting with, yep, you guessed it: setting up a new world, its rules, and any new characters or plot beats.

You'll have the following three plot points of Section 4 to accomplish this setup and a chance to explore the new circumstances. Thus, Section 4 has the main responsibility to establish the new status quo of Act 2.

Section 4 has double duty. Hear me out: just like Act 1, Section 1 sets up both the ordinary world of the protagonist's central character arc and the first act's purpose. Section 4 sets up both the central conflict of the narrative and the new world of Act 2 itself.

See, your protagonist has left the first act and the world they once knew. By leaving that old world, they're entering a new world that has different contexts and circumstances. This new world doesn't have to be a physical location; it can be an emotional, spiritual, or mental one. Again, the new world isn't limited to being another new location, although it can certainly be one—a character could leave New York and enter LA, and that's completely fine.

## The 27 Plot Point Outline: When Plot Meets Story

However, it doesn't have to specifically be a change in location. Instead, play with their new circumstances. For example:

In a romance, Act 2 features two characters at the start of their new relationship together. Act 1 saw them living separately; then they had a meet-cute, dated a little, and now in Act 2 they took a leap and started a committed relationship.

Wait, let's play with the romance plot a bit more. Maybe Act 1 ends with them saying those three magic words, "I love you," after making love for the first time. This brings them into a new world, filled with new circumstances. Such as new emotions, context, and potential opportunities for character development. In other words, they're entering a new world.

Section 4 is also an opportunity to get creative in their new world.

How about a thriller?

Act 1 tells the narrative from the primary protagonist's perspective, but in Act 2's new world, it switches to a secondary protagonist.

Of course, you'd have to establish the secondary protagonist in Act 1 to earn the switch, but as you can see, it's not a new location; it's a new circumstance.

Whatever is established in the new world of Act 2, remember, the whole point of Section 4 is to lay out the new context, the status quo of a narrative, and the protagonist and other characters.

Another aspect of Section 4 to keep in mind is the emotional truth that carries over from Act 1. Yep, whatever happened at the conclusion of Act 1, it must follow the narrative into the new world of Act 2.

And sure, things are different now; they have to be. After all, this section is where the protagonist's world has changed. That and stakes are raised, tension should build, and you should toss the characters around a bit. I know you don't want to hurt them, but you can push them around a little. Besides, it keeps Act 2 interesting and from having a saggy middle, keeping readers turning the pages.

So push on the protagonist and other characters to keep it interesting.

*Section 4: The Protagonist Explores The New World*

Ultimately, Section 4 has a very important job:

To explain the new world, the new status quo of the protagonist, who any new characters are, and the potential for what comes next. Remember, this section must also set up the context of Act 2 itself.

# PLOT POINT 10
# THE PROTAGONIST IS INTRODUCED TO THE NEW WORLD (NEW WORLD)

Since Section 4 is the exploration of Act 2's new world, PP10 sets up its context. Hear me out with this: you'll have all three plot points to explore the new world. This includes exploring a new status quo, the characters, and circumstances. But again, you're meant to explore all of that over the course of Section 4 and its three associated plot points. You do not need to front-load exposition.

And PP10, well, it has the privilege of setting up that new world, taking it slow, and giving it all time to breathe. Basically, don't rush into Act 2 with guns blazing, though you could. Hell, you could have dragons blazing fire. My point is, you don't have to. Let things unfold with some breathing room.

Remember, you know your narrative and where it needs to go, but your readers don't. So slow narratives down to give your readers a chance to take in the context; otherwise, they won't know what's going on.

Now, keep in mind: PP10 sets up Section 4, while Section 4 itself sets up Act 2. So give the chapters within PP10 a chance to establish the new world, but use Section 4 to establish Act 2's narrative thread.

But, Thomas, what if I don't know what I need to set up?

You can write in hindsight.

Hindsight?

Yes, hindsight. As an outline develops, you'll notice certain elements that can now be seeded and distributed across earlier plot points, chapters, and scenes.

So if you originally wrote out a section, and now it must change, so be it. After all, great writing is rewriting. When you finish PP14, take note of what new world elements must be explained to pay off in the midpoint conflict.

## The 27 Plot Point Outline: When Plot Meets Story

What's fun about introducing the new world is that both the characters and readers don't know anything about these new circumstances. Characters will learn as they explore this new world (readers too), so give the characters a chance to react to this new information as they discover it—even have them question it.

But, Thomas, how does this all play out narratively?

It's time to revisit our alien narrative. Last we saw our protagonist, they learned that their city had been taken over by aliens, their building was safer than the streets, and their boss is an alien.

> PP10: The protagonist accepts the new reality of their boss being an alien, his best friend is hesitant about their chance for survival, and the dynamic with the alien boss has changed.

The new world sets up those themes and ideas to now be explored. Plus, the protagonist accepting the new reality gives them agency and a chance to make choices and choose to not give up yet. Besides, they have an ally in the alien boss, who might have insight into what's to come.

And knowing that the best friend's skeptical about potential survival, it means this position (belief) can now be challenged in Act 2. Ah, yes, the power of knowing a character's position. Muhahaha! Oh, um, of course I don't want to see the characters killed... I... I love them. More aliens!

Notice how all the alien invasion narrative ideas are written with broad, general statements. I'm not writing anything too fancy or complex. My goal is to simply understand the rhythm and movement of the narrative.

But, Thomas, I also notice the stakes don't feel raised. You said the stakes need to rise with each plot point, section, and act.

That's correct; the outlined beats in PP10 lack action, have low stakes, and are slow-paced. Raising the stakes doesn't always mean going crazy. Stakes are what the cost is for loss. The alien example shows the stakes raised by the increase in the alien's presence. This doesn't mean the protagonist can't breathe. It means they are now in a situation above their pay grade.

And remember, the protagonist just learned that his boss is also an alien at the end of Act 1, and that he must accept or push back on this truth.

*Section 4: The Protagonist Explores The New World*

Tension needs to release and build back up like a balloon to be effective, and it's these slower moments that build the context for the air to fill the balloon, or balloons, again.

Ultimately, the stakes have been raised because the aliens are in charge of the area now, danger is all around them, they don't understand their new world, and can they trust their alien boss or not? These are stakes, because all they knew has changed. This raises the stakes for the situation.

Oh sure, the protagonist accepted the new reality of an alien boss, but that dynamic can now be explored in the next chapter, or chapters within Section 4, PP10. It's not one scene, though it could be, but it's really about exploring the emotional truth of this information.

In fact, PP10 might have three chapters; in the first, they'll mull the new information over. In the second, the protagonist finds common ground. Finally, in the third chapter of PP10, the protagonist accepts the new reality of their boss being an alien.

To be fair, it could all happen in one chapter or one scene. Think of this nugget of wisdom as me opening the many doors for you to explore your outline beats. In fact, no one's forcing you to fly past ideas, dump massive information on the page, or push through character growth. Take your time when you must.

My point still stands: let things breathe in plot points, sections, chapters, scenes, and acts. You can still have a fast-paced chapter, but you must allow things to be present on the page when they appear on said page; otherwise, what's the point of them being there in the first place?

## PLOT POINT 11
## THE PROTAGONIST CAN TAKE A BREAK AND HAVE A LITTLE FUN (FUN & GAMES)

Welcome to the middle of Section 4, where the fun and games begin. PP11 gives a protagonist a break to have a little bit of fun. More importantly, it'll give readers a chance to learn a bit more about who the characters are and their backgrounds, maybe even meet a new character or two.

## The 27 Plot Point Outline: When Plot Meets Story

To be clear, "Fun & Games" doesn't mean characters are going to clock out of the narrative and go play ping pong (Balls of Fury says otherwise). I mean, yes, if you really want them to play ping pong, they can, but that's not the point of PP11. Even when they're having fun, what happens on the page needs to move the narrative's plot and character arcs forward.

A quick aside: The point of any plot point is to move things forward and not just be about things, an environment, or a parlor trick filled with fluff. A parlor trick creates spectacle for spectacle's sake, which only slows down a narrative, let alone adds anything to the plot.

But, Thomas, how would I know if it's a spectacle of importance?

Okay, picture this: Aquaman is walking toward the ocean and swigs alcohol down as rock music plays over his slow-motion strut before he slams the bottle on rocks and ocean water pops up around him.

That's spectacle. Spectacle can look cool, and honestly, often it does, but rarely (if ever) does it add anything to a narrative. Besides, spectacle will easily eat away a good chunk of your word count fast.

I'll say this much: there's a rule that breaks this rule, the Rule of Cool. Basically, the audience's willingness to suspend disbelief is directly proportional to how awesome/exciting an element in the narrative is, regardless of its logical or realistic consistency.

Back to PP11, a protagonist must take a break and have a little fun. But, as always, the second plot point in a section is its middle, the conflict. Again, not all conflicts are negative. They can be positive and still challenge protagonists.

The challenge might explore the protagonist's past, trying to get them to open up and talk about it, even though it's hard for them to deal with. Or they can learn a new skill. Find a mentor. These things challenge their status quo. Even a mentor, who comes with new lessons and ideas to think about challenge protagonists in new circumstances.

But, Thomas, how does that work with the alien invasion?

*Section 4: The Protagonist Explores The New World*

PP11: Our protagonist is given enhanced abilities due to a device his alien boss has with him. Gaining the abilities, he must learn to use them. However, there's a learning curve, and the abilities themselves don't last long (limitations).

This is a positive challenge; I mean, abilities are fun! It shows growth for the protagonist and gives them a new obstacle to overcome. Most importantly, it shows the limitations of these new abilities.

So yes, even though it's a conflict, it's not forcing characters to get hurt, threatened, or deal with near-death experiences. However, as you can see, their conflict does explicitly place them in an unfamiliar situation that challenges their capability to adapt, learn, and grow.

I'll add that this plot point has the distinct advantage of being more than a chance to go deeper into protagonists or other characters. PP11 introduces new rules to the known world, exploring additional worldbuilding and its history to expand the depth of a narrative's purpose.

Readers might even learn about the antagonist and potentially discover that one of the characters is the long-lost son of Bootstrap Bill Turner, who can end the curse in exchange for a ship.

Basically, the whole point of the fun & games plot point is knowledge, growth, and developing characters, all while moving the plot forward.

# PLOT POINT 12
# THE PROTAGONIST COMPARES THEIR CURRENT WORLD TO HOW THINGS WERE AT THE BEGINNING (JUXTAPOSITION)

"It was the best of times, it was the worst of times…" Ah, that old juxtaposition.

It's in this plot point where the protagonist compares their old ordinary world with their current, new world circumstances. Bear in mind, it doesn't need to be explained through actual conversation. In fact, I recommend staying away from comparing the differences of their worlds outright in conversation. That'll get old real quick, and not old juxtaposition old, but old old.

## The 27 Plot Point Outline: When Plot Meets Story

The strongest way to do this: show the difference. Show, don't tell. Yeah, I know, it feels cliché, and it is; therefore, I'll reframe it to show, sometimes tell. Telling is for context, but the truth remains: show the difference.

But, Thomas, um, this might be a stupid question, but, uh, what is...

Juxtaposition? First off, there are no stupid questions. Second, if we don't know something, it's our job to ask questions for clarity and also to research any new information that we learn. Because the truth is, knowing something and understanding it are not the same. With that said, here's the definition:

> Juxtaposition places two elements side by side, highlighting them in contrast to one another. E.g., a big, strong character beside a much smaller, weaker one. Or an internal emotion contrasting an external action: doing something brave while being afraid inside.

In the grand scheme of writing, you'd be surprised how often a moment of juxtaposition in general shows up randomly in a narrative—a comparison that exposes differences: a poor character walks through a wealthy neighborhood, or a character stands in a castle ruin they were forbidden to enter as a child.

However, PP12 is straightforward, and its juxtaposition will focus more on the macro differences of the narrative than the micro. This plot point is meant to specifically compare the differences between the protagonist's ordinary world (where they started) and where they currently are in Act 2.

In closing, here's how it looks in the alien narrative.

> PP12: A group of aliens attacks the protagonist. He and his friends run. And in the chaos they survive a major explosion, causing them to get hurt and realize they're not equipped to handle this. It's revealed that too much use of the abilities device could also kill them.

The juxtaposition: He was a miserable accountant who didn't even have the courage to ask his dream woman out. Now he has superpowers, fights aliens... And is literally in a whole new world... a new fantastic point of view... No one to tell us... Um, where was I? Oh yes. PP12 shows rather than tells the difference.

# CHAPTER 12

## The Crisis of the New World

**SECTION 5: THE CRISIS OF THE NEW WORLD**

This is the big, intense section of your narrative, where the outline is at its highest point of stakes, conflicts, and tensions. Section 5's three plot points build up to a midpoint conflict, present it, and cause a narrative reversal in its fallout.

The crisis of the new world isn't only the middle of the second act; it's also the middle of the protagonist's central character arc. This is when everything that was set up in the first half of the narrative is now challenged. Everything a protagonist believed, knew, or understood up to this point will be challenged, forcing them to see the truth of the lie they believed.

Of course, we'll go over what the truth of the lie is in PP14, but for now, understand that the truth of the lie is what a protagonist believes, so seed their belief into the narrative enough to prepare for the impact when they reach PP14.

But, Thomas, what am I preparing?

To flip the narrative on its edge. Okay, that sounds a bit darker than it is. A midpoint conflict doesn't necessarily need to be a significant event, but it'll always be a turning point in a narrative. And it's doing double the work in PP14: challenging what was set up in Section 5 and the protagonist's central character arc.

## The 27 Plot Point Outline: When Plot Meets Story

As the turning point for the narrative, it'll place characters in a position to question what they've believed to be true or thought possible.

Here's the thing: a midpoint conflict can be soft, just like in The Empire Strikes Back when Luke confronts Darth Vader in a vision on Dagobah. It's here that he learns that he might be on the path to the dark side.

Another soft midpoint is after years of writing letters to the state, Andy receives a donation for his Shawshank Prison library. It also came with a nice vinyl record player. Andy locked himself in the warden's office and broadcast Mozart's "The Marriage of Figaro" over the prison's PA system.

This moment is soft but deeply impactful, giving him and the inmates a moment of shared hope and beauty. However, this small act is the catalyst that triggers a series of events, which ultimately exposes the truth of the prison system and leads to the downfall of Andy's value within that system itself.

Take note of how this example directly challenges what was set up in Act 1 and Act 2's beginning. Throughout the first half of the narrative, Andy's hope is established, and he's shown walking on clouds in the courtyard. Basically, he lives in his own world, "like a man in a park without a care or worry in the world," as if something awaited him in the future.

Oh, and as a reminder, Section 5 challenges new world circumstances set up in Section 4 (the beginning of Act 2).

But, Thomas, what's set up in the beginning of Act 2?

Andy's agency leads to several important setups: he asks Red for a poster of Rita Hayworth, he's beaten by Bogs, leading to Hadley avenging Andy getting beaten, and, the biggest change, the warden takes an interest in Andy.

All of these things are set up in Section 4 as Andy tries to become part of the system. It's in Section 5 where Andy does the guards' taxes, helps the warden start an illegal infrastructure, gets thrown into solitary confinement, and has his hope challenged (but he had music to keep him company).

So use Section 5, The Crisis of the New World, to push back against the first half of the protagonist's central arc and Act 2. This turns the middle of your narrative into an emotionally charged beat that specifically flips it on its head. And you need this moment to reverse the truth of the lie, creating a new problem, one the protagonist must find a solution for in Section 6.

Section 5: *The Crisis of the New World*

# PLOT POINT 13
# THE BUILDUP TO THE MIDPOINT CONFLICT
# (BUILDUP)

Now that we understand the purpose of Section 5, let's break it down one plot point at a time, starting with PP13, The Buildup to the Midpoint Conflict.

As this is the beginning of the section, it's time to set up the context for these new circumstances. Keep in mind, beginnings are a chance to establish new elements: new changes, the status quo of the protagonist, and their emotional, physical, and mental states.

However, it's important to note that PP13 is the buildup to a narrative's midpoint conflict. Every action must have a natural cause and effect that propels the narrative and its characters toward PP14. This places weight on PP13 to set up enough context on where things are and where they're heading to earn the payoff of the midpoint conflict.

But, Thomas, how would I set up the narrative to get it to PP14?

> Jacob lifted the letter, brown and old, to his nose. He squinted in the thin veil of candlelight, orange and flickering. "Meet me where this all began, and I'll tell you everything…" The words stood out, written in a rust red, dried over months, and signed by David Hallo.

Let's pull it back a bit. "Meet me where this all began, and I'll tell you everything…" is the final beat of PP13. But getting to that letter, taking the steps to find it, is the buildup to PP14, the midpoint conflict.

It does a lot of work for a final passage in a chapter, but that's the point. In a single chapter, or multiple chapters, it must lead up to a moment that pushes the narrative forward, nudging the narrative closer to its midpoint conflict.

My example is tight and to the point for dramatic effect; a letter is found, signed by David Hallo, etc., but it also allows for questions to be answered while leaving some unanswered questions. Who's David Hallo? Where did it all begin?

When writing out your narrative, you might find yourself at the answers, getting right to the point, sort of like that passage example above. Your job is to

## The 27 Plot Point Outline: When Plot Meets Story

figure out how to get there by giving PP13 a bit more strength to push things forward in motion, narratively.

However, what if we reverse it? What if that passage starts off PP13? Ah, now the protagonist and fellow characters can spend this particular plot point figuring out those very questions: who and where.

Now you have options. That's right, narratives have options, and you're the writer who gets the chance to ask the questions and make the choices to keep things moving, flowing, and working together.

For example, starting with that passage at the beginning might take the narrative one, two, or even four chapters to explore and discover only where it first began, or both who David Hallo is and where it all began. Each chapter gives deeper context, pushing characters closer and closer toward the midpoint.

What about a third option? They won't meet David Hallo or get to the location during PP13. However, they'll discover how to get there by the end. The benefit of this option is now allowing the narrative to move forward, and PP14 is a chance to let meeting David Hallo be the reveal once they get to the location.

See? Options.

But, Thomas, I'm writing a romance novel, not a thriller.

Okay, first you must understand what the midpoint conflict is going to be and what led the characters to this point of the narrative in your romance. You might say you're a pantser and you're trying to figure out the narrative as you go. Meaning that you don't need to or know what the midpoint conflict is. Which means... How do we figure out what PP13 would look like for a romance?

In a romance, the midpoint conflict could be their first big kiss. It could be a surprise visit from an ex-boyfriend/girlfriend (no one wants that). It can be a major job opportunity for one of the characters, and it's across the country.

That's the beauty of any narrative; it can be anything you want it to be. But, once you know what it is, go back and adjust what you have to so you can play with the buildup to the midpoint conflict.

So, let's play with one or two of those as an example.

The midpoint conflict will be the big first kiss. PP13 can now be a series of perfect dates.

But, Thomas, why didn't they kiss before PP13?

## Section 5: The Crisis of the New World

That's a great writer's question. Why didn't they? Maybe they want to take it slow and get to know each other. Or a kiss on the lips is really important to them. In Pretty Woman, their first kiss is a major turning point in the narrative and for their relationship. They go from a business arrangement to something deeper. The kiss solidified their relationship, which means it must now be earned through the events of PP13.

This can even lead to the big day. A day that plays out in PP14.

How about one of the protagonists gets a major job opportunity across the country: do they take it or choose love? PP13 leads to this reveal. In doing so, the buildup happens through scenes/chapters: they have a meeting as a favor to a friend who set it up. The initial meeting goes great; nothing is finalized, it's just a meeting. Afterwards, the protagonist goes home, fantasizes about the job, but also thinks about their current relationship.

PP14? That's when the job is offered to them. Now it's not a daydream.

These examples build up to a midpoint conflict, setting up the context but also challenging their positions and feeding the lie they believe. Even though you challenge them in PP13, the midpoint conflict of PP14 directly challenges it even further—revealing the truth of the lie: the job IS their dream job.

In our alien narrative, we see that:

PP13: The alien boss has a device they can use to communicate with other sympathetic aliens. The protagonist and his group need to get it, but it's at the alien boss' apartment. It also turns out that when he used the ability device on the humans in PP11, giving them powers, it also activated a beacon of their whereabouts.

This context creates the details for their mission, a mission the narrative can play out over one, two, or even three chapters during PP13.

Chapter 1 might have them heading to the apartment, and random alien attacks affect their journey as a consequence of being on the antagonist's radar.

Chapter 2 adds another challenge; they're making sure the apartment of the alien boss is clear to head into. This could take the full chapter, searching and checking things out. Basically, they're trying to make it through the city safely.

*The 27 Plot Point Outline: When Plot Meets Story*

# PLOT POINT 14
# THE MIDPOINT CONFLICT
# (MIDPOINT)

We're at the middle of an outline, tackling both a protagonist's central character arc and Act 2, Section 5. The protagonist must deal with the crisis of their new world as a result of learning the truth of their lie. This reveal will fundamentally change things, challenging some, if not all, of what a protagonist had believed.

The challenge hits against what the protagonist understood, shifting it into a new light. It's not a twist or pinch per se, though the reveal of the truth can be those things, but narratively, it alters what was believed for the protagonist.

To be fair, the protagonist's belief can be as simple as having confidence in themselves, believing they can beat the villain, only to realize the antagonistic force has a much larger army, or as complicated as them finding out they're dying of AIDS, having believed it was something less serious.

What makes PP14 an important moment in the narrative is how it shifts two elements of your narrative: the protagonist's central character arc (CC) and Act 2's middle, Section 5. So, let me explain this with some examples.

To do this, let's look at the alien invasion. For clarity, I'll explain what two things were set up at the beginning of Act 2. This'll be the protagonist's central character arc and the purpose of Act 2, based on what Section 4 set up.

> Protagonist's Central Character Arc: The protagonist makes the shift to lead his friends to survive this alien invasion, and gaining new abilities means he might have a chance—discovering that he needs to practice using them, but using the device more could kill him.

> Act 2, Section 4: They gain the use of powers from an alien device. Having never used powers before, there's a learning curve. Ultimately they must flee an alien attack, and in an explosion during the attack, they realize they're outside their depth.

## Section 5: The Crisis of the New World

These two things are leading the narrative to the midpoint conflict based on what was set up at the start of Act 2 in Section 4. Basically, it boils down to a desperate mission to retrieve an item while being pursued by a powerful enemy, and the protagonist must master their powers to succeed.

Now, let's look at what was set up in Act 1.

Protagonist's Central Character Arc: They started out as another ordinary accountant, working as a passive observer, if you will, who was too afraid to ask out the woman of his dreams. Aliens arrive, pushing him to make desperate decisions to save his friends. In the chaos, he learns that his boss was an alien hiding as a human.

Act 1: An alien invasion is thrust upon the building and becomes a city-wide event. The protagonist's initial goal is simple survival, as would be expected from any sane person, but that changes when they learn the true identity of their boss... who is indeed an alien too.

So, now begs the question, what truth does the midpoint conflict reveal about a specific lie? Well, let's look at what happens in PP14 of the alien invasion.

PP14: The protagonist, his friends, and the alien boss arrive at the apartment. It's an ambush led by the alien commander, who is angry about their soldier's betrayal (the boss alien). A battle breaks out after he orders his execution.

The humans overuse their abilities and are weakened. Overwhelmed by the forces, the boss alien tells them to find his life partner, who also believes in humanity. He gives them proof of his message before sacrificing himself.

The Lie of Act 1: The protagonist believed that their boss couldn't be trusted and that their professed fondness for humanity was a lie.

## The 27 Plot Point Outline: When Plot Meets Story

But, Thomas, can you explain the truth of the lie?

Yes. By willingly giving their life to save the protagonist and friends, the alien boss proved that they genuinely cared for humanity. Their betrayal against their own species wasn't a lie. Their sacrifice convinces the protagonist, shifting their perspective of the lie they believed.

> The Lie of Act 2: The protagonist believed they were being hunted because "aliens kill humans." To keep themselves and their friends safe, the protagonist has to retrieve the communication device.

The truth of the lie is that the protagonist realizes that the conflict is far more personal and complex than he originally thought. The ambush was meant for the alien boss for betraying their own species. The alien commander is angry about a soldier who defected from their rank and mission.

As a little bonus, we learn there are other sympathetic aliens who don't want to take over Earth with the mention of their life partner.

Things to keep in mind when working through PP14:

1. How does the truth of the lie reshape the protagonist's beliefs?
2. Was enough context and information seeded to earn the reveal?
3. In what way does the protagonist's belief change completely, somewhat, or not at all?
4. If the protagonist's position doesn't change, how do they double down on their belief of the lie?

Whatever your answers are, know that there are more questions you can always ask yourself about every plot point in your narrative, including PP14. The trick is to think about the questions that best elevate your specific narrative goals.

At the end of the day, PP14 must allow the midpoint conflict to directly cause a shift in the narrative for the protagonist's central character arc. That shift, also known as the reversal, will then be explored in PP15, leading the protagonist to try and find a solution to that shift in Act 2, Section 6.

Simply put, a midpoint conflict disrupts the course of a narrative.

Section 5: *The Crisis of the New World*

# PLOT POINT 15
# THE IMMEDIATE REACTION
# OR CONSEQUENCE OF THE MIDPOINT CONFLICT
# (REVERSAL)

PP15 is known as the reversal, focused on the immediate reaction or consequence of the midpoint conflict. The events of this plot point unfold as a direct reaction to what physically, mentally, or spiritually happened in PP14's midpoint conflict. The protagonist must now deal with the reversal caused by the truth of the lie.

The truth of the lie challenges some or all of what the protagonist had believed up to this point in the narrative. Keep in mind they don't take action on that truth's reveal, at least not yet, as they're still processing and reacting to what had happened and what was revealed in PP14.

> A quick aside: Keep both urgency and stakes raised, maintaining a narrative's momentum. Use urgency and stakes as opportunities to challenge the protagonist—any time characters are forced to respond and make a choice is worth the word count of your narrative.

These choices show readers who characters really are. In fact, it's through pushback that you, the writer, will figure out who a character really is, what they are or aren't capable of, and if they're up to the task to reach the narrative's end.

Because PP15 is the third plot point of Section 5, it must resolve any and all context established in Section 5, moving the narrative into Section 6. However, Section 5 is considered The Crisis of the New World, making the conflict in PP14 much heavier than any other conflict or middle plot point before or after.

But, Thomas, what gives this plot point so much weight?

PP14 is both the midpoint conflict of the protagonist's central character arc and the middle of Act 2. Whatever happened in PP14 must leave a lasting effect on a protagonist that follows them into PP15.

In PP15 the protagonist explores that effect; they might try to get away from it (to regroup) or work on dealing with the narrative reversal and everything in between. The narrative goal is to keep things moving forward into Section 6.

## The 27 Plot Point Outline: When Plot Meets Story

When I say lasting effect, that doesn't mean it must be world-ending. And remember, it's all relative to the protagonist's narrative journey. Sure, their world could blow up literally or figuratively, but the truth remains: what's lasting for one person might not be so lasting for another.

PP15 is where a protagonist deals with the reveal. And again, they're not trying to solve the problem yet, just dealing with the reversal and getting far enough away to regroup: physically, mentally, or spiritually.

If we take a glance at the alien invasion, we'll see in PP15, they're dealing with the fallout of the midpoint conflict of PP14.

> PP15: The protagonist and friends are weakened after a major loss against the alien commander. As the apartment building collapses, they retreat. They hide in the rubble and appear dead to the aliens. The protagonist discovers their power device is destroyed.

As you can see, the protagonist and friends don't try to fix the problem. They're too busy dealing with the direct and immediate fallout of the midpoint conflict: being ambushed, the alien boss sacrificed, and trying to stay alive.

Writing that narrative beat out in an outline could be a few lines, maybe a paragraph. Writing it long-form? That could be one, two, or even three chapters.

You're not beholden to write a narrative out quickly or rush to the next plot point. Remember, a plot point is as it needs to be narratively in the sections and acts. The goal is to hit emotional truths, physical responses, take breaths, etc. In the case of the alien invasion, how might it all unfold?

> Chapter 1: The protagonist and friends rush through a building as it collapses, trying to avoid more aliens. Aliens search the rubble and leave when they can't find bodies. The protagonist and friends push out of the rubble and must get to safety and find refuge.

But, Thomas, isn't that a lot for one chapter?

It could be. In fact, let's cut the chapter up and control the pace a bit more. Keep in mind, shorter chapters speed up the pace; longer ones slow it down.

## Section 5: The Crisis of the New World

Chapter 1: The protagonist and friends rush through a building as it collapses, trying to avoid more aliens. The chapter ends as they're crushed under the destruction.

Chapter 2: Aliens search the rubble and leave when they can't find bodies. The protagonist and friends push out of the rubble and must get to safety and find refuge.

As you can see, I broke up the rhythm by context. The first chapter is all about the escape, keeping the focus on the action. In the second chapter, I kept it centered on the emotional response to that escape and trying to find safety.

However, both chapters keep PP15's purpose of the immediate reaction or consequence of the midpoint conflict.

If you didn't know, you can write a book that takes place over the course of one hour and still be in control of the pace using twenty-seven chapters. Each chapter would cover X amount of time. So the immediate reaction could still unfold over the course of one, two, three, or even four chapters.

It's all based on how you play it out, and is it accomplishing the needs of the plot point? If yes, great! If not, you'll have to work on the narrative within each plot point, making sure you're writing out the purpose of that plot point.

Ultimately, PP15 resolves and wraps up the crisis of the new world and pushes the protagonist forward into Section 6: Finding a Solution. So if any new and relevant points of information or context are introduced in Section 5, they need to be resolved. If they're not, then anything unresolved can be explored in the next section.

# CHAPTER 13

## Finding A Solution

**SECTION 6: FINDING A SOLUTION**

Act 2's resolution must lead a protagonist and narrative into Act 3. The narrative needs to find a solution to the problem formed from the midpoint conflict: this is the truth of the lie that was revealed in Section 5, PP14. By finding a solution, the protagonist officially moves into Act 3, ready and able to take on the final battle.

The protagonist will spend Section 6 finding a solution to the problem created by the midpoint conflict. Act 2, Section 6 ends when the protagonist has what they believe will solve the problem in Act 3's climax.

Again, a protagonist doesn't solve the problem at the conclusion of Act 2. The protagonist finds the solution or the necessary tools/information needed to potentially solve the problem in the third act (weapon, information, etc.) This solution will help them win (or sometimes lose) in the third act climax.

Over the course of Section 6's three plot points, the protagonist will find a solution to the truth that's revealed in the midpoint conflict. It was at the end of Section 5 that the protagonist learned the truth and either completely believed it, somewhat believed it, or didn't believe it at all.

## The 27 Plot Point Outline: When Plot Meets Story

Section 6 will directly challenge the revealed truth, reframing the lie the protagonist believed as they explore the new truth. If the protagonist believes the truth, their goal is to figure out how to fix what the truth has done to their world and the problem the truth created. As an example:

> A protagonist believes the city is safe, but in the midpoint conflict, it's revealed that the occupying armies are far more dangerous than they realized. Forced to fight to survive, their father is badly hurt.

The truth leaves them in a new problem: the protagonist must get their father help, or he'll die, and then get them home alive and gather their people.

> Romance: a protagonist goes on a fake date with a co-worker; while dancing and having fun, they kiss. She realizes she actually likes him.

The truth of the lie is she thought they were just having fun, being silly, and completely friends—even though in Act 1 she didn't even like him. But now the truth reveals that they're perfect for each other.

But, Thomas, what's the solution she finds?

Ah, I know, right? Romance. She doesn't want to have those feelings, so she focuses on work and vanishes (always busy). Trying to push away her growing feelings, she realizes that he's the one. She finally admits to herself and her friends that she's truly fallen in love with this guy.

As a reminder of just how a position can change completely, somewhat, or not at all, a protagonist will double down if they don't believe the truth of the lie. If they double down, they try to find a solution by trying to prove that it's not the truth and to prove to themselves (or others) that their belief is right.

In that situation, the solution usually, but not always, will result in them realizing they were wrong. In realizing this, they must now deal with the fallout of the real truth, as their lack of preparation causes more issues in the third act.

And please keep in mind that whether they believe the truth or not, it's perfectly fine for a protagonist to go into Act 3 believing what they believe. The idea of a solution is that they "believe" they have found one, not that it is one.

*Section 6: Finding A Solution*

# PLOT POINT 16
# THE PROTAGONIST REFLECTS ON THE LONG-TERM IMPACT OF THE MIDPOINT CONFLICT (CONSEQUENCE)

But, Thomas, consequences? Isn't PP16 the starting plot point for Section 6?

Yes, PP16 does start Section 6 off, setting up the new circumstances. But, you have to remember that Section 5 presented the crisis of the new world. Once all of that unfolded, a new status quo for the protagonist must be set up in PP16.

So yes, the consequences are what remain after the protagonist dealt with PP14's midpoint conflict and its fallout. Now in PP16, they must deal with that fallout, and thus Section 6, PP16, must establish what a protagonist needs, is dealing with, any and all emotional fallout caused by the midpoint conflict, etc.

After all, a protagonist could have just gotten their legs blown off in the midpoint conflict, or maybe they had their heart broken, or they married the tall, blond elven prince with the perfect abs.

Like all plot points, PP16 is an opportunity to raise the narrative stakes and force protagonists to make choices and deal with consequences. That and the solution to their midpoint problem isn't going to be easy; well, it shouldn't be easy. But the protagonist isn't just yet going to find a solution in PP16. Besides, they're still trying to accept the truth of the lie that befell them. So do they accept it somewhat, completely, or not at all? Well, that's what PP16 explores... in part.

Whatever they do, their choices will set the tone for Section 6 altogether.

But, Thomas, what does a protagonist do here?

That's the magic of narrative development; they can do anything. Really, they can literally do anything: they're in a hospital, stuck in outer space, dancing on a star, carrying moonbeams home in a jar!

However, as per each plot point's title, there are rules for them—rules that help guide a narrative, setting the foundation of what must happen, what to focus on, and the emotional truth of the narrative beat. Even if it's a protagonist teaching a class, giving birth, or riding a bike, it must be present in the context of the plot point's purpose (its rules).

Let me explain.

## The 27 Plot Point Outline: When Plot Meets Story

Plot points come with basic rules; for example, PP1 must introduce the protagonist in their ordinary world before the disruption of it all. It establishes a foundation: who the protagonist is, their motivations, the rules of the world, etc.

As a reminder, please don't go ham and present every detail you think of in one singular scene, chapter, plot point, section, or act. Let things breathe and unfold naturally over the course of a narrative.

But, Thomas, what are the rules of PP16?

> Having just learned about the truth of the lie from the midpoint conflict, the protagonist must now reflect on the long-term impact of its consequence.

And sure, those consequences can be physical: the loss of a leg. And if it ends up that way, what's their reaction to having no leg, what must happen now, what does this mean for their future, and what's the solution to fix this issue?

Looking at the alien invasion:

> PP16: The protagonist and friends find a group hiding underground after they had left the collapsed building. Hurt and wounded, these people take them in, introducing them to others who are fighting the cause and meeting those in charge of the resistance.

Ultimately the protagonist deals with their injuries, wonders if they can fight back since the device was destroyed, and learns they're not alone. They must also honor the alien boss' final wish: find their life partner.

By the way, this shouldn't be a direct scene of dialogue, though it could be, but rather a show of PP16's rules. The protagonist doesn't talk about the way their injuries are affecting them or how they need to be healed. In Star Wars EP 5, Luke heals when he's in the bacta tank. But the narrative doesn't spend time explaining what's happening or how it works.

Instead, the protagonist is in a situation where people are wrapping him up. This shows what is happening and establishes the physical consequences of what had happened to him.

## Section 6: Finding A Solution

Keep in mind that PP16 is also an opportunity to seed the potential of what's to come and a potential solution to fix the problem created in PP14—the midpoint conflict's truth of the lie being revealed.

Additionally, this plot point sets the tone for the alien invasion. Basically, they're not alone anymore and they're thinking about how it played out, the fact that their powers are gone, and their alien boss friend is dead.

But, Thomas, what does that mean for PP17?

You're jumping ahead, but I'll say this: what's set up in PP16 must then be challenged in PP17 and resolved in PP18. Simple. That's basically a reminder of the Rule of Threes. It's important to note that outlining is about knowing the finer details of what's to come and how to set up what needs to be challenged and seed how the protagonist might resolve it all. And, most of all, whatever happens in any plot point, remember, it must influence the narrative forward.

## PLOT POINT 17
## THE PROTAGONIST TAKES ACTION TO RESOLVE THE PROBLEM CREATED BY THE MIDPOINT CONFLICT (TRIALS/TESTED)

All section middle plot points are action beats: a protagonist does something or something happens to them. More often than not, the protagonist takes actions. Not that they must take action; things could happen to or around them. I'd add that when possible, giving the protagonist agency will benefit a narrative. Passive protagonists can become boring.

The action taken creates movement and narrative momentum. In PP2, the inciting incident, action creates change, disrupting the protagonist's ordinary world, forcing them to react. The midpoint conflict of PP14 actively challenges the lie the protagonist believes, forcing them to confront a new truth. In PP17, a protagonist is put through trials, testing who they are.

In Section 6, PP17, the protagonist actively tries to find solutions to the problem created by the midpoint conflict. Trials push back on the protagonist, making it difficult for them to find the solution to the problem. Of course, don't make it too easy, but also don't make it impossible.

## The 27 Plot Point Outline: When Plot Meets Story

If it is easy, at least allow the consequence of PP18 to be something they have to truly earn. It's fine if it's impossible and they're reaching their limits. All this means is that you need to give them a win in PP18. At the least, let them get through with a bit more ease.

To be fair, you need to push back on your protagonist, whether it's their positions, their behavior, or even their choices. Reader engagement comes from a protagonist's response to being challenged. If protagonists aren't given a chance to respond to challenges, it's hard to see growth and, more importantly, for the reader to root for them.

But, Thomas, what exactly are the trials that test a protagonist in PP17?

Have you heard of The Twelve Labors of Hercules? It's a series of tasks imposed on the hero Hercules by King Eurystheus. He's tasked to take on these trials and tested as penance for killing the king's family. Through each of these labors, Hercules' strength, courage, and wit are tested.

If you've ever read or watched any version of Hercules, you know Xena: The Warrior Princess is a much better show. Oh wait, no, that's not what I was going to say... I was saying, if you've ever seen any version of the twelve labors of Hercules, you know he's pitted against mythical creatures and challenging tests.

Am I telling you to have your protagonist fight the Nemean Lion or the Cattle of Geryon? No. Am I telling you that your protagonist should have twelve trials, testing them as they try to find a solution to the problem introduced in the midpoint conflict? Maybe. But really, it can be one major trial that tests them, or it can be three, six, ten, twelve, or whatever your narrative needs it to be.

You're the author; it's up to you on how your protagonist is tested. And again, a plot point isn't the length of a chapter. A plot point is the guided rules of what must happen in chapters within that plot point.

> A quick aside: Who is your character? What are their strengths and weaknesses? What are their positions? How did they react to the truth of the lie being revealed? Their trials and tests should challenge these things and help them find the solution itself.

Basically, use what you set up in the narrative to influence the trials.

## Section 6: Finding A Solution

Still, my advice is to not go overboard, but don't make it so easy that the protagonist walks into a room with a minotaur and tells them, "Hey, minotaur, I need to, uh, you know, get the Sword of Bloop Bloop over there to stop the big, evil, scary, and strong villain, Bob," and the beast smiles, handing Sir Derrick the Sword of Bloop Bloop. Oh wait, this is an epic fantasy: Sir Derrhick.

Taking a look at our alien invasion:

PP17: The protagonist stands with human reinforcements, who are ready to head in and attack the aliens—the goal is to rescue the life partner. The attempt leads to the humans losing, most killed in the debacle, and the best friend is captured.

For the record, the protagonist could have easily done all of this in one chapter. But what if they had extra trials to test their mettle? How about this:

Chapter 1: Trial one is them trying to obtain plans to attack the base.

Chapter 2: Trial two is to find the life partner's location.

Chapter 3: The final trial is them running in to save the life partner, only for the narrative to play out as originally written above.

That's three chapters, maybe even four if we break things up a little more. Another tool at your fingertips is that you can do it in more chapters if you have multiple scenes and like using chapters to create smaller cuts to those scenes. It really comes down to the pace you're looking for narratively.

My point is, whatever you choose to do for your narrative, a plot point is at minimum a single chapter, but it's allowed to be more for the protagonist's central character arc. And remember, you can have more than one trial challenge your protagonist.

Romance novels might have the trials showing the protagonist trying to win back the affection of the woman/man they lost. Crime gets an investigator to experience clues through the hardest reveals. It's all relative to your narrative.

## PLOT POINT 18
## DESPITE THE SETBACKS, THE PROTAGONIST
## DECIDES THEY WILL SUCCEED NO MATTER WHAT
## (DEDICATION)

PP18 has a double resolution: Section 6 and Act 2. Each pushes the narrative into Act 3. How they resolve it is based on the specific setup in your outline. PP18's conclusion is attached to the protagonist's central character arc—a direct link to the problem created by the midpoint conflict.

Section 6's double resolution prepares a protagonist for Act 3. It's at this point a protagonist believes they've found the solution to the problem created by the midpoint conflict. In this belief, they're committed to fixing the problem in Act 3. This choice works best when driven by a protagonist's agency. What they don't realize is that it'll take way more effort to solve the problem in Act 3.

Things to realize about PP18. A protagonist is working through having just passed a series of trials that challenged them and their new beliefs (or lack of). Whatever a protagonist's emotional, mental, or spiritual status is, PP18 ends with them completely dedicated to fixing the problem with the solution they found.

Again, they may've found an actual solution, but fixing the problem will take a lot more effort to accomplish in Act 3. However, they may not believe the truth of the lie. Therefore, they're going into Act 3 under false pretenses; their lie is correct. The consequences in the third act prove to the protagonist that they were indeed wrong.

This new perspective comes from a protagonist learning something new, gaining new skills or information, or accepting that their next step is going to be a sacrifice for the good of all life. By accepting this new reality, they truly commit themselves to the final confrontation—no matter the cost.

I love how PP18 reframes what happened in the narrative. Good or bad, positive or negative, a protagonist must and does find a new way forward. As the first act has a point of no return due to circumstances, this plot point has one due to a protagonist making a conscious decision and following the path to the end. It is here that they control the agency to that commitment. Therefore, it's a truly powerful narrative moment to think about and not just another "beat."

## Section 6: Finding A Solution

I know, it's a lot. It should be. A lot is riding on this moment. Okay, not a lot-lot, but enough for you to say, "They were forced over a point of no return earlier, but this time they're making a choice knowing it could end forever."

But, Thomas, that sounds drastic. I'm writing a romance with a happily ever after. I'm not sure it's going to be so dark.

That's true. Here's an important detail: what seems dark is actually more about a deeper commitment or dedication. To be blunt, in a romance, maybe the protagonist doesn't care if they fail miserably when they go to confess their love because they have to try no matter what. The need to try no matter the cost to their ego, peace, or self-worth is what PP18 brings to the table.

It's time to give it my last shot, professing my love to them.

Sure, your narrative will have its happily ever after romance. Everything's in place, except the woman decided to play it safe and marry a wealthy guy, since their parents really love him. Now the protagonist, the bad boy author with long, flowing hair and a thick beard, crashes the wedding and professes their love.

He knows his choice is a massive risk. She might say yes, but if he fails, he knows there's no coming back. When he shows up at the temple, in front of all those friends and family, and says, "I love you," only for her to say no... Well... it has ended forever.

But, Thomas, that's not a happily ever after.

Correct. It's not. But the protagonist doesn't know the outcome. They didn't get an advance copy of the manuscript beforehand. All they know in PP18 and their heart is that they're committed to the worst potential no, hoping she'll give them a life-changing yes—no matter the cost.

"Claire, I'm not standing here asking you to marry me. I'm just asking you... not to marry him. And maybe take a walk."

See? It'll all work out for your narrative's happily ever after.

However, maybe you're writing the next version of Rocky... or Rambo. In that case, PP18 could be as straightforward and easy as gathering resources, a final training montage, or a quiet moment of resolve where they dedicate all they are to the cause (no matter the cost).

After all, most times, you want the character to have a sense of potential in them as they head off into Act 3. It keeps the energy up and adds to engagement.

## *The 27 Plot Point Outline: When Plot Meets Story*

But, Thomas, what about the alien invasion narrative?

Oh, yes, I almost forgot. We last left our protagonist sitting in a loss, and their best friend had been taken prisoner... oh, and the friend learned that the life partner was working for the antagonist. This leaves us with PP18:

PP18: The protagonist emotionally deals with the fact that his best friend was taken and he lost his human allies. Despite wanting to go in alone to keep more people from dying, the remaining humans create a distraction so he can infiltrate the alien headquarters.

The best friend is processed, surrounded by aliens, and led by the life partner. The best friend talks with her, trying to convince her that they knew the alien boss she loved. She doesn't trust him and eventually decides to search for the protagonist and help him.

But, Thomas, where's the double resolution?

Protagonist's Central Character Arc: They meet a human resistance group underground (setup), he attacks the aliens head-on, and his best friend is captured (challenge). With the help of the humans, he infiltrates the alien headquarters to save his best friend (resolution).

Section 6's resolution is tied directly to PP16 and PP17:

Act 2, Section 6, PP18: The protagonist must find the alien boss's life partner, save his friend, and defeat the aliens. The act concludes when the solution is in place for Act 3 as he heads into the ship.

In closing, remember that no rule is a law written in stone, and all rules are meant to be broken once you understand them. So experiment with ideas, play with rules, break stuff, and mold them into what's needed.

Now, just like the protagonist, it's your turn to get ready and commit to the next chapters in this book, learning about Act 3! You got this.

# CHAPTER 14

## Act 3: The Resolution

### ACT 3: THE RESOLUTION

The first rule of Act 3 is "you don't talk about Fight Club…"

Now that I have your attention, the inevitable just happened, and I did it on purpose: new information made this chapter opening confusing. This means that rule numero uno is "don't add new information to Act 3."

Act 3 isn't the time for big exposition dumps, new missions from out of nowhere, or new characters popping up from Bumble Funk, Nebraska. Oh sure, it's nice this time of year in Bumble Funk, Nebraska—but new information, new characters, all of it, should've been learned about during the narrative's first half, up to the midpoint of Act 2.

But, Thomas, I can't introduce anything new in Act 3?

Correct. Don't add anything new unless it's been seeded, foreshadowed, or hinted at already. Basically, stick with what the protagonist and readers know.

That doesn't mean you can't expand on what information came before a third act. Just don't add new, unexplored information. If the fall of the first war is introduced in the narrative's first half and mentions that it led to the downfall of an ancient civilization of giants, then you can use it in Act 3.

## The 27 Plot Point Outline: When Plot Meets Story

Yep, that's right. Now giants can come in during the climax. After all, it's basically Chekhov's gun. Clears throat: setup and payoff.

The third act must focus on resolving existing conflicts, not introducing new ones. Adding new information means you'll have to rush the context to pay it off, which feels unearned. You can't or won't be able to maintain a strong pace if dense information needs to add extended context in a short time.

In the end, literally, keep the momentum forward, avoiding unnecessary exposition dumps (unless you put $2 in the exposition jar). Doing this can, and most likely will, derail the emotional impact of the climax.

Which leads to rule two: resolve the narrative in the third act, wrapping things up. You don't have to go home, but you can't stay here.

Act 3, like all acts, raises the stakes, tension, and urgency, keeping things moving fast. Fast movement is one of the reasons Act 3 is traditionally half the size of Act 2 (most times): fewer chapters, fewer words, and less of everything, really. It's about getting to the point and paying everything off.

It's never the time for new things that were never mentioned.

Besides, Act 1 might be as long as Act 3, at times longer, but it's dense. It introduces a protagonist, their world, characters, and a central conflict, which is usually, if not always, the protagonist's central character arc.

Act 2 is typically twice as long as the first and third acts and broken into two parts: the rise to and the fall from the midpoint conflict. It has a lot of work to do, challenging the protagonist and other characters and creating the problem in the midpoint conflict. After a midpoint conflict, the protagonist must find a solution to the problem created by the midpoint conflict.

Basically, a lot happens in Act 2. Therefore, it's a large part of a narrative.

Act 3? The heavy lifting was accomplished in the first act and challenged in the second, leaving the narrative to do one thing: focus on a resolution. Yep, it's time that every third act chapter, scene, and choice the protagonist makes leads a narrative to resolve, resolve, resolve.

P.S. The resolution should have a major payoff.

But, Thomas, I want to add color to my plot, characters, and world.

Do it. Have fun. In fact, I recommend doing what you want as a creator. All I'm saying is limit new exposition or worldbuilding to narrative momentum.

*Act 3: The Resolution*

But, Thomas, what's narrative momentum?

The protagonist runs up to the spaceship's control panel, opening three of them, and presses buttons, trying to turn off the alarm.
"If we don't get this alarm to stop, the whole ship will blow up."
"Wait, are there any escape pods?" his friend asked.
They check a control panel, and the protagonist looks up. "One."

Not only does this situation elevate the stakes, as one must stay behind, but it also keeps the narrative momentum moving forward. As you can see, this is technically new information. The escape pod wasn't introduced until this very moment. However, a quick seed in Act 2 about planet jumper ships sucking for only having one escape pod would have a stronger impact.

If you feel that you must absolutely add new information without any seeding (I recommend seeding), then do so, but keep things moving as I did with the example, and continue raising the stakes with each tidbit of information. Act 3, without raised stakes, is like a pool on a hot desert summer day with no water.

However, Act 3 should feel like it's getting hot since it's the most intense and suspenseful moment of a narrative. It's the moment with the highest stakes for a protagonist in a narrative. And yeah, you want to challenge them in Act 2 to test the limits of what Act 1 set up, but the third act is where you challenge the protagonist's mettle, pushing them to their breaking point and beyond.

I know I'm repeating myself, trying to drill it in about stakes, urgency, and the importance of keeping things moving to resolve, resolve, resolve. But you must remember, Act 3 is the end of your narrative. And you can't keep it going, no matter how much you want to. And despite the name, The NeverEnding Story isn't actually an infinite amount of pages; it ends, just like your narrative should.

But, Thomas, In Search of Lost Time, written by Marcel Proust, had a word count of 1,267,069.

Yes, and he's in the Guinness World Records. Yet, that book is still often published in multiple volumes and not one massive tome. The next largest book is Poor Fellow My Country, written by Xavier Herbert, with 852,000 words. But let's be clear, outliers aren't the norm, and I'll be the first to say, "Write the book's

## The 27 Plot Point Outline: When Plot Meets Story

first draft without looking at its word count. Once you're finished, edit down the book if its count is over the moon."

You'll have to resolve the book sometime. When you do, make sure it's a strong resolution, not just at the very end, but throughout Act 3. Pay things off, deliver on any promises you set up, and allow the last third of Act 3 to focus on the protagonist's central character arc's resolution (the climax).

When you do get to the very end, offer closure, real closure. Not, "They beat the antagonist and lived happily ever after!" Okay, you can do that if you want. It's your book. I'm just advising that you should provide a sense of closure for the protagonist, but most of all, the reader. You want them to feel good about reading your book, even if it ends on a down note.

The good news is, a narrative's resolve can leave room for interpretation, and it should always leave a sense of future potential. I mean, trilogies are a thing, as are sagas and series. However, beyond that, always resolve a book in a series or saga as if it's a standalone book. Every book should feel complete.

It's true, some authors have series or sagas lined up. Hell, you might have one. And still, you want to have closure to the narrative you're working on, but where you can, feel free to set up sequels. You're allowed to. All this means is to conclude the narrative you're telling while leaving room for potential sequels or spin-offs, and... have the ending feel complete yet expansive.

The reader should think, "This is complete, but I know there's more."

Before I move onto the five things every third act should have, I want to add another point: not everything must be explicitly spelled out. I'd implore you to allow readers to ponder the deeper meaning and implications of the narrative's conclusion. It's okay to have a deeper meaning to it all: themes are a thing for a reason. Readers can understand how a narrative ended, that it ended, and why it ended, and yet still walk away thinking, "What does it all mean?"

Act 3's job is to resolve, resolve, resolve the central conflict. The third act is the culmination of everything that has come before it. It's the final push where the major conflicts and character arcs collide. Even more so, a protagonist should be transformed by their journey, having faced their ultimate test in the climax.

But, Thomas, all genres resolve? Even an epic fantasy, romance, or crime novel? Isn't The Wheel of Time like fourteen books long?

*Act 3: The Resolution*

Whether a narrative is a crime thriller, epic fantasy, or romance, the third act resolves. That's right, the central mystery must be solved, the antagonist must be confronted, and the final profession of love must be made. And yes, each book within the Wheel of Time series has its own resolution, as does the series itself.

But, Thomas, all of that sounds like the climax needs to be epic.

Epic is relative. For a love novel, losing a partner would be the most epic loss they'll deal with. A crime novel ends with an arrest, not a fight to the death.

Remember, a strong resolution is that a protagonist's climactic battle, or revelation, doesn't have to be an actual fight against a big dragon (though it could be). In fact, they don't even have to win. Yep. A protagonist can lose in the end, fail miserably, and lose the girl, or get their arm eaten off by the dragon.

Though, in losses, always let a protagonist learn something from their loss. Think about how Luke Skywalker in The Empire Strikes Back loses but still learns a valuable lesson, one that he'll never forget (and grows from in Episode VI).

But, Thomas, what about flat arcs?

Even flat arcs must have a resolution to the narrative itself. Jack Reacher, Sherlock Holmes, and other crime novels solve their cases in the resolution. Sure, the protagonist returns back to their status quo, rarely learning any life-changing lessons. Yes, they can grow, but those books are more about mysteries being solved.

Dan Brown's The Da Vinci Code has a flat arc. Robert Langdon doesn't change from one book to the next but provides a very satisfying ending. Okay, maybe he might change slightly in the next book, but that's usually established in the new ordinary world of another book. All I'm saying is that you must end a narrative, resolve character arcs, and bring everything to a nice close.

## RESOLVING THE NARRATIVE

Closure is the name of the game, and the name of the game is closure. There will always be nuance to any rule, but ultimately, you must resolve a narrative in the third act. Below are five things every third act should have in some shape or form. Each thing will guide you to resolve, resolve, resolve. At any given moment in the third act, you're heading toward the resolution, resolving subarcs, tying up loose ends, and working your way to the denouement.

*The 27 Plot Point Outline: When Plot Meets Story*

# 1. RESOLVE THE CENTRAL CONFLICT

Whether you want to or not, the narrative needs to end at some point. To do this, you must resolve the central conflict of a narrative. Yes, before you ask, things can have a future, but even a romance novel working up to a wedding scene will end at the wedding, knowing that they have a potential future together.

In the romance example, the narrative is about them meeting, falling in love, and getting married. Of course they have a whole life and potential narrative after the wedding: honeymoon, living together, kids, first year married, but those are their own narratives (ones you can write about in another book).

With that said, a third act must bring the central conflict to a head, with the goal of providing a solid resolution. It doesn't matter if your narrative has the protagonist fighting a villain, a final confrontation with a personal inner demon, or a race against time to save the world—conclude the central conflict.

Readers can tell when a narrative has ended but hasn't ended. There's a magic stopping point in every narrative. No, really. As you develop your craft and understanding of narrative, you'll start seeing natural conclusions. Not just in the third act, but in scenes, chapters, acts, and, of course, the narrative itself.

Over time, natural endings will become second nature to you. You'll see them coming and also feel when narratives aren't ending when they should and instead lull or meander. It's an aspect of the writer's mind, discovery writers and plotters alike. But until you start seeing them, you'll have to do the work to spot them. You'll have to figure out when and where it should end, or in some cases, should've ended.

When you do resolve the central conflict, it should feel earned and come as a direct result of the protagonist's agency, actions, and growth. You don't want it to be anticlimactic.

Stay away from your protagonist running up stairs to kill the antagonist in their evil tower, and then when Bob reaches the top step, the tower collapses out of nowhere, killing the antagonist.

How's that end? We follow Bob walking down a thousand stairs. He is not tired when he reaches the lower floor, walks outside the destroyed castle to see his three friends, and asks them, "Want to get a beer?"

*Act 3: The Resolution*

Actually, that sounds amazing. Visually, maybe? Maybe a comedy? But the point still stands: an adult epic fantasy must pay off the ending for the reader. A reader who's been following a protagonist through life and death choices only to have the tower randomly collapse on itself... yeah, no. Not satisfying.

And not worth it for a laugh... maybe.

I'll add the following: a central conflict doesn't have to be an actual big fight—it can be internal, mental, emotional, or spiritual. A climax must end with a character arc that pays off emotionally and is earned, showing growth or change.

Unless it's a flat arc.

## 2. CHARACTER DEVELOPMENT

Outside of crime and noir, traditionally, narratives won't have flat character arcs. There will usually be some form of growth and/or change for a protagonist by the end of a narrative. Believe it or not, this is something you can look for yourself.

But, Thomas, how do I see growth and change in a character?

The short short answer is simple: at the end of your narrative, does your protagonist feel identical to who they were in Act 1 or somewhat to completely different in Act 3 or on the last page of your narrative?

If they feel the same on the first fifty pages as they do on the last fifty, it's a flat arc (if that's what you want). However, characters feel more accessible when they somewhat or completely change by the end.

As you develop your craft, you'll notice this more consistently. Watch Star Wars: The Empire Strikes Back for a real-time change.

> Luke Skywalker starts that narrative confident, naive, and ready to take on the world. He doesn't even know the depth of the world yet.
> At first he treats Yoda like crap before he knows it's Yoda.

Do you remember this moment? "Do, or do not. There is no try?"

This tells you everything you need to know about Luke up to this point. The cave scene challenges this too, where Yoda tells Luke that he won't need his weapons, yet he takes them anyway.

## The 27 Plot Point Outline: When Plot Meets Story

But, Thomas, how does he change by the end of the movie?

That's your homework. I'll let you experience how he's changed from the beginning to the end of the film. Pay attention to the emotional reveal of how he behaves and where he ends up internally and externally.

Here are some more great films where the characters change by Act 3's resolution: Braveheart, The Godfather, Schindler's List, and Good Will Hunting. You want more? The Matrix, Up (I cry every time), Shrek, Iron Man, and one of my favorites, Groundhog Day.

But, Thomas, why does the protagonist change (do they have to)?

They don't have to change. It's your narrative—you have control of it. A growth arc (especially a positive one) is generally the most common approach for popular literature and books alike. Readers want to feel an emotional conclusion to a character they've been following for 81,000 words. It doesn't mean a flat arc isn't highly accepted or you won't see success with it.

Besides, this book is focused on writing a narrative and giving you the tools to make choices when outlining that narrative.

However, Act 3 does bring the ultimate test for the protagonist, one that has built over the narrative, heading toward a final showdown. It's in that climax the protagonist is going to deal with internal or external circumstances that could change them.

Remember, protagonists began their journey with specific positions and a lie (or lies) they believed, and each position and lie had been challenged. These things will result in change for their ideals, morals, and what they believed in.

It doesn't matter if it's epic fantasy, romance, science fiction, horror, or any one of 40-plus genres: characters are challenged and molded through the fires of life. A simple death of a parent will be as powerful as a profound love or the sight of seeing a dead body for the first time in a crime novel.

People change under the crucible of time. Your protagonist will change; the lessons they've learned will be the catalyst for the growth they'll experience over the first two acts. These experiences should culminate in their ability to face and overcome the final challenge, leading to change.

But, Thomas, what if my characters don't change until the end? Like, what if they aren't flat arcs, but nothing has changed them by the end?

## Act 3: The Resolution

In that final battle, a protagonist should change, more often than not, and won't be the same person they were at the start of Act 1. The transformation should be present in their behavior, choices, and actions during the climax.

But, Thomas, what about with a flat arc?

In flat arcs, the plot unfolds. That's the ever-changing reality. In a crime, they discover the clues that lead them to the solution. Thus, they solve the crime. At the end of the narrative, Sherlock goes home, having won, and drinks a little, plays some violin, and then waits for the next case. That's his life.

It's elementary, my dear Watson.

## 3. TIE UP LOOSE ENDS

The third act provides closure for all loose ends. Basically, all significant subarcs, mysteries, and questions raised earlier in the narrative are addressed and wrapped up by the end of Act 3.

Not every detail needs to be explained. Major narrative threads should be woven into a cohesive conclusion of completeness. Oh, an alliteration; say that sentence three times fast.

> Here's an insider truth: wrapping things up will fail if there's a lot going on in the background. It happens to all writers and can come out of nowhere if you're not paying attention to it.

I mean, how many subarcs do you have? Did you add a bunch of random but much-needed mysteries? What about introducing interesting worldbuilding or history? Is something not paying off and you can't figure it out?

Look, it really does happen to the best of us. It's inevitable as narratives get bigger, the cast larger, and details become more complex. It's more likely you end up missing things as it expands.

I'm not saying don't have a big, massive narrative (write those epics). I'm saying to keep track of things within narrative threads and wrap them up. It's a matter of just being aware of what you're putting onto the page.

But, Thomas, how many narrative threads could I really have?

## The 27 Plot Point Outline: When Plot Meets Story

If people have a friendship or relationship, this starts a narrative subarc. Are characters dealing with a flaw? Narrative subarc. Trust me, they add up. Does that mean they all must be addressed? Yes and no. Go with the rule of importance.

For example, did a character lose a necklace? Sure, it can just be a piece of jewelry, but how important is that necklace to the central conflict? Maybe it's not important, but it belonged to a secondary character's mother. It's all they have left to remember a parent they lost. So, how is their behavior affected if they don't find the necklace? Do they find it? If so, how does that affect them?

My point is, sometimes a lost necklace is just a necklace that got lost. It's a novel, not a movie or television show. Novels get more space, a lot more space, and this extra space allows you to add little nothings to the page.

A novel allows for more worldbuilding, character depth, side quests, etc. A lost necklace leads to character development; we learned about them and their parents. The real question is, do they need to find that necklace? No. I mean, they can, but at the end of the day, does it matter?

Well, the truth is, that's up to you. You're the writer, and part of being a writer is keeping track of what is and isn't important.

I personally keep a spreadsheet, outlining each new thread that's formed, writing a quick summary of what it is and maybe where I want it to go. And as I mention things, even if it's a short sentence or a dialogue line, I mark down that I mentioned it in XY & Z Chapter.

If I look at my sheet and see threads mentioned only a few times, I know it might need more page time, since there's no way it'll get wrapped up in a few mentions... well, maybe it could. One of those, I lost my necklace... nope, found it.

It's about keeping track of the threads on a readback and marking where I need to add more (or less sometimes) to it. Great writing is rewriting, and this includes doing the work of adjusting and readjusting what you wrote.

This all comes to the very important point of tying up loose ends in your third act. The majority of threads should be wrapped by PP24, but we'll go more into that when we get there. For now, just know that the minor narrative threads should be dealt with before the last three plot points arrive. Remember, the last three plot points should let a narrative focus on the protagonist's central character arc's resolution.

*Act 3: The Resolution*

# 4. DENOUEMENT

Day-noo-mah, French, meaning untangling or unknotting. In the magical world of literature and drama, it refers to the final part of a narrative where the conflict is resolved after all the loose ends have been tied up. A resolve comes with a sense of closure to the narrative—a new normal, if you would.

PP27 is a literal resolution, the denouement. This is the narrative's final plot point, where tension subsides, revealing the consequences of the climax.

As mentioned above, not all loose ends will be tied up by PP24, and so it rests on PP27 to address any unanswered questions, reveal secrets, and show how the protagonist and characters were affected by the climax.

This is important because it brings a resolution to the narrative.

Oh, and remember, every element within a third act should be working towards resolving the narrative. The denouement is no different, as it's the new status quo. The moment should give a narrative a sense of finality, giving readers a clear understanding of what had happened, where the characters are, and the potential for tomorrow.

At this moment the readers don't need to read a second book, but still, they should have an idea about what's next for your characters.

Did you see The Transporter? At the end, he stops the antagonist, the cops show up, and the credits roll. We don't need to see what's next for Frank or even get a hint of it. He's going to keep being Frank, and the audience knows this.

Now Titanic, it ends with a clear finality when Rose tosses the Heart of the Ocean over the railing—no, I promised myself I wouldn't get upset over that again. 1997 was a long time ago... Move on, Thomas... move on.

Sorry, where was I? Yes, wrapping things up... bringing a resolution to it all. Which, by the way, if you have an epilogue, that's not the resolution of a narrative.

Epilogues aren't the end of a narrative. Like prologues, they have a very specific narrative job. But ultimately, it's important to distinguish an epilogue from the denouement. Epilogues usually show a future for characters after the central conflict itself has ended, been resolved, and hinted at a potential future.

But, Thomas, what would be examples of a denouement?

*The 27 Plot Point Outline: When Plot Meets Story*

Romeo and Juliet: When both families discover the two lovers dead. This leads to remorse when they realize what their feud has done.

The Shawshank Redemption: Andy escaped, crawling through 500 yards of shit smelling foulness to reach his freedom. Red is finally released, finding hope, and eventually the two friends meet up.

The denouement isn't a climax or resolution. Rather, it's a moment that happens after the climax itself. It's the part of a narrative that shows the lasting effects of all that had unfolded. After all, a protagonist's world has permanently changed internally and/or externally, as it should've.

With that, I want you to think of the denouement as the new status quo. Just like Act 1 starts with the protagonist's ordinary world, and Act 2 gives us the new world, it's here in the end where you must show the status quo of the world to come for the protagonist. The potential of tomorrow. The world that is hinted at, even if this is the only book we'll see these characters in.

Whether it's happy, tragic, or something in between, the denouement leaves a narrative with the sense of a clear path of future potential. That feeling of what's going to happen next. It should feel like a definitive conclusion, yes, but it must show that a protagonist's life doesn't end when the reader closes the book. It continues on, giving readers an idea of what life for these characters will look like moving forward.

## 5. CLOSURE WITH A PLANNED FUTURE

You might be writing a ten book series, saga, or romance that goes on and on as it shows the later years of your romantic couple into old age. And that's fine, but a narrative must still resolve in the current book you are writing, giving it closure.

However, closure can have a sense of a potential future.

There's a large chance you watched a movie, and it was a big, massive hit, a summer blockbuster, if you will. Two years later it happens: a sequel comes out. Who wasn't expecting a sequel to The Predator? But, as you can tell, the first Predator movie had a beginning, middle, and end.

## Act 3: The Resolution

Not many novelists or screenwriters plan for their next project. In fact, often, we write and focus on a single narrative, one that means a great deal to us. In essence, it's our passion project—one we've dreamed about for years.

That's the thing: it's a one-off project. We didn't know it was going to be huge and go anywhere other than being a one-and-done.

But, Thomas, are you saying I shouldn't plan for a sequel?

You should, could, or would be able to if you only knew it was coming. Think about it: you have one really great idea, and it sells two hundred thousand copies. Of course the publisher will ask you if you can keep it going. Sure, pay me. You wrote a hit... but your protagonist lost their legs at the end—prequel!

Listen, it's okay if you didn't plan for a sequel or prequel. Every book you write (planned sequel or not) should feel like its own, contained narrative. In fact, you're more likely to give a narrative closure when you don't have another book in mind. After all, you did just spend five years working on this one book.

So let every book in a series feel like it concluded. However, and I say this with caution, you could, and should, drop pebbles of potential future all within the book itself, even seed things in the third act. Those little "did you catch that" moments that'll pay off in the future.

But, Thomas, you said not to add new information in Act 3.

I said not to add narratively important information into Act 3. You can add little nothings all you want in a narrative. Especially when you're sure there'll be other books in the series. A strong epilogue, for example, can be a window to the next book of your series. I'm just saying.

Look, as long as you allow the current narrative to feel complete on its own, you have plenty of room to add worldbuilding, potential plot points for the future, and character growth that doesn't pay off until next time.

For example, a protagonist searches for a Medallion of Bloom, and while in the Cave of Wonders, a secondary character takes a few bags of gold. However, in the sequel, the secondary character tries to sell their gold and realizes there's an item that's also a map to something else.

The bag of gold wasn't narratively important to the central conflict. The central conflict was to find the gold in the first place. And you know what? They found it! So there's no need to resolve it and show them taking the gold home.

## *The 27 Plot Point Outline: When Plot Meets Story*

We get it. He took the gold—selling it is for the next book.

The reader isn't concerned about the gold coming home. A reader does, however, care if a protagonist overcomes challenges in the narrative connected to the inciting incident and its midpoint conflict.

All I'm saying is if you have a sequel planned, there's no harm in seeding what's to come. Readers will appreciate a second read, connecting the continuity. So I recommend doing both: give closure on the current narrative and reward the readers with hints of future potential.

But, Thomas, isn't introducing potential plot points for a sequel leaving things unresolved?

Technically, yes. Those new, future plot points aren't resolved, and they shouldn't be—since you have a sequel coming. Again, if a plot point is narratively important to the central conflict, it must be resolved. However, the next narrative will have its own inciting incident. So focus on letting your characters fix their current situation, even if you seed for the future.

# CHAPTER 15

## Victory Seems Impossible

**SECTION 7: VICTORY SEEMS IMPOSSIBLE**

Ah, yes, victory seems impossible in the opening section of Act 3. And it should, because it's time to set up your protagonist's emotional and narrative low point before the climax. Section 7 is all about "can they…" or will they fail going into it, whether their climactic final battle is an actual battle of feats, a deeply emotional journey inward, or a will they/won't they end up happily ever after.

Section 7 lures the protagonist (and hopefully the reader) into thinking they have a shot, then pulls the rug out from beneath them. The short of it is, this opening section of Act 3 prepares a protagonist for a final battle, one that must feel hard-earned and, if possible, uncertain.

But, Thomas, if my protagonist's victory feels uncertain, wouldn't that undermine their capability?

You'd think so, but challenging a protagonist, and characters in general, is what makes an engaging narrative. Sure, you shouldn't write a narrative for the reader, but you shouldn't keep their experience out of mind. You want readers to feel like a protagonist could win, but it's going to be difficult. This keeps readers turning the page.

## The 27 Plot Point Outline: When Plot Meets Story

Again, don't write creatively for readers. Write for you, for the narratives you want to read yourself, and for the ideas and characters that compel you to sit down and write. The thing driving you should be the narrative idea boiling up inside you, needing to get out and blast across the page. In a nutshell, think of the reader when it comes to the presentation, not the concept.

With that said, I've found clients (and fellow writers) afraid to hurt their protagonist and their characters. Often it comes down to pushing on them, but not hard enough to make it life-threatening. It's okay to have your characters fail, and fail often. Just remember to give them victories, the ones that matter.

However, it's important that even in their failures, you must allow your characters to grow and learn from them—giving them the earned knowledge for later victories in Act 3 (and some in Act 2).

This is the part that makes Section 7 so interesting; it sets up a potential for failure, and yet, the protagonist doesn't know it's coming. So who are they in this feeling, believing they'll solve the problem caused by the midpoint conflict? How does a protagonist respond emotionally and behave as this failure unfolds?

See, the thing is, Act 1 establishes the potential of a protagonist and the other players around them. It's in the first act where we learn about who they are, what they can do, and why they would, could, or should do it.

"It" being sword fighting, casting a fireball, or being an excellent lover. But it's also learning about them being brave, cowardly, smart, shy, or proactive.

Act 2 challenges what was set up in Act 1, pushing a protagonist to their limit and giving characters a chance to showcase their capability through choices, trying to get through circumstances and situations. You know, through action and behavior. However, those skills should be pushed to their limit, a limit they'll eventually have to overcome in the third act.

Oh, your warrior knows how to fight with a sword? Great, let them win some, lose some, and realize they still have lots to learn. Maybe they'll realize it's not always about the sword but about their friends helping them.

Your mystical, magical wizard can cast a tiny fireball in Act 1? Well now in Act 2 they blast a large fireball down a whole room and hallway, hurting their friends and themselves, realizing they have a ways to go in controlling magic.

But, Thomas, where does the wizard go from there into the third act?

## Section 7: Victory Seems Impossible

The wizard's friends are hurt, unable to follow. The wizard must now go to fight the dragon alone, afraid to use magic to their full capacity now.

How about a protagonist who's an excellent lover? In Act 3 he realizes women have been using him for his body. Now he wants to prove his worth, that he's more than a body and long flowing hair. He works to refine himself and become someone worth marrying or growing a life with.

As you can see, each example has them going into Act three determined, and it's in the beginning of Act 3, Section 7, where you're going to slowly chip away at this determination, confidence, and hope.

And you know what? Use all three plot points of Section 7 to establish the beginning of Act 3, giving them a sense that maybe, just maybe, they're going to do it before hitting the protagonist with another plot twist/pinch to make sure they are left sitting in their darkest moment. Muhahaha!

By the end of Section 7 it should feel like the sun won't come out at all tomorrow. Like there's no point to anything—it's impossible, and a protagonist is at their literal lowest point.

## PLOT POINT 19
## THE PROTAGONIST FACES DIFFICULT AND SIGNIFICANT TRIALS, SOMETHING THEY HAVE NEVER EXPERIENCED BEFORE (CALM BEFORE THE STORM)

The calm before the storm places a protagonist in the fray and mercy of difficult trials. Ones that'll be significantly more difficult than anything they've previously dealt with or never experienced before.

Remember, while they've never experienced these types of trials before, they still go into PP19 with a sense of potential, possibility, hope, and a great deal of determination. They believe they cannot fail (even if they know they could still "die, get rejected, or lose").

Act 1 was their ordinary world, a world intimately familiar to them. It's in Act 2 where that ordinary world is messed with—changed. Still, protagonists will understand something familiar about the new world. As if they were able to bring something real and truthful with them from Act 1 into Act 2.

## The 27 Plot Point Outline: When Plot Meets Story

However, in Act 3 the protagonist falls into a new, unknown territory, one that pushes hard against them during their trials. This new, unfamiliar world can be a physical, mental, or spiritual new circumstance.

During the trials of PP19, protagonists still believe they have a chance to succeed. Therefore, as a writer, you want to show protagonists working hard to get through each trial—whether they succeed or fail. In either case, give them some kind of victory. And honestly, they really should win in PP19 (it doesn't have to be a major victory); it should allow a protagonist to feel they'll make it through.

But, Thomas, do they have to win? Like, what if I want them to lose?

You can do that. It's your narrative. I'd suggest not letting a protagonist lose in PP19. If you do, it might unintentionally shoot your narrative in the foot.

Plot points guide narratives and you as the writer, making sure certain things, certain movements occur. Though suggestions are still only suggestions, I'll point out that a protagonist is meant to succeed in PP19. Their victory makes it seem possible—in reality, it's a false sense of hope in the grand scheme of things.

Section 7 ends in a major loss, so the losing part is coming soon in PP20 and PP21. For an emotional impact to hit harder, PP19's beat gives a protagonist a sense of possibility at the beginning of the third act.

Once you set up the protagonist in PP19, then feel free to knock them down in PP20 and again, even harder, in PP21.

Honestly, do what you want in a narrative; break the rules, adjust them, and refine it all, but at the end of the day, being a writer is controlling how things play out. If there are too many losses leading up to the final battle, it might be a lot harder for readers to believe the protagonist can win at all.

Even in a loss, readers must believe characters can win.

I'd go as far as to say that the beginning of Act 3, Section 7, PP19 isn't about a loss or a win; it's about setting up the emotional context to challenge it in PP20, pushing a protagonist into their darkest moment in PP21.

The 27 Plot Point Outline is here to guide how you move the emotional throughline of character arcs of a narrative's plot. Even in a plot-driven narrative, characters need to feel real, authentic, and three-dimensional. If characters aren't dealing with hope, failure, regret, loss, or any number of emotional truths, then they won't stand out on the page.

## Section 7: Victory Seems Impossible

Readers can't connect to action alone or perfection. Watching plot play out over and over again is boring. Show readers a narrative's story, having the plot unfold through the emotional experiences and choices of your characters.

This is why a protagonist should be entering Act 3 with a sense of hope, even if they're experiencing new trials they've never encountered before. I mean, the characters just left Act 2 with a sense of accomplishment, firm in a dedication to succeed no matter what. Kicking them down now, as soon as they enter Act 3, would knock their momentum off the rails.

That's right, a protagonist should be feeling good right about now. They entered Act 3 with the belief of having found a solution to the midpoint conflict. PP19 is where protagonists should feel like they'll come out on top, even though ultimately, they will not by the end of Section 7.

So, what does this mean? First, let's remind ourselves that every section needs a beginning, middle, and end—context to challenge and ultimately resolve. If you don't set up the fall to come, the fall itself won't feel earned. I'd argue that three bad losses in a row slow the pace, falling short of an earned resolution. One loss, two losses, and a third loss... where's the resolution?

Going back to our alien invasion, we know the narrative must set up the beginning of Act 3 and Section 7 in this first plot point. We know PP19 must end with a sense of potential, perhaps a victory, or there's a possible victory coming.

The last we saw the protagonist, they were entering the headquarters of the alien commander. His goal: to find and rescue his best friend.

> PP19: The protagonist sneaks around the headquarters while other humans create a distraction. Surviving several near-death situations, the protagonist fights a powerful alien in a control room. Winning, he uses the control panel to find his best friend's cell location.

PP19 ends, leaving the protagonist with a sense of hope. Sure, they need to escape the headquarters, and they need to survive any other threats, but they're in a position of potential: they're going to accomplish their goals. But this victory still leaves the narrative with hope. He's won a few battles. He found his friend's location. And he might get through this after all. Might.

*The 27 Plot Point Outline: When Plot Meets Story*

Could they have lost? Absolutely, but only if it still ends with a sense of hope. For example:

> The powerful alien beat up the protagonist and left them alive, and the alien commander demands the protagonist be brought to him. Even in their "loss," the protagonist believes, "I can end all of this by getting close enough to the alien commander to kill them."

The point to all of this is that even in the loss, they're ending PP19 with a sense of hope. This elevates the potential of success and also sets up the coming fall the protagonist is about to experience... twice.

## PLOT POINT 20
## A SECOND MAJOR PLOT TWIST OR PINCH WHERE THE PROTAGONIST EXPERIENCES A COMPLETELY UNEXPECTED EVENT, MAKING IT ALL WORSE (PLOT TWIST/PINCH)

"What happens when everything a protagonist relied on is stripped away?"

Ah yes, the fundamental question PP20 asks of a narrative. However, I should add that this particular question does come with a great deal of nuance.

Again, here's a quick reminder on what a plot twist and pinch are.

A plot twist is a significant and unexpected turn of events that drastically changes the audience's and protagonist's understanding and perspective of the narrative, fellow characters, and/or the previous events.

A pinch, on the other hand, serves as a reminder of the existing conflict, increasing a sense of urgency and danger. A stronger pinch will show, rather than tell, the power of the opposition.

Now that we have that reminder, whether you use a plot twist or pinch, it's not going to be a small or simple event for a protagonist. It'll be something that changes their whole circumstance. Unlike the first act's plot twist or pinch, the protagonist will experience a completely unexpected turn of events. And it will make everything worse.

## Section 7: Victory Seems Impossible

Which brings us back to: "What happens when everything a protagonist relied on is stripped away?" Of course, like I said, there's nuance to this question.

The nuance is different for every narrative. However, let's break up that nuance into two very important general questions to ask yourself, both of which will add perspective, showing you the depth of your narrative.

Question #1: What's your protagonist's current situation?

Starting with their situation and analyzing it gives you a chance to figure out how to disrupt it, tossing it around and making everything worse. The worse you make it, the better. Hear me out: think about what's currently happening to them in the narrative, try to dismantle it, corrupt it, or switch it up—anything to throw a pickle into your protagonist's life?

Additionally, if you're using a pinch, hit back on the protagonist hard, showing how their situation is beyond their capability and there's no way out of this one. Besides, this is a chance to show the antagonist force (whether internal, external, or otherwise) is still in control of what's happening right now.

Question #2: What's your protagonist's current emotional state?

Not every narrative is action-packed or a Shadow Daddy dark romance where a perfectly timed sex scene solves everything. The first question did center on the external, whereas this one dives deep into a protagonist's emotional truth. That's right, you're allowed to disrupt their emotional or spiritual truth.

This could be a heartbreak (death or a breakup), the betrayal of a trusted ally, or the revelation of a horrifying truth. Personally, there's nothing worse than a protagonist sacrificing something, anything, and the results being futile.

Yep, when a protagonist makes a massive sacrifice all for nothing to save a love interest, only for them to die anyway. Or a sought-after item that's found destroyed after a full narrative exploration for it. Talk about a plot twist...

The point is, both questions are valuable to the outlining process. I'll always be the first to say that a protagonist's mental state is as important as the physical, external circumstances of their situations. Know what they both are.

## The 27 Plot Point Outline: When Plot Meets Story

A quick aside: I'd even argue to take note of all points of mental and physical states within narratives and not just in this moment. PP20 is one plot point. Give them all a good look as a way to decide how you could push back on your protagonist and their circumstances.

Before I get to the alien invasion example, know this: whether you write a plot twist or pinch, the results will have a profound influence on the situation. These results will negate all of their hard-won victories, reinforcing emotional or environmental conflicts of the protagonist, leaving them without hope.

Now back to our regular broadcast showing: the alien invasion. Here's a playful approach to everything I've explained about PP20.

Our protagonist moved through the alien headquarters during PP19 and fought off a bunch of aliens as they discovered their best friend's location.

PP20: In the famous words of Admiral Ackbar, "IT'S A TRAP!" A hopeful plan is in motion as our protagonist arrives to save his best friend, discovering there's an alien in disguise as the friend (seeded in the first act with the boss alien and employees that looked human).

Oh no! What a twist! That and the protagonist is zapped, and the alien commander orders his men to bring the protagonist to him. This plot twist leaves their fate uncertain; is this death? We don't know. It's in the air.

Here's the thing: at the end of PP20, the protagonist thought they were going to save their best friend, but instead, they were taken prisoner themselves.

There is a touch of a pinch here, but it's mostly a plot twist. Their sense of hope is torn from them when they realize their best friend was actually an alien waiting for the protagonist. Not that his actual best friend was an alien. But does this mean his best friend in the whole world is... is... dead?

A quick aside: let things fall apart in this plot point. Start the process of knocking them off their throne of hope and into a pit of despair, even though it's going to get worse before it gets better.

Section 7: Victory Seems Impossible

# PLOT POINT 21
# A FINAL MAJOR PLOT TWIST, OR PINCH, LEADS TO THE DARKEST MOMENT, AND SUCCESS FEELS INCOMPREHENSIBLE (DARKEST MOMENT)

There are always three narrative moments where a plot twist or pinch will occur: PP8, PP20, and this one, PP21. Of those three, this one is the worst, the one that will lead a protagonist to their darkest moment. Dun Dun Dun!

Okay, maybe not that melodramatic, but it'll still put them in the worst situation yet. The darkest moment is literally rock bottom, where all hope seems lost for a protagonist, and defeat feels inevitable (feels). They are forced to face an ultimate despair before a potential final fight or tragic end.

If you're trying to figure it out... think about this moment in one of the greatest films ever made.

> A pale man entered a cave, lit by candlelight and chandeliers. His white hair flopped at his shoulders as he descended a small flight of stairs. He reached a man, unconscious and locked to a wooden table.
>
> He grabbed a washing cloth and tapped it over the Man in Black's wounded shoulder.
>
> The Man in Black's head rotated up, waking, groggy.
>
> The Albino continued washing the wound, dabbing away; a small crease to the side of his mouth grew at the man's opening eyes.
>
> "Where am I?"
>
> "The Pit of Despair. Don't even think—" He said in a raspy mess, coughing out phlegm. "Don't even think about trying to escape," the Albino said, his voice now a clear posh timbre. "The chains are far too thick. And don't dream of being rescued either. The only way in is secret. Only the prince, the count, and I know how to get in and out."
>
> "Then I'm here till I die?"
>
> "Till they kill you, yeah."

## *The 27 Plot Point Outline: When Plot Meets Story*

The Princess Bride. A 10/10 film. This scene does what Plot Point 21 must do and accomplishes it with ease. The Man in Black, Dread Pirate Roberts, is literally at his lowest, darkest moment, waking up on a table he is locked to, and the Albino tells him outright, "Don't even think about trying to escape." Followed by, "Till they kill you, yeah."

Yeah, it shouldn't look good for them. But that's okay; protags are going to protag, which means they'll win, just not yet, nor in this plot point.

Wait, let me clarify that for those in the back seats. Not all endings need to be a victory or happy ending, but we'll talk more about that for Section 9.

For now, let's jump right in with the alien invasion before I explain it in a bit more depth and go darker and deeper with PP21.

PP21: Our protagonist is now brought before the alien commander. The life partner comes out, revealing they were involved in the best friend switch trap. But, while the alien commander monologues, he mentions the alien boss who fell in love with the human species.

The life partner realizes the best friend was telling the truth, and she decides to do right by her lover's memory, causing a distraction, and saves the protagonist. The life partner knows where the best friend is. They run through the ship, find, and rescue the best friend.

But, Thomas, that doesn't sound like the darkest moment.
Correct. PP21 is not over yet. There's still more to come; in fact, now it's time for a narrative double gut punch: a twist and a pinch.

The life partner's betrayal causes the alien commander to demand his people kill her, the protagonist, and Earth. He angrily activates a nuclear bomb to drop after other alien ships depart Earth.

This moment creates a countdown for the nuclear weapon, the group being chased down to be killed, and the potential end for Earth, causing, wait for it, the darkest moment in the narrative for the protagonist.

## Section 7: Victory Seems Impossible

But, Thomas, so, why's it a twist and a pinch?

The life partner's act of betrayal is a plot twist. Her actions are both shocking and unexpected, drastically changing the protagonist's understanding of her character. Thought to be only an enemy, she revealed herself to be an ally, helping the humans. This reveal shifts their entire perspective on past events and the current situation.

And yes, this isn't the darkest moment; there's still plenty of PP21 to go around. If anything, this appears to be a well-earned victory. However, the cause and effect of their actions cause a pinch; the alien commander emotionally reacts and activates the nuclear bomb sequence and orders his men to kill the life partner and the protagonist.

Now this is a clear and powerful reminder of the conflict. It's here in this moment that the urgency and danger have increased, showing the power of the opposition and starting the countdown to destruction (play the Megadeth song).

PP21 ends with the darkest moment: Earth, and everything on it, will be destroyed. Notice how the plot point has both a plot twist and pinch, influencing the antagonistic force, the protagonist, and surrounding characters.

> A quick aside: When writing a darkest moment, the situation itself doesn't have to be world-ending like my alien example. It certainly can be, but I'm using it as an extreme example.

In romance, a protagonist says goodbye to the love of their life; she must move across the country for a dream job. The protagonist wants to go, but they must stay close to their dying father (as caretaker). The job is a once-in-a-lifetime opportunity, and the love interest can't give it up.

A horror narrative might have the protagonist and their friends hiding in a barn, and the protagonist hidden under the floor. Michael Myers comes in, and one by one they hear their friends being killed. There's nothing they can do but wait for Michael Myers to find them hiding, alone, and in a small space.

Crime and thrillers are my favorite narratives; rarely, if ever, will there be a world-ending event in a crime novel. Especially in a noir. In a crime narrative, the darkest moment might be when the protagonist is framed for a crime they didn't

## The 27 Plot Point Outline: When Plot Meets Story

commit (and the audience knows they're innocent), but all the evidence points to their guilt. Nothing works to prove their innocence. All efforts to clear their name fail, and they get life for a crime they didn't commit.

When writing your outline, remember, you're allowed to play with rules and try things out, adjust them, shift them within the plot point parameters, and break things. After all, they're only rules and suggestions.

Obviously you'll have to pay attention to a narrative and figure out what works specifically as you develop it. Results must be relative to what's happening within and around your protagonist.

The fact remains, though, whatever you choose, you want PP21 to end with the protagonist at their lowest point. As Section 7's title suggests, this lowest point should feel like victory... seems... impossible.

# CHAPTER 16

## The Protagonist Finds The Power

### SECTION 8: THE PROTAGONIST FINDS THE POWER

Section 8 is when a protagonist finds the power within and keeps going. Since all acts have a beginning, middle, and end, Act 3, Section 7 had set up the third act's context and placed the protagonist at their lowest point. Essentially Section 7 establishes the emotional, mental, and physical starting point for the protagonist that will be explored through the remainder of Act 3.

Which means now it's time to introduce the conflict of Act 3 in Section 8. The protagonist will take action, challenging established context. In our alien invasion, context defined their new status quo: victory seems impossible because the alien commander set the countdown to destruction (headbangs to metal).

The point of Section 8 is to challenge the established context and push back on the new status quo. This pushback shows a protagonist working to break the chains that bind them.

Even if you're writing romance, action adventure, horror, or straight-up epic fantasy, you'll need to show how your protagonist acts with agency. Agency shows a proactive protagonist instead of a passive one. A good, strong, proactive protagonist pushes their arc and the narrative's plot forward.

## The 27 Plot Point Outline: When Plot Meets Story

In Section 8, use agency to show a protagonist taking action and, by the end, accepting what's to come, what it'll take, and braving the potential outcome of consequences to achieve success or failure. This is the emotional and narrative turning point where a protagonist chooses to rise.

And sure, they hit rock bottom in Section 7, but now they'll uncover a deeper strength or truth that reignites their will to act in Section 8. Ultimately, their choices will be influenced by a deeper clarity and purpose; they set the plan in motion, and all storylines tighten toward the inevitable final clash.

Remember, like all sections, Section 8 has three plot points to show the protagonist coming to their senses, finding a strength within, and taking action. You don't have to rush the revelation of this inner power in the first plot point or even the first two of the section. In fact, I implore you to take all three plot points and show the stages of that transformation.

One other thing: don't give protagonists the ultimate victory in Section 8. Save that for later, letting them earn the biggest victory in the next section. In fact, think of Section 8 as an opportunity to begin the protagonist on a journey to find the strength within. A strength that will lead to action and finally end this section with a sense of potential to win the coming battle. Have the protagonist head into Section 9, PP25, The Final Battle, with the will to win.

## PLOT POINT 22
## HAVING HIT ROCK BOTTOM,
## THE PROTAGONIST FINDS A POWER WITHIN TO SUCCEED
## (POWER WITHIN)

Another beginning; time to set up context and reveal the new status quo of your protagonist. Oh sure, the narrative's plot showed them dealing with their literal lowest point. And yes, it's clear they're not in a good place, so show protagonists in their new internal and external circumstances.

But, Thomas, didn't PP21 establish their external circumstances?

No. PP21 showed readers where a protagonist was. It's time to go deeper and show where a protagonist presently is. This gives readers enough context to know what's going on. Always make sure readers know what's going on.

## Section 8: The Protagonist Finds The Power

Remember, this plot point is when a protagonist finds an inner strength within to resolve the problem caused by the midpoint conflict. This inner strength is important for fueling protagonists with renewed determination to fight back.

A narrative, and a protagonist, need that renewed determination to fight back for many reasons, one being to keep protagonists moving forward. A second and third reason is that Section 7 ended on a down note, so things need to pick up for Sections 8 and 9. It's all about keeping things moving.

Let me put it this way: having this renewed energy also engages the hope for the reader and, of course, your protagonist. It lifts the narrative into a sense of possibility. Sure, "will they, won't they" is still on the table (and should be), but you need that spark to light the fire of interest and excitement.

But, Thomas, you said not to write for the reader.

I did say that, and I did remind you in a previous chapter that you never write creatively for a reader. That part is reserved for you and the passion you have for writing. However, it doesn't mean to ignore a reader's experience.

The difference between what you want to write and what you think the reader wants to read can make or break your book. Write for the reader, and you won't find your voice nor an audience because no one person is the same.

What connects your books to an audience is your authentic voice as an author and writing about the things that matter to you. George R.R. Martin had an idea about a group of people, a family, that finds a dead Direwolf mother with five... I mean, six pups—the rest is history.

Game of Thrones became his passion. Sure, he probably was passionate about his science fiction stuff too, but he said in interviews that it all started with one scene that he needed to write. So write for you, and an audience will find you. Write for an audience, and you'll always be trying to find them.

Getting back: the 27 PPO is designed to help you create movement, slow things down in a narrative, let moments breathe, and direct you when and where to spark some action. And you might be asking, "Why is that important?"

See, part of being a writer is knowing how to tell a narrative in a way that gets people to lean in. Don't get me wrong, there are poor storytellers who write great narratives and great storytellers who write less ideal ones. A great storyteller can make any poor narrative sound good. But a poor storyteller?

## The 27 Plot Point Outline: When Plot Meets Story

Imagine sitting around a campfire, the crickle crackle of wood breaking and popping under the warmth of thrashing fire. Friends to the left and right as the storyteller settles in and begins... And then it happens: they don't know how to tell stories or when to sit in beats, or they rush through others, and worst of all, they don't allow for tension and suspense.

It's like reading a book that's filled with all the parts they really like at the beginning (or the straight details). There's nothing less exciting than:

> It was March 3rd, 1801, and she found the love of her life that night in a house, the one she entered on a dark and stormy night as the clock struck thirteen. Love at first sight, they kissed, got engaged, and before the end of their second year, had a family.

Writing is knowing when and where to move narratives around to create reader engagement. Otherwise, it's not a story; it's a lecture being told to a person who'll probably put the book down. Even great narratives can have a truly poor presentation. Which leads me to my closing before the alien invasion.

PP22 is the spark. It's the slow rise of music and the discovery of a deep fire within, a power to take a chance on making things happen by making things happen. A protagonist should come out of their darkest moment with a sense of renewed purpose, maybe even a plan.

But, Thomas, why?

Because PP23 is when they finally take action to end all of this.

For our hero fighting aliens:

> PP22: The protagonist still has their alien abilities inside them, but if they use them, they could die, draining their life force, making what they have left inside of them life-or-death.

> The protagonist decides to stop the bomb as the life partner goes to start the ship's self-destruction countdown. The best friend heads off to get others underground to safety (in case the plan fails).

## Section 8: The Protagonist Finds The Power

The setup for this situation might take a chapter or three, but the reality is as follows. PP22 sets up what the three characters must do within PP23. We also now understand the stakes (one more ability will kill the protagonist, warn humans about the coming launch, and get them underground, or they'll die if the protagonist fails).

All this sets up PP23, but it also shows that the protagonist is using their agency and getting ready to take action in the next plot point. If they do nothing, they die, so why not die trying to save Earth and the people they love?

That's the basic motivation of the once mundane accountant.

## PLOT POINT 23
## THE PROTAGONIST TAKES ACTION
## (ACTION TO RALLY)

Alright, let's pull back a bit and give you the tools to control the narrative. Right now, your gut might have you believing Act 3 should be flying down the road at three hundred miles an hour. It shouldn't. In fact, I'd suggest that no narrative needs to be balls to the wall (though it can be).

What you need to realize and reevaluate often is relativity—relativity to your plot, the characters, and the pace of the narrative you're telling. That's right, never rush toward a climax, nor should you rush a climax. However, there's such a thing as too slow. Just because a protagonist takes action to rally doesn't always mean they go all in, head down, and shoulder smash a door down.

For example: Pirates of the Caribbean: The Curse of the Black Pearl.

> Trapped on an island with Captain Jack Sparrow, Elizabeth Swann burns all the rum to create a massive fire, hoping James Norrington will catch sight of it, since the entire Royal Navy is looking for her.

What's actually happening in PP23 is that Elizabeth takes action. She's not fighting anyone; there's no war or battle, nor is she hanging by the neck from a rope. None of that is happening. In fact, in the scene before this, she's drinking rum with Jack Sparrow, trying to get him drunk so she can enact her plan. They

## The 27 Plot Point Outline: When Plot Meets Story

were just abandoned on an island, and all hope was lost. PP22 was about finding her power within. PP23 is her taking action to live.

And she did. She knew if she could get Jack drunk, she'd be able to light the fire (but why the rum?), and James Norrington Borington would find them. And he does. It's relative to Swann's situation.

Section 8 has the protagonist discover a power within, take action, and give the narrative momentum, thrusting it closer toward the final battle. But even thrust doesn't mean a protagonist should be forced forward at ludicrous speed until everything turns plaid.

Here's the skinny: PP23 is a point in a narrative where the protagonist is both emotionally and mentally ready to take action and rally themselves and others to believe they'll win.

That action can be a small, intimate one or a big explosion of potential. Either should show a protagonist's agency, fueling them up with a renewed inner strength. Basically, the protagonist is now ready to do whatever they must to fully embrace their greatest strength.

This plot point is important to add and build onto the momentum of a protagonist's narrative journey. Think of Section 8 as a narrative triple jump, and PP23 is the middle stone they need to touch but not stop at. Because Section 9 is only a hop, skip, and a jump away.

Now, what about our alien invasion?

PP23: The protagonist tries to turn off the nuclear weapon all while fighting aliens. The life partner deals with destroying the ship before it leaves. And finally, the best friend finds the other humans, getting everyone underground to safety.

I love having three narrative points going on at the same time. We have the protagonist doing their thing, the life partner doing hers, and the best friend handling his responsibilities. They all take action, building narrative momentum toward what's coming their way. Though the final battle isn't around the corner, they can still smell it a mile away.

But, Thomas, what about the protagonist's love interest?

## Section 8: The Protagonist Finds The Power

I was waiting for you to be wondering about the love interest. The point of an outline isn't to get it all right on the first go-round. I'm purposefully leaving her out of the later plot points as an example of forgetting about characters.

Remember, one of the rules of the process is broad, general ideas that are built upon. That goes for the outlining process too. So as one of the fixes, I would make sure to add more agency, beats, and purpose to the love interest.

What is the lesson to learn? Great writing is rewriting. You can always go back and add, adjust, delete, change, and altogether play around with it. Outlining isn't writing prose; it's working out the narrative foundation and truth.

You'll learn over time that it's okay to go back in and get your hands a bit dirty, fixing what is there and connecting things by noticing what's not there. So, if you've noticed the missing love interest by now, or even earlier, that's a great writer's eye moment!

## PLOT POINT 24
## THE CONVERGENCE OF STORYLINES
## AND BUILDING UP TO THE FINAL BATTLE
## (CONVERGE)

This is the last plot point before the narrative heads off into Section 9. Everything that's been set in motion from the narrative's beginning will collide here. Okay, maybe not everything, but most arcs, threads, and themes will tighten toward a single convergence point. This convergence cleans things up before the chaos of the final battle and resolution of the narrative truly begins.

Keep in mind, PP24 does some heavy lifting to resolve Section 8 but also prepares a narrative and protagonist for a coming resolution in the final section. Most, if not all, subarcs should be concluded by the end of this plot point.

It doesn't always have to go that way, but the fewer distractions there are in Section 9, the better. Do what you can to naturally conclude as many narrative subarcs as possible in PP24 so the central conflict will have more room to play in during the three final plot points of the last section.

But, Thomas, are you saying that PP24 should focus on trying to set up Section 9? Doesn't PP24 have any other responsibilities?

## The 27 Plot Point Outline: When Plot Meets Story

PP24 isn't here to set up Section 9; it's here to wrap up as much as it can. The focus should be on wrapping up anything that isn't narratively important for the final showdown or the complete resolution at the end of the narrative.

For example: A secondary character is a coward and has been for the majority of the narrative. Within PP24, this character has a moment where they push through their cowardice and show bravery.

That thread isn't needed for the final battle (though it could be). But now you've earned a chance for a stronger return to Section 9. All because you wrapped up the "coward arc" in PP24.

Think about it: now that secondary character's new growth can be used to help the protagonist and the narrative come to a good, clean resolution in the final battle.

Yep, wrapping things up in Section 8, PP24 gives a narrative a chance to shine light on the secondary character arcs and subarcs in Section 9. This doesn't mean all subarcs are wrapped up in PP24, but most are. Some might have to go forward into Section 9. Others might connect directly to the central conflict in small, medium, or larger ways (even though they're still subarcs).

Of course, before you ask, if you have sequels coming up, some subarcs or threads won't or don't have to be resolved in this particular narrative, but they should still feel like something about the subarcs themselves has been resolved.

For example: A character lost their father at a young age, developing an internal conflict of self-doubt. They believe the world is against them. A resolve is them learning that their father is a conman, alive, and had left the family.

Their character arc wraps up when they accept that their father is alive and chose to abandon him and their mother. Sure, the character still has some of their self-doubt, but now they don't believe the world's against them, and they've gained some confidence, becoming more proactive. This'll follow over with them into Section 9 and other books: "I make my own destiny!"

## Section 8: The Protagonist Finds The Power

Alright, now let's jump into the alien invasion example for PP24.

PP24: The life partner activates the self-destruction sequence on the ship. They end up fighting and killing the alien who drew the killing blow to the alien boss (who she loved).

The best friend fights beside other humans, attacking any fleeing aliens as they try to reach the remaining ships. Believing they're going to die in the explosion anyway, why not fight!

Our protagonist finds the nuclear weapon, fights off a few random aliens, and learns that the alien commander has the remote that can turn the bomb off. The protagonist feels his powers running out; he knows what he must do to save Earth, and it'll cost him his life.

It's a loss with a potential for victory; they finally accept all of the power within, stand confident, and have the courage to do what they must for victory. That's the point of PP24: to end on a high note of potential.

With that said, here are some notes to summarize PP24: Give subarcs and minor narrative threads a chance to narrow into natural resolutions to close out character arcs, giving the narrative a chance to focus on the protagonist's central character arc.

Of course, Section 8 should resolve with the protagonist getting hit with a final stroke of power from within, solidifying their confidence going into the final battle and final section of the narrative.

And remember, PP24 must end on a high note; even if it's a loss, keep it positive, allowing a protagonist's momentum and agency to keep that narrative's forward momentum filled with potential.

And yes, these are just rules and suggestions. You're always allowed to go in and break stuff, make things up, and play with rules; after all, writing is all fake. It's fiction. That's why we call it that. I mean... dragons, wizards, murder, crimes, gods, demons, witches, and the power to move through time (though you need a gem for that, Sassenach).

## *The 27 Plot Point Outline: When Plot Meets Story*

Look, the truth is, story is the fun part, the stuff unfolding through the emotional experiences and choices of your characters, and plot, well, plot is what needs to happen no matter what. But still, at the end of the day... it's all made up.

So try things, find your author voice; you never know, you might change the landscape of the narrative world, the creative writing of it all, and the genre conventions we all thought it needed to be.

After all, where would writing be today without authors like Miguel de Cervantes, Jane Austen, James Joyce, Virginia Woolf, or the Godfather of epic fantasy, J.R.R. Tolkien?

Each of them explored writing in their own ways, changing and evolving the art and landscape of creative, long-form narratives.

# CHAPTER 17

# The Protagonist Fights And Wins

## SECTION 9: THE PROTAGONIST FIGHTS AND WINS

Section 9 has one job and one job only: resolution. That's right, its purpose is to resolve all narrative threads, plural, more than one, because there are three plot points in this section, a few select subarcs remaining, and, among other things, the central conflict and character arcs. It must all come to a natural conclusion in this final section, this final act, and these three final plot points.

Let's get right to the nitty-gritty, shall we? The first resolution to resolve is the established narrative thread of Act 3, Section 9; the second is the protagonist's central character arc. Both of these narrative threads must be resolved by the end.

Every narrative element of Section 9 must push the protagonist's central character arc and Act 3's narrative thread forward. This section specifically must ensure that every narrative beat leads to the resolution of it all.

> A quick aside: Every page should move a narrative forward for each act, section, character arc, and plot point. I'm not saying every page must move all these elements forward. Only that every page should move at least one or more of those elements forward.

## The 27 Plot Point Outline: When Plot Meets Story

For a five-page chapter, maybe it's broken up like this:

The act's narrative gets pushed forward on page one. On page two, it pushes the section forward. Pages three, four, and five give weight to each a little, pushing the act, section, arcs, and plot point forward.

After all, Section 9 has the protagonist doing what they do best (at least they're trying to do their best), and in doing so, they'll fight and win. This victory can be a literal win physically, mentally, or spiritually. Though, they could lose too (anything is possible), but then they'd learn a moral lesson in the process.

It's in Section 9 where a protagonist engages in a final battle: whether to take the promotion, propose to their dream partner, or have a big fight with an alien commander—this is where everything they've learned is tested.

At the end of narratives, the climax must resolve core, central conflicts to a definitive and well-earned moment. Yes, the final battle resolves the climax but not the final resolution. A final resolution, or rather, the denouement, happens when the protagonist's central character arc is concluded in PP27.

I'll add that one or two-ish secondary characters will get any needed page time to tie up loose ends, revealing a new normal for everyone, forged by sacrifice, growth, and a hard-fought victory.

But, Thomas, that all sounds pretty dramatic.

It is, but then again, sometimes a new normal, forged by sacrifice, growth, and a hard-fought victory, could be a simple, soft, and low-key narrative about an old man living on a farm.

The man finds love, gets married, has five kids, inherits his parent's farm, walks two daughters down the aisle, sees his sons start their own lives, buries his eighty-year-old wife, and one day, sitting on his porch, he dies peacefully after a long, fruitful existence.

A resolution doesn't have to always end in a big explosion or triumph. It can be a simple human story. For even that old man died happy, knowing he was going to see his wife again in the afterlife.

*Section 9: The Protagonist Fights And Wins*

# PLOT POINT 25
# THE PROTAGONIST BEGINS THEIR FINAL BATTLE
# (FINAL BATTLE)

Act 3, Section 9, PP25 means only one thing: the ultimate confrontation begins. The protagonist and antagonistic force directly clash, testing the protagonist on what they've learned and fought for to get to this final, high-stakes (hopefully) central conflict struggle with significant consequences.

That's a mouthful. Let's break it up. PP25 begins a final battle, but it's not the climax of the narrative. It's the start of the climax. Final battles can be a physical duel of the fates, an emotional reunion of lovers or parents with a child, or just about anything your mind can conjure up.

Keep in mind that this plot point is the beginning of Section 9, as well as the final battle itself, not its middle or end. In the immortal words of the one and only Shang Tsung, "It has begun!" That's the reality of PP25; the protagonist has one last battle, one that'll start them down the road toward the narrative's climax.

I'd also add that it doesn't actually have to be a battle to the death. It can be the moment a character hands someone a letter, professing their love to them. The final battle can be a surgery. A protagonist's final battle can be them kneeling down, preparing for the marathon they've been training for their whole life.

But, Thomas, a marathon sounds like a long start to a final battle.

Again, it's not about the length of the plot point; it's about what's going on within a plot point. In this case, PP25 could end up being three chapters long:

Chapter 1: They kneel at the line and run off across their first mile.

Chapter 2: The protagonist is in their tenth mile, feeling good.

Chapter 3: How are they doing on their twenty-fourth mile?

These chapters show their mental, physical, or spiritual state at different, specific mile markers as each chapter drives... runs a narrative forward. But each chapter does something important: it builds context to be challenged in PP26.

## *The 27 Plot Point Outline: When Plot Meets Story*

PP25 is Section 9's first plot point. It must set up context leading to the climax. Yes, readers need to know the protagonist's mental, physical, and spiritual states. They must know the stakes, the situation, and what a win looks like in the final battle. Readers need to know this as much as you do as a writer, as much as the characters (especially the protagonist) need to know.

But, Thomas, why do the characters need to know?

Characters need to know what they're fighting for, up against, and what it'll take to win (if they win at all). And as always, in section openers, context is king. Without it, you can't properly challenge anything in the section's middle plot point. Which, by the way, means you can't resolve it. And as we all know, Section 9's plot points need to constantly work toward resolutions.

Alright, let's summarize a few things.

PP25 sets up what the final battle is, how a protagonist could win (even though a victory or loss happens in PP26), and the final battle's stakes.

You should really only have major plot points to wrap up in PP25 (though some subarcs can still linger). The goal is to let the protagonist's central character arc be the focus of Section 9.

I mentioned that Section 8 should have the majority of subarcs resolved by PP24; if they aren't, it's here in PP25 that narrative beats should resolve any and all smaller subarcs. Again, this doesn't mean all of them—there's leeway to get them to resolve in the final twenty-seventh plot point (leeway).

> A quick aside: If there's too much going on in Section 9, check if the alpha or beta readers are able to keep track of everything. If they are unable to track it all, what character arcs/subarcs aren't mentioned?

I get it; some narratives are massive epic fantasies. But even A Song of Ice and Fire, Book 1, A Game of Thrones, has a few narrative threads near the end:

> Eddard's final chapter is shown through Arya, and then Bran, Sansa, Tyrion, Jon, and Catelyn get a chapter in the last seven chapters of the book. Daenerys Targaryen gets two chapters in those last seven, one of which is the final chapter of the book.

## Section 9: The Protagonist Fights And Wins

Interestingly enough, Arya's chapter isn't the final battle plot point. I'm using the last seven chapters as an example to show you how multiple threads are still resolving after the win or loss of PP26. I'm simply trying to explain that you can break rules when wrapping up subarcs or other POV narratives.

Here's the thing: Eddard might have been the protagonist, driving the central conflict forward as the Hand of the King, having learned of the previous Hand's death and the royal children's true bloodlines, but the central conflict still gets pulled to the end of the book by other characters.

However, those other characters still have narrative threads that need to either be finalized and resolved or seeded to lead to the next book.

My point is, in PP25, the final battle, any remaining subarcs or threads should directly connect to the central conflict, helping to truly elevate and drive the narrative forward. Though, the fewer subarcs you have roaming around in Section 9, the better.

Oh, sure, you could have untethered subarcs from the central conflict, but try to keep them from pulling attention away. After all, this is the start of the coming narrative crescendo.

Now that we know about PP25, let's check in on our alien invasion.

PP25: Our protagonist battles the alien commander and some of his minions. He defeats the alien guards and struggles against the much stronger commander. With the nuclear bomb close to detonating and on the verge of defeat, he uses his abilities regardless of the cost.

The life partner wins her fight, and the humans and best friend kill other aliens. The best friend nearly dies but is saved.

As you may notice, the central conflict stays on the protagonist and their fight against the alien commander (which will lead into Plot Point 26).

The life partner won their fight, ending their moment, leaving the focus on the protagonist in PP26. Additionally, the best friend and other humans win their fight... leaving lots of room and space for the protagonist to get the spotlight in the next plot point.

*The 27 Plot Point Outline: When Plot Meets Story*

# PLOT POINT 26
# THE PROTAGONIST WILL SUCCEED OR FAIL
# (CLIMAX)

It's time for the climax where a protagonist will succeed or fail in a battle against the antagonistic force (internally or externally).

But, Thomas, shouldn't the protagonist win in their own narrative?

There are many ways to win, even when it's a loss. In truth, your endings can all be victories (you're the writer). My pushback: nothing says you must have a positive ending. It's fine to have protagonists fail or lose their climactic battle. If they fail, it's usually (not always) a fatal flaw in their character or a tragic virtue.

If you haven't had a chance to see Joker and Joker: Folie à Deux, spoiler alert, he technically loses in those films. If you didn't know, Luke Skywalker loses in one of the greatest films in cinematic history: The Empire Strikes Back.

But, Thomas, is watching the protagonist lose something people enjoy?

I mean, if we're talking just hits, you have Thelma & Louise, Braveheart, Gladiator, American Beauty, Saving Private Ryan, and I Am Legend. By the way, those are films where the protagonist dies. Losses would be Se7en, Rocky, and if you like horror, Halloween.

It's not uncommon for a loss or death to occur in the ending climax. But remember, if they do lose, it must be earned, have a massive payoff, or potentially show the protagonist learning a moral lesson in the process.

Besides, if the protagonist does have a fatal flaw, it adds to the earned end of a much bigger narrative. Though, they don't always have to have a fatal flaw; it could be that they have a tragic virtue.

And if you don't remember...

*"Maximus Decimus Meridius, commander of the Armies of the North, general of the Felix Legions, and loyal servant to the true emperor, Marcus Aurelius. Father to a murdered son. Husband to a murdered wife. And I will have my vengeance, in this life or the next..."*

Wow, okay, even on the page I just got chills.

## Section 9: The Protagonist Fights And Wins

Sorry, my point still stands; Maximus didn't have fatal flaws in the sense of being like Joker. He had tragic virtues: his deep sense of pride, honor, and true loyalty to his emperor and family. He lost not because he wasn't capable or he had fatal flaws; he died due to his need to avenge his family and the Emperor, a father figure he lost.

He was loyal to the end, and it cost him everything. Even though he won and got everything he wanted, he still perished.

All I'm trying to say is, you have options when approaching a climax. It doesn't always have to be a win as much as it doesn't always have to be a loss. My suggestion is the same as always: remember the rule—it's relative to the narrative you're trying to tell.

Win or lose, the fundamental truth remains that all narratives must have an earned climax before the resolution. In a climax the central conflict reaches its narrative peak, fulfilling the final battle's purpose: can a protagonist achieve their goal or face ultimate failure?

Alien invasion time.

PP26: Fighting against the alien commander, the protagonist had to use his abilities (knowing he'll die as his powers run out) and was able to match the commander's strength. The two fight toe-to-toe, with the protagonist holding his own.

Going toe-to-toe, the alien commander uses his own enhancement device, but the protagonist breaks it free from him, overcharging it as he enhances his own power tenfold, killing the commander with a powerful eye beam, and finally collapsing on the ground himself.

The life partner hits the ship's self-destruction sequence and escapes the ship as it explodes. The life partner jumped to safety, knowing in their heart that the protagonist "dies" in the blast. Everyone watches the ship blowing up.

But, Thomas, you killed him!

## The 27 Plot Point Outline: When Plot Meets Story

Oh no! That's okay. It happens to the best of us. Besides, he still won, and Earth is safe—for now. We just have to wait for the sequel. Wait, we still have Plot Point 27: The Resolution. But, let me conclude PP26 for you.

PP26 is Section 9's middle, its conflict. This conflict elevates the stakes, pushing back on any and all context set up in PP25. Use this plot point to finish the final battle, ending the central conflict of a narrative. Whether that final battle is internal or external is up to you, and you have choices.

A romance might end with a big wedding. Horrors would see at least the protagonist (sometimes) defeat a monster. An FBI agent searches for the killer in a house, walking in a dark room, and kills Buffalo Bill. An epic fantasy adventure, where two hobbits finally toss a ring into a volcano after one of them just lost a finger from Gollum biting it off... Okay, that's a more specific example.

My point is, climaxes have room to play with them; genres will influence how much of it might be a physical fight, an emotional journey inward, or hell, a plethora of ideas can literally be pulled out of a hat. That's what makes writing so amazing; you can think of anything, and you need only follow the rules of the 27 Plot Point Outline as a guideline.

But, Thomas, you can't just make anything up? Doesn't it have to have some semblance of "interesting" or purpose?

A young fawn sees his mother get shot by a hunter. Our protagonist is a deer. He must figure out how to survive in the forest with no mommy. He makes friends with animals, let's say a rabbit, who introduces the deer (yes, the animals speak) to other animals of the forest. What is the climax? Well, it must be relative to the narrative.

A forest fire started by people camping. During this fire, the deer is shot in their leg, but before that happens, he saves his friends, love interest, and a deer friend... a... deer... friend... No? Just me? Anyway, a fire intensifies, and Bambi (yep, that Bambi) flees the blaze with his father. They escape to an island, where they find Faline and the other animals have also taken refuge.

It's all fake. It's all made up. Writing: the power of imagination. Literally, you can make up anything from humans falling in love to animals to germs living in cities inside a body as they keep a human body healthy.

Wow. All that freedom. What will you come up with? Oh... PP27!

*Section 9: The Protagonist Fights And Wins*

# PLOT POINT 27
# THE RESOLUTION OR THE IMMEDIATE REACTION TO THE RESULTS OF THE CLIMAX (RESOLUTION)

We're finally at the world's end. The final plot point of the 27 Plot Point Outline. A protagonist, by this point, should've gone on a magical adventure filled with a slew of trials and tribulations in a full and eventful narrative. Along the way, the narrative should've given us new characters, a world to explore, and pushed the narrative forward.

But it's time to wrap things up in Act 3, Section 9. The central conflict is most likely over in PP26, but if it's not, it needs to say goodbye in PP27. Ah yes, 'tis the denouement, the world after a climax, the world after a protagonist went through it all. This is it, the resolution beyond the results of the central conflict, giving the narrative and characters a new status quo and future potential.

Keep in mind, future potential doesn't mean a sequel or a series, though it could. A future potential is the life we believe they'll live beyond the resolution of the narrative.

> Willow: We know that Madmartigan and Sorsha will be a king and queen. We know that Willow Ufgood does make it home to his wife and becomes a name of importance among his village. And we know that Fin Raziel is free of her animal form.

And yes, in the grand scheme of narrative construction, there's plenty of nuance. Simply put: introduce a central conflict in Act 1, PP2 (inciting incident), and it concludes in Act 3, PP26 (climax). Now that the central conflict is resolved (potentially), the narrative must show a world after said central conflict is over.

However, let's look at the construction of the narrative's central conflict. If you notice, the central conflict was sandwiched between The Ordinary World of Act 1, PP1, and The Resolution of Act 3, PP27.

That's a narrative in a nutshell. It shows the world before the chaos of change, its disruption, after its disruption, and the journey of chaos to its end.

## The 27 Plot Point Outline: When Plot Meets Story

Now, in PP27, any remaining loose ends will get tied up. This is your last chance to wrap it up with a nice bow. Though, as mentioned, PP27 does double duty, it resolves Act 3 and the protagonist's central conflict. I know; that's a lot.

But, Thomas, how am I supposed to fit that all into one chapter?

Well, you don't have to do it in one chapter; however, that doesn't mean you couldn't fit it into one long chapter. Look, the reality of narrative is that you can do more than one thing in a sentence, let alone a passage, scene, or chapter.

But, Thomas, wouldn't doing more than one thing reduce the effect?

No. In fact, having a strong word economy comes from learning how to give each sentence, scene, and chapter a chance to pull the weight of a narrative.

I'll say this: one sentence could do one thing while the scene does a single other thing as the chapter itself does a third thing.

Oddly enough, easy-to-understand sentences (and chapters) are quite commonplace in middle grade and young adult books for a reason. But, you can still break things up and create rhythms and nuance in your work.

With that said, it's about having a command over your craft, which takes practice and time, leading you to give moments, like PP27, a payoff for both Act 3 and the protagonist's central character arc.

If you don't give those things a resolution, the whole manuscript might not feel finalized. Readers really do want it wrapped and finalized. Besides, your central conflict is easy to conclude; it's basically handled in PP26.

But, Thomas, how do I do that?

Obviously it depends on your narrative. A romance tries to resolve its happily ever after; maybe a job offer finalizes, and, of course, somehow Ben Stiller ends up with Jennifer Aniston. Oh, that's right, he's the producer.

However, let's look at the resolution of PP27 for the alien invasion, and then I'll show you how PP27 wraps up Act 3, Section 9, and the central conflict.

We know our protagonist was unconscious in the ship when it blew up...

PP27: The best friend and love interest celebrate with the humans, watching the ship explode. The life partner reaches the ground and looks back up at the explosion to see the protagonist floating in air.

## Section 9: The Protagonist Fights And Wins

The explosion combined with using the device at the same time gave the protagonist unlimited power, so he doesn't get weakened when he uses it. This ends the resolution with the reunion of characters, the defeat of the alien invasion, and Earth safe.

Wow, I'd read that book. What a triumphant return and victory. Oh, I'm sorry, I was getting caught up in the fun of the narrative. Where was I? Yes, I need to show you how to wrap up Act 3 and the protagonist's central character arc.

Let's talk about Act 3 first.

Act 3, Section 9, PP27: The protagonist fought the much stronger alien commander and struggled against him, only to risk his life to save Earth. The resolution is that the protagonist survives, the alien ship is destroyed, and everyone is safe on Earth.

Protagonist's Central Character Arc: From a mundane job and boss he hated to aliens showing up and changing his life. He changed and grew, having fought for the honor of his dead boss (who he hated), and the aliens were destroyed, freeing Earth from their invasion.

But, Thomas, what if I have sequels?

Wow, okay, we're just moving to the next question. That's okay, I get it; we're at the end, and we need to wrap things up.

What if there are sequels... Well, a resolution must wrap up the current narrative, even if it sets up a series or its sequel. It doesn't matter if there will be another three or ten more books, or if it's a standalone. Books must be a complete and contained narrative. Yes, you can seed future storylines, and yes, you can hint at things to come for the next narrative.

What you should never do as a writer is focus on anything that's not going to be narratively important to the current book. Oh, or worse, stand your ground on... "Oh, that'll pay off in book five." Pay off the book in their hand.

To be clear, you can include things that'll be in future books, especially if they influence the current narrative too. The secret to that is to make sure that

## The 27 Plot Point Outline: When Plot Meets Story

things pay off in the current narrative (even if it's going to keep going in the next books). And yes, the resolution of a narrative thread can hint at the next step.

For example: (Stop me if you've heard this one before), a character is told they're the heir to the throne, and in book one, this character proves that they're the king. However, in the next narrative, you can now explore them being the king.

But, wait, there's more.

In the first narrative, something is mentioned about their birthright and how the protagonist is connected to Bob. But Bob is presumed to be dead. Sure, the protagonist is connected to Bob, and Bob was royalty. Therefore, the protagonist is able to become king.

Though, in book two, Bob is still alive. So, Book 1 dropped Bob's name, connecting it to the protagonist, which was narratively important, helped resolve the central conflict, and seeded future threads for the next book's narrative.

Give me a moment to take a breath. We just finished the final plot point to the 27 Plot Point Outline, and I'm tired. Wait... ugh, let me wrap it up for you.

Remember, PP27 must resolve all narrative threads and give a sense of a potential future we may never see but believe the lives of the protagonist and other characters will go on, and, of course, feel like no threads are left unturned.

But, Thomas, what happens if I do leave threads open?

If they're for future narratives, that's fine. If not, then you have to do the work. Go back to the outline (or drafts), and seed information or create plot beats to pay off those threads in the narrative.

Once that's done, you'll have a complete narrative outline. Now it's time to play with the outline and have fun.

But, before you start outlining, I recommend you finish this book. After all, now you know what the 27 Plot Point Outline is and what all of the acts, their sections, and plot points do. So let the second half of this book show you how to use this newfound knowledge.

# CHAPTER 18

## Prologues and Epilogues

### PROLOGUES AND EPILOGUES

Nowadays, the word prologue is a stain on the tongues of writers. A place few are willing to venture, and even more have stayed completely away from. The reason? Readers. Yep, and it's not uncommon for readers to be wary of prologues, to the point where they skip them altogether.

But, Thomas, most prologues aren't even good.

Ah yes, the not-so-good prologue is a problem. Especially when it's used to drop a long, constipated info dump onto the page, forcing it into a frontload. No one enjoys reading backstory that could've easily been woven into a narrative. Over the years, those backstories have pushed the joy out of potentially awesome, amazing, and unique prologues, and... I get it.

We're not writing Lord of the Rings prologues anymore. Don't get me wrong, it's a fantastic prologue for what it was, setting the stage for epic fantasy and changing the known literary stage forever. You know, he is the grandfather of epic fantasy for a reason. Unfortunately, or fortunately, the reader and writer climate has vastly changed since July 29, 1954.

## The 27 Plot Point Outline: When Plot Meets Story

However, are prologues really still a no-go zone, or can we use them and not feel dirty in the morning? Who knows, but I'll try to make an argument for it, taking the position that prologues are still something to think about as an option.

Which brings us to the second part of this chapter: Epilogues.

Oddly enough, an epilogue is still generally seen in a more positive light than the dreaded, evil prologue. There's something about how an epilogue adds to a sense of closure, giving us a peek into the future or a character's life after the narrative ended. It's not too crazy to say that epilogues have a highly anticipated appreciation by readers, especially in genre fiction.

Though, I'd add that just because epilogues are fondly adored, it doesn't mean they're always used correctly. Nor does it mean that a great narrative can't be ruined by a poorly executed epilogue.

The truth remains: a prologue or epilogue can still ruin a narrative, but a poor one could destroy a reader's desire to continue to chapter one. The overall feeling is that prologues and epilogues must justify their existence. Basically, are they even really doing anything?

This question and others will be explored in this chapter, as I give you more than a list of what prologues and epilogues need. I'll give you a deeper why and what you should look for with either. With that, let's start the dive into what they are, how to use them, and why you should or shouldn't even bother.

## PROLOGUES

But, Thomas, what is a prologue, and what should you do in it?

I love this question, and I get it often from clients, writers, and random curious readers. Honestly, there's a long-winded answer and a short answer.

> Short answer: Is there information readers must have to set the tone, themes, author voice, and future elements that absolutely can't be explored within the narrative?

If your answer is "Yes, Thomas, I need to do all of that," then go on and write a prologue. Sometimes a prologue is great for doing the heavy lifting.

## *Prologues and Epilogues*

Okay, now the longer answer.

The long answer could end up being a list of clichéd rules and extremely generic explanations found in any book on writing or outlining. But if you need a quick list and have zero idea of what a prologue is, here's the list.

1. Hook the reader
2. Provide essential context
3. Introduce a different point of view
4. Set the tone
5. Foreshadow future events

But, Thomas, what does any of that mean? A hook? Set the tone?

If you've used social media or watched a "Five Reasons Prologues Fail" YouTube video, argh, well, them, there be hooks, matey, and not pirate ones.

Hooks catch an audience's attention by creating a question that needs to be answered in the full narrative, promising things to come or adventure (did you show magic in the prologue?). Or maybe it's just a massive action set piece.

Being vague but informative is a great way to hook a reader. It's a magic trick that answers just enough questions for context so readers understand what's going on. It then creates intrigue by leaving some questions unanswered so they lean in, wanting more. For example...

Prologue: Two men walked in the dark, guided by the limited warm orange hue of torchlight. It crackled over their conversation about the coming assassination of the queen—

But, Thomas, you said not to use prologues for exposition.
Correct. Keep following.

The two discussed the potential attempt coming, and deeper they walked into the darkness of the castle's underdeep. Wearing full armor, swords hung at their sides—both bore thick beards. A shed of light reached them from a close distance.

## The 27 Plot Point Outline: When Plot Meets Story

Stepping into a large room, a hum radiated from the presence of an open portal. Three robed men stood around it, chanting. One of the robed men turned, asking them if they brought the amulet.

The larger of the two handed the amulet to him, and he broke the gem from it, wrapping it in a red lock of the queen's hair. He handed it back to one of the knights.

"Once you walk through that portal, you'll forever be lost there, never to return to this moment."

"For the honor of Queen Abella and to save our kingdom," they said at the same time.

The two knights stepped through the portal as it closed after them.

Chapter 1: A redheaded woman finished up a client's dog; the client loved the work she did. She gave the client her business card.

"Tell your friends about Opatra's Wag and Groom—the first wash is ten percent off."

The bell above the door rang as the lady left.

The redhead entered her office and hopped over the arm of a torn-up leather couch. She tossed her feet up and spread her legs out.

She looked over at her large bag filled with books and papers. She pulled out an old, worn book and opened it to a bookmarked page.

"Queen Abella Opatra..." are the first words out of her mouth.

This prologue sets up questions, ends with some answers, and has both a hook and a cliffhanger. And the first chapter also hits with a hook. It went from knights to a dog groomer, ending with her reading a book about a queen bearing the same last name as her shop, connecting the chapter back to the prologue.

Look, not all narratives need a prologue, but if you're going to use one, have it feel like it's doing something. In fact, have it actually do something. If it's providing essential context, then do so by showing the world in motion, any, if at all, of the historical information, and, of course, showing who the characters are.

Some prologues start with different points of view, setting up a character the audience will meet in Act 2. POVs are great for setting narratives up through

## Prologues and Epilogues

the lens of another character and personality. Best for giving context to the world before the protagonist reaches it (or is introduced).

For me, an important aspect of a prologue is setting the tone, not just for the genre (though that's important to do—after all, romance has to romance as much as fantasy will fantasy), but to teach the reader who you are as a writer.

But, Thomas... Am I really supposed to explain who I am in my book?

Not with a short bio, but with your words you can tell readers who you are as a writer. Your style, the tense you'll use, themes, and how deep you go with immersion. See, part of reading is getting used to the lyrical or mechanical prose throughout the narrative.

There's a rhythm to your author voice, but also in what you're willing to write about. A good prologue sets the tone of how you'll present war, love, good, and evil. Is it a grand adventure or an intimate one? Will there be politics? Maybe add to the mood and atmosphere of your book, or set the simple cozy mystery up? All of this comes to light in the way you write a prologue (and the book in general).

However, keep in mind, this style must be kept up in the narrative too. My point still stands: a prologue sets the tone, as does it establish genre—whether it's a sense of dread, murder, any magic (fireball!), or a fun, lighthearted romance. These things can help foreshadow future events to come, doing so by showing or hinting at what has or will happen.

For example, the knights mentioned that there's a chance the queen will be assassinated. So... there's a potential that'll happen or has happened.

Alright. That's a lot of information—a thousand words explaining what a prologue is. Let's wrap it up:

Do you need a prologue?

What determines if you need one or not?

Fundamentally, a prologue is an opportunity to open with a segment of a novel that traditionally (and should) sit outside the narrative's timeline. I'd say that at its best, it sets the tone, stakes, or context needed for readers before diving into chapter one. At its worst, it's an infodump or a "chapter zero" that could've been folded into the actual narrative.

But, Thomas, should I have one or not?

It depends on what you're trying to do. And if you can do it elsewhere.

## The 27 Plot Point Outline: When Plot Meets Story

Honestly, I believe prologues shouldn't be for information. Prologues should avoid worldbuilding, history, or prophecy. But do you need one or not? I'd ask myself this question for my own prologues: Can this stuff be revealed much later and more naturally through flashbacks, conversation, and showing?

If the answer is yes, then you probably don't need the prologue. At the end of the day, your job as a writer is to ask questions and make confident answers to those questions. But a superpower writers can develop is when you're able to notice when things are happening but nothing is happening.

If things are happening but nothing is happening, it means a narrative's plot isn't being played out through the story, or rather, the emotional experiences and choices of your characters, but more so, it's just straight plot.

Just plot means you don't need the prologue—nothing is actually even happening on the page. True discovery is watching prologues live on their own, showing things, and letting it all happen through vague but informative moments.

I'm saying this because over the years, readers have been burned by these bloated prologues that feel like homework. So, some skip them entirely, and most publishers (literary agents) often advise against them. That's why we see more adult epic fantasy novels dropping prologues altogether. Which, by the way, upsets me personally, because I love a good prologue. Especially when it adds to a narrative, and a well-done one will change the reading experience for the better.

But a great prologue? It can be incredible. Epic fantasy thrives on scale, mythology, and intrigue. A prologue can drop readers into a pivotal event in the past that casts a shadow over the present-day narrative. Introduce a perspective or event that never returns but sets the tone. A great prologue can establish tension or mystery that frames the entire narrative.

So embrace the ideas you have in your head and see if a prologue is right for you. If not, remember, you can always cut up the information and seed it into your narrative with flashbacks, dialogue, and/or physically showing your world and how it was influenced by past events that left a lingering mark on the present.

A quick aside: Use prologues to add some narrative texture, and not to be a general "you should know this stuff first" experience.

*Prologues and Epilogues*

## EPILOGUES

If you've seen a Marvel movie in the last twenty years, you already know what an epilogue could be. We've all waited, watching long-winded closing credits scroll by, keeping you in your seat until you get a fun little extra treat at the end.

Of course, not all epilogues have to be like that. They could easily be so much more. The truth remains: epilogues do have a purpose and aren't just there for you to keep the narrative going.

Before I became a novelist, I studied film and television. I had a passion for screenwriting and developing projects. It's my love of film that probably leans me toward using epilogues and prologues like I'm writing a feature. I'd even say I write with a cinematic, third-person limited rotating style, moving my prose in a mixture of lyricism and clarity. I'm always searching for a camera angle, tracking shots, close-ups, and establishing shots.

Like all things, there are many ways to use epilogues and plenty of rules to break once you learn them. Therefore, I'll give you the short-short version of what an epilogue is, then go into much greater detail.

> Short answer: By design, epilogues are completely separate narrative plot points that sit after a narrative has run its course. It occurs after a central conflict has been resolved and often shows how a narrative left a lasting impact on the characters and their world. More so, it's used to tie up loose ends, offer a glimpse into a possible future, or set up a potential sequel.

Now it's time for a long-winded explanation. You want a list first? Yeah, you probably want a list to look at.

1. Provides a sense of closure
2. Ties up loose ends
3. Highlight any character growth
4. Can release tension after a big climax
5. Often used to set up a sequel

## The 27 Plot Point Outline: When Plot Meets Story

Lists are pretty... but they don't explain what things are. As we all know, my brain won't allow me to leave it at a list. Also, this list isn't a complete one. It's complete enough for this chapter and what you'll need to start your journey into making choices. Choices to change the game by changing the brain of writing.

Alright, enough inspirational talk; let's dive into it.

I said earlier that epilogues all have a purpose, and they do, to provide a... Well, you saw the list above, but it's more than that, much, much more than that. However, epilogues can fall into the same pitfalls as prologues. They can feel like a next chapter, another info-dump so thick it clogs the reader's mind toilet.

Can we just do a quick aside: don't do info-dumps. Okay, rant over.

But, Thomas, what if I need information to be told to the reader?

Seed exposition in the narrative and allow it to be delivered in piecemeal. Prologues and epilogues should never be exposition dumps. Chapters—well, I'd say you should hold off on dumping information. It's more economic to deliver exposition in action, character dialogue, and narrative movement than to have it come off as a stop-the-press, a heavy aside coming through.

Besides, do you really have enough money for the exposition jar?

Okay, moving on. My point is, you don't want exposition or epilogues to do what just happened in the above passage: stop the narrative flow to explain things. So when narratives are over, they're over, and epilogues should be their own nice moment that shouldn't sludge through to another ending.

Bad epilogues feel off from a narrative or mess up pacing and its tone by taking a resolution and keeping it going—keep an eye on pace and tone. Oh, and adding new plotlines out of nowhere can feel too vague and confusing.

If you notice those things in an outline or even a draft, there are simple fixes. For now, one is to keep consistency with the overall tone and pacing of the book. Another is that epilogues shouldn't feel like the beginning of the next book. This happens when new characters or the "ordinary world" are introduced from out of nowhere. Basically, an epilogue isn't meant to tease another book with the first chapter.

But, Thomas, all that sounds great, though what's a good epilogue?

## *Prologues and Epilogues*

This next part isn't what makes a good epilogue (that's subjective), but these things are what an epilogue can be, do, and explore. Let's play out of order from the above list and go into releasing tension after a big climax.

Deadpool (the first movie) plays with the audience and gives them a Ferris Bueller's Day Off after-credit epilogue.

This does a great job in releasing the tension after the big climax, as well as teasing what's to come (Cable). For a narrative, you can use your epilogue to do the same thing as the hit, Deadpool. You can do this by letting the epilogue be a fun, relaxed scene that says that everything's going to be alright.

By the way, an epilogue doesn't always have to come after the credits in a film—and yes, I know this book is for outlining long-form narratives, but I'm telling you this so you know what to look for as you study a film with the 27 PPO.

For me, I do enjoy using epilogues to set up sequels, giving the reader a peek into what's to come. Not that I do this every time, but it's nice to say, "Hey, if you come back, you'll know what's to come."

Of course, don't break the rule of setting up the next book by starting the epilogue off in a new ordinary world. A fun example of doing it right was in The Curse of the Black Pearl. I'm talking about the scene with Hector Barbossa dead on a pile of gold, and his monkey shows up with the cursed coin. It tells the audience that things might not be over for Hector or the series. What it doesn't do is give us Barbossa waking up and trying to figure out what's going on.

If epilogues present new information, orient the characters to figure out what's next, etc., the epilogue is basically another chapter. It's stronger to have the epilogue feel like it's in the middle of something else, not the start of it.

Another strong use for epilogues is giving the narrative a sense of closure or show character growth, maybe even tying up loose ends by giving the reader a glimpse into their future.

For example: After a mighty warrior defeated an evil antagonist, the epilogue shows them living a calm life on a farm with a family. And no, his name isn't Thanos (that was PP27 in Infinity War).

## The 27 Plot Point Outline: When Plot Meets Story

I'd say another example of this is a jump forward, showing a character getting ready for another crime, meeting up with a character that was introduced in Act 2, etc.

But, Thomas, you said don't set up ordinary worlds or a new plot point.

Correct. In this example the character was introduced in Act 2, and the protagonist's original ordinary world showed them breaking in to rob a house, only to meet up with a seller for the items they stole before the inciting incident happens. Ultimately, this example shows that the character's still doing what they do, and it's all good for them (they continue being a criminal).

However... What if the protagonist arrives back on the island and shows up to a character introduced in Act 2, saying, "It's time we talked about the Dial of Fortune"? And the returning character says, "I thought you'd never ask."

This introduces the future, a potential sequel, and provides a sense of closure, telling us that the character continues to do what they do.

What about tying up loose ends or giving a protagonist a bit of character growth as they're ready to tackle a difficult crime? In fact, a narrative could have a character introduced in Act 2 ask the protagonist to help them with a big crime, but the protagonist says it's far too dangerous. Only for them to come back in the epilogue and say... "It's time we talked about the Dial of Fortune."

Which brings us to the end and a final touch of wisdom. Remember, an epilogue should be distinct from the rest of the narrative while still connected to its tone, pace, and themes, giving both a sense of closure to what has come before without saying we're starting over even when it's setting up the potential for the next big thing.

At the end of the day, have fun with epilogues, even in a horror or crime novel, and also, not every narrative needs an epilogue. But if you end up having one, keep it concise. Sure, a prologue can be longer; in fact, it can have more than one (right, Brandon Sanderson?), but epilogues should be brief. If it becomes too long and contains too much new information, it might turn into the next chapter, or your narrative might need more space.

Either way, prologues and epilogues can be a magical part of a narrative, adding to it and the reader's experience. My final note of advice is to use either of them purposefully and wisely, giving them a sense of belonging.

# CHAPTER 19

# Pirates of the Caribbean: The Curse of the Black Pearl

**PIRATES OF THE CARIBBEAN: THE CURSE OF THE BLACK PEARL**

To say that Pirates of the Caribbean shouldn't have found any success as a movie is an understatement. It's based on a Disney ride, and sure, it has star power, a list of talented unknowns, and great performances—but it still screamed failure.

Who knew this pirate ride movie would start a billion dollar franchise?

Well, the truth is, and I'm proud to say it, I love this movie. I have almost nothing bad to say about it. I can't help it; my brain even analyzes perfect movies. The Shawshank Redemption is my favorite film, and still, I point out things that don't really matter, but, hey, the lesson is that in this world, nothing is perfect.

If you've not seen The Curse of the Black Pearl yet, it's absolutely a ride worth taking. With that said, if you've not seen it, please skip this chapter. A few spoilers are going to pop up as I analyze this fantastic experience, start to finish, breaking down the 27 PPO's narrative beats, acts, sections, and plot points.

If you're still here, then read the chapter first, take notes, and then watch the film. As you do, check your notes and make adjustments based on how each scene connects to one of the twenty-seven plot points. Yes, plot points can have more than one scene to them, just as plot points can have more than one chapter.

## The 27 Plot Point Outline: When Plot Meets Story

## PROLOGUE

Characters, themes, tone, and history are all shown in a brief, effective prologue. We meet our protagonists, William Turner and Elizabeth Swann, see how he got to Port Royal, and meet Mr. Swann, the governor. Our final introductions are James Norrington and Mr. Gibbs (he returns in Act 2).

What's nice about this opener is that the pirates, the Black Pearl, and the destruction they leave behind are placed before us, the audience. We now know how ruthless the pirates are, Gibbs is superstitious, and a single cursed medallion is on William Turner's person. Who takes and hides it? Elizabeth Swann.

The audience is presented with questions and answers to know what's going on and enough relevant context to understand who the characters are, their reactions to things, and dialogue. As you can see, an ordinary world isn't set up here. But the prologue gives context to history without doing an info dump.

A fantastic prologue that gives us mystery, plot seeding, tone, theme, and character introductions. It does everything it needs to in a tight four minutes and fifty seconds. And the Black Pearl is the last thing seen in Elizabeth Swann's POV, looking at it and transitioning to a present day version of her waking up (hook).

As a movie, it does it all in a few minutes. However, in a novel, you can go beyond a brief scene. Prologues have wiggle room, and they can do more than one thing in them, so play around and find out.

## ACT 1, SECTION 1
## SETTING UP THE ORDINARY WORLD (SETUP)

```
PP1: The Ordinary World Before the Disruption (Introductions)
```

PP1 sets up context for the central conflict, protagonists, and world rules, desires, wants, and some positions (challenged and changed throughout the narrative).

This first plot point establishes the status quo and what developed since the prologue. A leap forward, if you will, to give us a peek into William Turner's new ordinary world and his life as the blacksmith's assistant. He has unrequited love for the governor's daughter, Elizabeth Swann, a woman trying to navigate

## *Pirates of the Caribbean: The Curse of the Black Pearl*

aristocratic life. Mr. Turner delivered a sword (that he made) to Mr. Swann for James Norrington's promotion with the British Navy.

In these first few scenes of the movie, we're given a great deal of context without it being explained to us. We see William's shyness, Elizabeth's boldness, a bit of life they've grown to have in Port Royal, and an everyday, ordinary world of these characters. William loves Elizabeth but won't take action on it; she wants adventure, and her father and James Norrington have other plans for her.

### PP2: The Disruption of the Ordinary World (Inciting Incident)

This scene shall disrupt and change their lives forever. And well, it should, as the inciting incident sparks the central conflict into motion.

If this moment had never happened, the characters would've continued on in the world they knew, at least until another inciting incident hit.

Port Royal is given the pleasure of welcoming Captain Jack Sparrow's arrival. His arrival activates a potential for future possibilities. If he never arrived, William Turner wouldn't have taken action like he does later in PP8.

As for Elizabeth Swann, James Norrington proposes to her, but due to her father's gift, the dress she received in PP1, she can't breathe and falls into the sea. Her medallion signals the Black Pearl, setting the stage for the coming attack.

What's fantastic about the scenes in Plot Point 2 is the character work in every little moment. Jack's arrival on the ship, the imagery, and the grandness, only to realize he's on a tiny sinking dinghy, and his moment of silence for other pirates shows who Jack is. Then we get the treat of his coin moment, paying two coins before stealing a small pouch of more coins.

Study these scenes, and take note of how you too can say so much with so little exposition simply by showing characters making choices, being put into situations where there's a little conflict, even if it's not a battle, and moving the narrative forward. Conflict/tension equals engagement and movement.

A quick aside: Yes, Captain Jack Sparrow arrived in PP2, and still, he got an ordinary world (introduction). A narrative is driven by the central conflict, but secondary character arcs still get their own PP0.

## The 27 Plot Point Outline: When Plot Meets Story

### PP3: The Protagonist Reacts to the Inciting Incident (Fallout)

The first reaction is a shifting wind for both the central conflict and the coming Pearl. Another reaction is Jack Sparrow… I mean, Captain Jack Sparrow jumping in the water to save Elizabeth Swann from drowning.

A series of events lead to Jack being arrested, using Elizabeth to run off, and eventually fighting William at a shop.

What I love about these scenes is the cause and effect. Jack shows up to port, Elizabeth falls into the water, Jack dives in, saving her, which leads to James Norrington arresting Jack, only for Jack to run away with cuffs on… Which leads him to the blacksmith to break the cuffs off… ending with him fighting William.

This is great writing. Nothing is convenient. Each small scene detail adds to the narrative, escalating and leading to bigger reveals or pushes later. Sure, we see William's skill with a sword, his boss sleeping drunk, and Jack doesn't want to use the bullet on William (it's for someone else), costing Jack to be knocked out.

All these moments unfold in the first three plot points, pushing forward the narrative's plot through story. Yes, in a long-form creative narrative of a novel, your first three plot points might take five to fifteen chapters. Writing prose gives you time to sit in the characters' heads, play in immersion, and give texture to the overall narrative itself. A film or TV show will always feel faster.

My point is, even when you're writing a book, you want each scene to be more than only a scene doing only one thing. Connect cause and effect, seed, and foreshadow for payoffs, ones that don't pay off until a chapter, two, or ten later.

This is possible by going back after you finish your first outline draft and seed connecting minor details to previous plot points.

Alright, let's speed things up and get through these plot points, sections, and acts so you're not reading this chapter all day. You have an outline to get back to once you're finished reading and learning from this book. Besides, if I break it all into finer details, how will you learn while watching this fantastic movie?

*Pirates of the Caribbean: The Curse of the Black Pearl*

# ACT 1, SECTION 2
# A PROBLEM DISRUPTS THE PROTAGONIST'S LIFE (CONFLICT)

PP4: The Protagonist Reacts to and Reflects on The Long Term Impacts of the Inciting Incident (Reflection/Choice)

Sparrow is in a jail cell, trapped in his new circumstances. Swann gets ready for bed, reflecting on her near-death experience and James Norrington's proposal. Swann reveals feelings for William.
"Turner is a fine man too."
"That is too bold..."

PP5: The Protagonist Takes Action (Action)

The Black Pearl arrives, attacking Port Royal. William fights pirates, "killing one" (shows he's not afraid to kill to protect). During all of this, two pirates make their way to Elizabeth, drawn by the power of the medallion. They find her, and she asks for parley.

PP6: The Immediate Consequences of the Action Taken By The Protagonist (Consequences)

Turner is knocked out during the battle. Swann is taken aboard the Black Pearl. Enter Hector Barbossa, Captain of the Black Pearl. She bargains, claiming to be a Turner. Barbossa agrees—his people leave the port. Still in a cell, Jack learns the curse is real (connecting him to the pirates, curse, and history).

A quick aside: Each movement in Section 2's three plot points does something specific. Basically, it sets up the context, establishing the circumstances of the characters, challenging that context when the ship arrives, and giving each character a clear resolution forward.

*The 27 Plot Point Outline: When Plot Meets Story*

# ACT 1, SECTION 3
# THE PROTAGONIST'S LIFE CHANGES DIRECTION (RESOLUTION)

> PP7: The Protagonist's Life Changes as a Result of the Action They Took, Creating Pressure and Stress (Pressure)

Elizabeth's on the Pearl (she's absent from this plot point). William wakes up on the street in the morning, realizing Elizabeth was taken. He challenges Commodore James Norrington to take action. James reminds him that he's not the only one who cares for Elizabeth.

> PP8: The First Major Plot Twist,
> or Pinch, Happens (Plot Twist/Pinch)

William Turner makes a bold move and heads to the cells, where he asks Captain Jack Sparrow for help (twist). After learning William's last name is Turner, Jack agrees (he knows William's father). William breaks Jack from his cell, and they escape.

> PP9: Because of The Plot Twist or Pinch,
> The Protagonist Is Pushed into a New World (Pushed)

There's one way out of Port Royal: Jack and William steal a ship. James Norrington underestimated Jack, losing the HMS Interceptor to William and apparently the smartest pirate he's ever seen. James must prepare a ship to chase Jack and William and save Elizabeth.

A quick aside: Context → Action → Consequence. As you can see, the pattern is constant in sections, as they are in acts. PP7 sets up the context, PP8 challenges it with action, and PP9 resolves the section, resulting in the consequences of their action, pushing it all forward.

*Pirates of the Caribbean: The Curse of the Black Pearl*

# THINGS ACT 1 SETS UP

Captain Jack Sparrow is a smart and savvy pirate with style. His goal and motivations are simple: reclaim the Black Pearl and use his one bullet for but one other person (but who?). Jack is a fully realized character by the time Act 1 ends, but we know who he is in Section 1.

Elizabeth Swann navigates her aristocratic life as the daughter of the governor. Her goals and motivations are to have a life beyond being only a wife, have adventure and passion, and save Port Royal, which backfires, so now she wants to get back home safe.

William Turner hates pirates, is a swordsman and blacksmith, and is deeply in love with Elizabeth Swann. But we learn that he's shy and still able to take proactive steps for what he believes in. His goals and motivations are to save the love of his life and bring her back home.

James Norrington is promoted to Commodore in the British Navy, hates pirates, and loves Elizabeth. His goals and motivations are to save Elizabeth, capture Jack and William, and stop the Black Pearl so he can then marry the woman he loves.

Hector Barbosa is equally cunning and intelligent. He's the Black Pearl's captain. His arrival means no survivors (well then, who tells all the stories?). His goals and motivations aren't clearly stated, but they are seeded to break the curse.

A quick aside: Act 1 itself set up the plot, characters, and the world. The viewer now has the context to understand what's happening, what's at stake, and who these characters are so we can follow them around for the next two hours and twenty-three minutes.

*The 27 Plot Point Outline: When Plot Meets Story*

# ACT 2, SECTION 4
# THE PROTAGONIST EXPLORES THE NEW WORLD (SETUP)

```
PP10: The Protagonist is Introduced
   To the New World (New World)
```

William and Jack sail the HMS Interceptor. William accepts that he must follow a pirate and is told that his father, Bootstrap Bill, was a pirate and a great friend. William doesn't believe Jack. Their next goal is to get a full crew before saving Elizabeth.

```
PP11: The Protagonist Can Take A Break
   And Have A Little Fun (Fun & Games)
```

William and Jack arrive in Tortuga. Jack gets slapped a few times (I don't think I deserved that). They walk around the party city. In comes Mr. Gibbs (returns). Jack tells him his plan to get the Black Pearl back—William is his leverage. Turner overhears them.

```
PP12: The Protagonist Compares Their Current World
   To How Things Were At The Beginning (Juxtaposition)
```

Hector Barbossa tells Elizabeth about the curse and that he needs her blood. Elizabeth stabs Barbossa and learns an important truth: she best start believing in ghost stories, because she's in one. The world she knew is no longer the world she knew (the difference is shown instead of told).

A quick aside: Before the narrative gets crazier in the coming chaos of the midpoint conflict, Section 4 establishes the new world of the second act, exploring it and establishing the... yep, you guessed it, the context so we can challenge it in Section 5.

## ACT 2, SECTION 5
## THE CRISIS OF THE NEW WORLD (CONFLICT)

PP13: The Buildup To The Midpoint Conflict (Buildup)

Jack Sparrow—sorry, Captain Jack Sparrow procures a crew, sailing off to Isla de Muerta to find Swann and Barbossa. They sail through a rough storm overnight. The pirates make it to Isla de Muerta with Swann, pushing her into the cave.

PP14: The Midpoint Conflict (Midpoint)

Mr. Gibbs tells William about Barbossa leading a mutiny against Jack and leaving him on an island. They reach Isla de Muerta. Barbossa cuts Elizabeth's hand and learns she's not related to Bootstrap Bill (the truth of the lie is revealed), and the curse isn't broken. William betrays Jack by knocking him out before he saves Elizabeth.

PP15: The Immediate Reaction or Consequence Of the Midpoint Conflict (Reversal)

Barbossa's men search for Elizabeth and find Jack wandering. Jack calls for...
"Par... par..."
"Parley?"
"Yes, that's the one."
Turner takes Swann to the HMS Interceptor and tells the crew Jack fell behind (stick to the code), leaving Jack there.

A quick aside: This section starts with one understanding and ends with another. Everything is turned upside down: William betrayed Jack, Jack is with Barbossa, and Swann wasn't the cure for the curse.

*The 27 Plot Point Outline: When Plot Meets Story*

## ACT 2, SECTION 6
## FINDING A SOLUTION (RESOLUTION)

PP16: The Protagonist Reflects on the Long Term Impacts
Of the midpoint Conflict (Consequence)

Jack Sparrow makes a deal with Barbossa: give him back the Black Pearl, and he'll tell Barbossa who to find to break his curse. William puts everything together after Elizabeth tells him the truth and gives him the medallion back. He's the secret to breaking the curse, and his father was a pirate—all he knew is turned upside down.

PP17: The Protagonist Takes Action to Resolve the Problem
Created by the Midpoint Conflict (Trials/Tested)

Hector Barbossa follows close behind the HMS Interceptor, but his Black Pearl is faster. There's no way to break free. Barbossa catches up to the ship. Barbossa has Jack locked in a cell before they reach the other ship. Elizabeth gets the crew prepared for battle, dropping anchor to attack the Black Pearl.

PP18: Despite the Setbacks, The Protagonist Decides
They Will Succeed No Matter What (Dedication)

The only thing left to do is fight to survive. William and Elizabeth fight alongside the crew, the Black Pearl pushes back on them, and Turner is trapped in the hull, drowning. The monkey finds the medallion and returns it to Barbossa. The crew is brought aboard the Pearl, and the HMS Interceptor blows up. Turner died!?

A quick aside: A problem was caused in the midpoint conflict; thus, this section must find a solution to it. William's is easy: survive. The other solution is getting the medallion and William (for Jack's plan).

*Pirates of the Caribbean: The Curse of the Black Pearl*

## THINGS ACT 2 CHALLENGES

Captain Jack Sparrow believed he had the upper hand on William Turner, using him for his plan to get his Black Pearl back. However, Turner betrayed Jack, forcing Jack to make a deal with a person who led the mutiny against him: Barbossa.

Elizabeth thought she was safe and in control, having given William's last name to Barbossa to save Port Royal. It pulled her into the valley of the beast, being used to cure the curse. She ended up in over her head and now might die in this ghost story she best be believing in.

William Turner doesn't like pirates and believes Jack is lying to him about his father, Bootstrap Bill Turner, being a pirate. It all comes together later, and he must accept the truth: his father was a pirate and a good man—he comes from pirate blood. He can end the curse.

James Norrington basically is gone for the second act. He vanishes from the narrative. It's assumed he's roaming the oceans, searching for Elizabeth. His positions remain: he still hates pirates and loves Elizabeth. Meaning he won't stop till he finds her and saves her.

Barbossa found the final coin and Bootstrap's kid, Elizabeth, or so he thought. The curse wasn't broken, and thus he must continue to find Bill's heir. Put into a position with Jack, he agrees to work with him to bring an end to the curse he's lived with for far too long.

A quick aside: Act 2 has challenged all the main characters, putting them in positions that push back on their positions. William, who is the main protagonist, specifically doesn't like pirates, but now he must work with one, is related to one, and makes choices like one.

*The 27 Plot Point Outline: When Plot Meets Story*

## ACT 3, SECTION 7
## VICTORY SEEMS IMPOSSIBLE (SETUP)

PP19: The Protagonist Faces Difficult and Significant Trials, Something They Have Never Experienced Before (Calm Before the Storm)

William is alive! He climbs up on the Black Pearl and holds a gun to his head. This pulls the power dynamic from Barbossa as he reveals he's Bootstrap Bill's son. He can break the curse. William demands Elizabeth and the crew be freed and left unharmed. Barbossa agrees.

PP20: A Second Major Plot Twist or Pinch Where The Protagonist Experiences A Completely Unexpected Event, Making It All Worse (Plot Twist/Pinch)

Barbossa leaves Jack and Elizabeth on the same island he marooned Jack on once, leaving them to die. Barbossa allows them to have one pistol between them. Jack can be a gentleman and decide who lives. This is a pinch and places the character on their back foot.

PP21: The Final Major Plot Twist, or Pinch, Leads to the Darkest Moment, and Success Feels Incomprehensible (Darkest Moment)

In their darkest moment, Elizabeth learns a deeper truth: Jack was on this island once before, stranded for a total of three days before a rum-smuggling ship arrived. But since the authorities have stopped the smugglers, it's unlikely anyone will be around to save them.

A quick aside: The takeaway is that each plot point in this section slowly leads the characters to their darkest moment. Hope is there in PP19, but by the end of PP21, they're trapped on an island.

*Pirates of the Caribbean: The Curse of the Black Pearl*

# ACT 3, SECTION 8
# THE PROTAGONIST FINDS THE POWER (CONFLICT)

PP22: Having Hit Rock Bottom, The Protagonist
Finds A Power Within To Succeed (Power Within)

Elizabeth drinks with Jack till he is passed out drunk. During this time, he talks about his passion for the Black Pearl.
"But what a ship is, what the Black Pearl really is... it's freedom."
Elizabeth has a secret plan to get them off the island.

PP23: The Protagonist Takes Action (Action To Rally)

Elizabeth burns all the rum. This creates a massive fire to hopefully catch the sight of Commodore James Norrington.
"The entire Royal Navy is looking for me."
"But why is the rum gone?!"
It works! They're saved. Elizabeth wants the navy to save William. She makes a deal with Norrington to marry him if he saves William.

PP24: The Convergence of Storylines
And Building up to the Final Battle (Converge)

Commodore Norrington and his crew settle outside the caves while Captain Jack Sparrow goes in to make a deal with Hector Barbossa. Jack does indeed make another deal with Barbossa, telling him about the navy. Jack secretly takes a cursed coin from the treasure chest. The pirates head out (take a walk). Elizabeth escapes the room of the ship she was on. She heads to the Black Pearl to save the crew.

A quick aside: Context, context, context. Context is king. These plot points set up the coming final battle. We know where the pieces are (characters), and now we sit back and wait for the fight.

*The 27 Plot Point Outline: When Plot Meets Story*

# ACT 3, SECTION 9
# THE PROTAGONIST FIGHTS AND WINS (RESOLUTION)

PP25: The Protagonist Begins Their Final Battle
(Final Battle)

The pirate zombies attack the navy's ship (a big fight). Jack Sparrow and William Turner attack Barbossa, and Elizabeth makes it to the Black Pearl, freeing the crew. James Norrington heads back to his ship to help fight off the undead pirates.

PP26: The Protagonist Will Succeed or Fail (Climax)

Barbossa stabs Jack in the chest, revealing Jack is cursed. The fight continues on, but now on equal ground. Jack's crew runs off after Elizabeth frees them. She heads off to help Jack and William in the cave. Commodore Norrington makes it to the ship, and they fight the pirates. Elizabeth joins Will and Jack in their fight, helping them. Jack kills Barbossa after breaking the curse, leading to Norrington winning against the pirates to take back the ship.

PP27: The Resolution Or Immediate Reaction
To the Results of the Climax (Resolution)

Jack is sentenced to death for being a pirate. Turner finally professes his undying love to Elizabeth before trying to save Jack Sparrow. Jack and William fight, eventually stopping. Ultimately Jack jumps into the ocean, and his old crew arrives, lifting him out of the water. Norrington gives Jack a head start and recuses his love for Elizabeth so she can be with William.

A quick aside: The final section works towards a resolution. It starts with the final battle, hits the climax, and resolves narrative threads.

*Pirates of the Caribbean: The Curse of the Black Pearl*

## THINGS ACT 3 RESOLVES

Jack Sparrow gets his Black Pearl back, a crew he can trust, and lives to sail on for another day of freedom!
"And really bad eggs. Drink up, me 'earties. Yo ho."

Elizabeth Swann returns home and is given the freedom to make her own choices to be with the man she really loves.

William Turner professed his love to Elizabeth and went out of his way to save a pirate... and a good man. Turner takes the punishment for all his crimes, only for Norrington to set him free to be with the love of his life. William no longer hates pirates.

Hector Barbossa... Well, he did break the curse, but he never got to eat his green apples because, well, he's dead now. Or is he?

James Norrington did what he set out to do: stop the pirates and the Black Pearl and, of course, save Elizabeth Swann from certain death.

A quick aside: From PP19 to PP27, every beat must move toward a full and complete resolution. As you can see, each plot point is tight and keeps the narrative momentum going. There is very little, if any, fluff being fed to the audience in Act 3. Save Will, get Pearl, and profess his love to Elizabeth.

## EPILOGUE

Back in the cave on Isla de Muerta, Hector Barbossa's body is there, lying on the treasure. His monkey's alive and well... cursed, holding a piece of Aztec gold.

# CHAPTER 20

## Start With Character

**START WITH CHARACTER**

It all begins with character. Everything we've gone over about outlining starts by understanding your characters. Earlier I said that plot-driven narratives still need to know who the characters are.

As a writer, you've probably heard about needing a three-dimensional character. This doesn't mean they're literally three-dimensional people living in a two-dimensional world. It means that they have depth. Depth will always be more interesting than another chess piece moving the plot around.

To find a character's true purpose, you need to understand who they are, but do you need a full list of their flaws, motivations, favorite fruit, or hair color? No. No, you do not. In fact, I'd say you can wait until you get into the nit and grit of your narrative's story before you worry about the "details." During the process of outlining your plot, you really only need to know their character arcs.

But, Thomas, shouldn't I know what their faith is, or race, or the color of their eyes to know what to write for their character arc?

No. Great character work begins and ends with internal truths driven by their emotional experiences and choices. Even an external conflict will take you so

## The 27 Plot Point Outline: When Plot Meets Story

far before their internal truths determine their behavior toward it. So it's best to understand who characters are internally before external aspects define who they are simply by what they are (or look like).

A six-foot-three Italian man with green eyes from Rome, working at the bank, doesn't tell readers or writers any real truths about them. Well, unless you want a two-dimensional character and a bunch of stereotypes.

All I'm saying is that being Italian isn't inherently interesting; it doesn't explain how they'll behave on the page. And behavior is both interesting and will tell you more about who they are internally than any external factor would.

But, Thomas, don't Italians behave a certain way?

No. However, growing up in Italy from the age of two won't guarantee they'll have the Italian culture of the region, even if they're French by birth. But even then, this won't define their behavior.

For example, a six-foot character means he's tall, but does it tell us he's brave? He's an Italian man living in Rome. But did he grow up there or just move there? Does living in Rome make them Catholic, or are they something else?

The thing is, what someone is isn't who they are. Even an Irish boy born in Utah, adopted by a Korean family at birth, doesn't make him American, Irish, or Catholic. Nor does it make him Korean. I mean, he's Irish by heritage, but was he raised around Irish culture or Korean culture? Yeah, and still, none of that will absolutely tell you how they behave.

Their culture could influence them, sure, but being Italian doesn't mean they're destined to speak with their hands, love pasta, or wear gold chains around their neck while praying to Saint Francis of Assisi, the patron saint of Italy.

However, their culture is more about who they are internally. The things that matter to them might connect to their culture. Then again, Irish heritage doesn't influence them being born in the United States of America and raised by Koreans. Nor does it mean they know anything about being Irish.

To be clear, when I say internal truths make up who a character is, I'm not saying you can't write about a culture, lifestyle, faith, etc. I'm saying that the outlining process begins with plot: what must happen no matter what, and how the characters will react to it. Once you write the drafts, that other stuff unfolds through the narrative's story.

*Start With Character*

But even the mystery thriller The Da Vinci Code by Dan Brown isn't about faith or Italian Catholics. It's about Robert Langdon uncovering secrets hidden in Da Vinci's work, exposing Jesus' bloodline (as per the book's world).

But, Thomas, how do I do what you're talking about?

Think about who a character is within. From there, figure out what they are and why they are. I'll go deeper into all of this below and explain the terms you may know of and a few new ones to help you better understand your characters.

## POSITIONS & MOTIVATIONS

Who are we? Like, who are we really? What makes us who we are? I know above I said it's the internal truths, but how do you figure out what those internal truths are? Well, how about we look at positions and motivations?

But, Thomas, it's only positions & motivations? Faith isn't internal?

It's not so much that they have faith or faith itself that'll determine their internal truths. Here, ask yourself, "What determines a person's faith?" Is it them having said faith, or is it what led them to their faith (or away from it) that's their internal truth?

If they go to temple solely to worship the Green Leaf Tree Gods, then yes, that's external. Is it a deep truth? Is there depth? No. It's just something they do on Montuesday at 2pm.

But a better question to get you closer to their internal truth is the "why" leading to the deeper reason they go to temple. Or what's their position on faith?

A position, and their motivation, leads us closer to a character's internal truths, giving insight into who a character is. For example...

> A protagonist goes to temple to spend more time with their mother because it's the only time they can spend with her.

That right there is a motivation.

Want to go deeper? Let's look at a position. Their position on faith will be that they don't believe in the Green Leaf Tree God. Want another position? They love their mother more than anything in the world.

## The 27 Plot Point Outline: When Plot Meets Story

These positions and motivations give readers and you insight into who a character is. Which means you have a clearer picture of how they react to certain things. If someone challenges their faith, they won't care… But, a kid from down the block shows up and says, "Yo mama so fat, God said, 'Let there be light,' and he had to ask her to move out of the way."

Well, a "yo mama" joke will push him to say something. His behavior is motivated to take action. The reason? He loves his mother more than anything in the world, as per his position.

And that's the truth: we are the positions we hold close to our hearts and the motivations that drive us.

But, Thomas, what are positions and motivation?

Position: A character's belief, from as simple as their favorite color or football team to their complex stances on killing people, faith, or morality. If they care about it, they have a position on it.

Motivation: A driving force behind a character's desire, giving them reasons to achieve their goals—a reason to act, or rather, the agency a character holds to take action. Their "why" before taking action.

Motivations are quite straightforward; they're the fuel behind their need to achieve something. A character works sixty hours a week, so they go to temple because it's the only time they can spend with their mother. She's getting older, so he needs to be with her as much as possible.

Of course, the character might never say that on the page. In fact, they don't have to say it on the page. That's exposition. Their behavior will do the real work, showing the readers character motivations and positions on the page. That doesn't mean you can't say it, nor does it mean that you can't allude to it.

Showing: A character can't hang out on Saturdays—the day they go to temple. The only time they can spend with their mother. When challenged to hang out on Saturday with friends, they say they can't because she's getting old, and they like spending time with her.

Another motivation could be a character wanting to be the best, or they don't want to be afraid anymore, so they train all the time. A character is lonely, so they have a makeover, buying a suit because they want to have a family one day.

Motivations drive characters to take action. However, when it comes to true behavior, it's defined by a character's positions on things—their beliefs. And characters have millions of positions (but you don't have to know all of them).

## POSITIONS FOR GROWTH

Positions affect character behavior on the page, causing reactions or a lack thereof to situations and presented choices. The reaction or choice they make shows who they really are by what they'll do or not do, say or not say. And to show who they are, you need to challenge their positions; you know, to get a reaction from them. And I suggest challenging them as often as you can (at least once a scene).

Challenges aren't necessarily making a choice to go left or right. Though it might influence if they choose to drink this brand of soda or that one (based on their position—and how it developed). How about a situation where a character is forced to drink Soda X instead of their favorite soda?

Do they drink it anyway or not?

That's not a major choice, but it could lead to them "developing" and/or changing their original position on their favorite soda brand.

See, in a challenge, characters develop because they make a choice against their position (belief). They should be forced to make a choice. Not at gunpoint, of course, but ultimately what the character chooses is based on their position.

How much characters believe in their position will be a direct reflection of how they choose to take action. And depending on the choices they make, it could lead to a reaction (small or big), which leads to a result that could then lead to character development and growth.

But, Thomas, how does this develop characters?

Using the soda example, they might drink brand X and end up changing their position completely, somewhat, or not at all. Any of those choices are fine, and each one has a different influence on the character's position itself. Yep, even if they don't change at all.

## The 27 Plot Point Outline: When Plot Meets Story

A complete change will become a new position. That new position isn't a switch to the opposite of what they believed (though it could be). It just means they've completely replaced their old position with a new one.

But, Thomas, how does a soda choice make a narrative interesting?

It depends on why they have that position in the first place. It could be a position that connects them to their father or a best friend that passed away, and drinking one brand over the other is their way of remembering them.

Let's go a bit deeper with a new example. Morality.

A character's moral position on killing is to not kill, ever, for it's a moral sin. One that leads to the Underworld of Blar. But how deep does this position go, though? Is there any leeway? Let's make a choice as writers.

We'll call this character Bob. Bob's rule on killing is that you shouldn't kill others no matter what. It's not a person's right to kill another human. They should be punished, yes, but not killed. Killing, even in defense, is murder.

If that's Bob's position, now it's your job to challenge it. But wait, does this mean we should go big? Put Bob in a situation where he has to kill someone? No. That's not character development. Big jumps like that are not earned. Maybe "he has to kill someone" could be a crescendo in their arc or a midpoint conflict.

Challenging Bob should happen in small position challenges relative to an act, section, or plot point's purpose.

PP1 would establish their position on killing, but it wouldn't force them to have to kill someone. They can still be challenged, but maybe, just maybe, they stand their ground and don't change at all.

PP1: Killing comes up in a conversation at a party for his favorite cousin's return home from war, and Bob finds it hard to look him in the eyes because he found out he killed people (to survive).

The challenge leads Bob to not change at all. He judges his cousin. Fine. But how he doubles down is by judging his cousin. How much he judges his cousin is reflected in how firm or loose he is with his position. Let's say he has a firm stance, which leads him to choose not to voice his opinion. Bob's behavior is to ignore his cousin.

See, when a character doesn't change at all, they double down. And Bob is forced to confront his love for his cousin against his firm position on a killing.

Bob can't believe his cousin would kill, let alone join the war. Bob is now upset with his cousin simply because of his own defined positions.

Does this mean Bob won't ever change? Maybe. That's up to you as the writer to make that choice. However, challenge characters, and challenge them as much as you want, and maybe, just maybe, they'll change... eventually.

PP2: Bob is walking around town with a friend, and guess what? He runs into his cousin. Because of his position, he treats his cousin like a douche (behavior). He struggles with his choice because they were once best friends as children.

His cousin calls Bob out on his behavior. An argument erupts, and his cousin explains he had to kill to get home to his baby daughter. To his family. To a life he can't return to emotionally and mentally because of what he did to get home.

This challenges Bob's position, and he might not change at all again. I'd say that if he did, the narrative would focus on reconciling with his cousin. But I want to say Bob heard his cousin, and his position changed somewhat. He listens to his cousin, and now he's questioning his own stance on things. Changing... or I might say, developing as a character.

These kinds of changes develop characters far beyond character arcs. It's in these challenges you'll earn a satisfying change by allowing subtle moments to happen over the course of a narrative. This shows consistent growth, taking place over many choices, leading to a lot of small changes that are earned.

And I'm not saying you need to avoid big changes, or that you couldn't save a big change for the grand climax. It's stronger to hold off on big changes. To see characters stand their ground. I mean, think about it. Captain America took ten years of smaller narratives to finally settle down with Peggy Carter.

Whether characters change completely, somewhat, or not at all, it's these changes that give readers insight into who they are. That insight helps to form an emotional bond with characters. Even more so as readers watch characters evolve, change, or sometimes, simply stand their ground and hold their beliefs. Captain America is a really great example of doubling down on a position often. After all, he knows what's right, and he will die for that conviction.

## CHALLENGE CHARACTERS

When you challenge characters, it doesn't have to be a major fight or a fisticuff. Make it a series of choices, a couple of disagreements, or quiet intimate moments. Build on smaller choices: what they ate for dinner, whether they leave early, and if they do, do they rush out or walk out?

However, challenging your characters doesn't always have to be choices to take action and make it physical. Knowing a character's positions puts them in situations that challenge said positions.

Does a character believe in loyalty above all? If so, put them in situations that challenge their own loyalty. Put them in a situation where they see someone they deeply trust betray another person, which in turn challenges their position on loyalty and their position on that character.

Does your character not believe in violence? Put them in a situation that challenges their position, forcing them to make a choice: will they fight back or stand their ground? Does their love for another character allow for change in their stance on violence if it means protecting them?

The point is to create opportunities to challenge characters. This gives them a chance to think about their circumstance to make truthful choices. Ones that push back on their established positions. As mentioned above, every scene should challenge different positions of characters, especially the protagonist.

But, Thomas, if I have five main characters in a room, do I really have to challenge each character's position at least once?

You can do anything you want. You're the author. What I'm saying is, a reader will be more engaged in a narrative if you're showing conflict, tension, and raising stakes. No one leans in on a page filled with perfection. Sure, who doesn't enjoy a cozy fantasy romance, but there's still stuff happening in a narrative too. That something is tension, stakes, and conflict.

*Start With Character*

But, Thomas, how do I create tension, stakes, and conflict on the page?

Challenge characters against other characters. Play them in opposition. Positions, shared or otherwise, are an interesting narrative tool to watch play out on pages. Watching positions get challenged, evolve, or double down leans your readers closer.

Readers love watching characters behaving and responding certain ways. And when those behaviors are defined by a character's position, it creates a much more natural debate, tension, conflict, conversation, action, etc.

Think about the who, what, when, where, and why of it all, or a challenge can feel unearned. For example, if you throw a monster into the corner of a room for the fun of it all, sure, it's exciting, but it also becomes merely plot happening. Instead, use a character's position to push back on them in any given scene.

> A quick aside: You don't have to know every position a character holds before outlining or even writing your first drafts. You can and will develop positions as your outline develops, and more so when you're drafting your prose.
>
> Honestly, it all changes during the writing process. But, I mean, don't get me wrong, you're welcome to figure out a handful before starting. All I'm saying is that a narrative is always evolving, so don't worry about holding on tight to certain positions or motivations.

However, if you've already committed to certain positions that influence the narrative, you might not want to change or adjust them (though you can). I'd say that my point still stands: you can't challenge a position you don't know.

So, back to challenging positions.

Know what you're going to challenge. Sure, the answers might not come to you right away. In fact, they might become clear during the writing process as you outline or in a zero, first, second, and third draft. As scenes present moments where a character must do something, they'll make a choice or react to it.

But, Thomas, are there certain ways I could look at my writing to figure out what I'm going to challenge or how characters will react and behave?

*The 27 Plot Point Outline: When Plot Meets Story*

Here are a few questions to get you thinking:

1. How does the character's position influence what they'll do?
2. What are three scenarios the character can make choices on?
3. What three choices can they make for that single scenario?
4. Does the character's position change after the moment?

These four questions are strong starting points to ask yourself whenever your characters are in a situation. Oh, I assure you, there are more questions than this that'll be based on your narrative and choices you'll have to make as a writer.

Nonetheless, this exercise is designed to get your brain thinking, figuring out options for scenes and choices for characters to make, and creating movement on the page. Once you figure this out, ask yourself questions about pushing back on positions, challenge them, and give characters a chance to make more choices.

## MARY SUE AND GARY STU

Now it's time to set some rules and boundaries to guide you from writing poorly developed characters. That's right, it's Mary Sue and Gary Stu time. These terms are part of the zeitgeist, alive in the deep darkness of our writing community. I'm sure you've heard of these terms. And I'm sure you have a... position on them.

For those unfamiliar with the terms, a Mary Sue/Gary Stu is a character, usually a young woman, who is portrayed as free of weaknesses or character flaws. Both female and male characters can be written as unrealistically capable. But the reason for writing perfect characters depends on the intent of the author.

Usually authors believe that capable translates to likable. I'd argue that a reader needs to connect to a character's deeper emotional truth. See, readers grow interested in characters when they see how they behave, think, and feel.

But, Thomas, what's wrong with having perfectly strong, capable female or male characters?

First and foremost, a strong character doesn't mean a perfect character. I would push further and say that a character who can handle any given situation doesn't equal a highly engaging narrative or show growth. When you hear about strong characters, it's about their resilience to overcome their shortcomings. This is how they fail, learn, and improve.

But, Thomas, shouldn't characters be capable? If they fail often, won't people not like them?

Well, let me say this: readers build emotional relationships when they're able to relate to a character and their lives. We don't relate to the Hulk in Marvel; we relate to how Bruce Banner struggles with the literal monster in him. More so when he makes a choice to let the monster out for the greater good, knowing that it might hurt innocent people.

The trials and tribulations of your characters build rapport with readers. This happens when a reader sees themselves in the characters. With that, let's go back to the Marvel Cinematic Universe, shall we?

I believe there's an argument to be made that most men might fantasize about having Captain America's power and strength. You'd get away with saying most women might fantasize about being with him, but that's not what makes his movies great, nor his character.

People root for Steve Rogers for his morals (positions) and this: "Even if the whole world is telling you to move, it is your duty to plant yourself like a tree, look them in the eye, and say, 'No, you move.'"

He's the best of us, and yet, he still has his trials and tribulations, room for growth, and is constantly being challenged on his positions. Also, watch how he often doubles down on his positions, occasionally changing somewhat, and in rare moments, accepting new information and making complete changes. Even still, at the end of the day, he has standards, ones he's willing to fight for.

Now secondly, Mary Sue and Gary Stu are probably annoying at parties, always able to juggle, sing the best karaoke songs, or bust a move on beat. Which means they'll be the same way if and when they show up in a narrative, annoying your readers and, let's be honest, some of the characters.

Give characters at least one flaw or tragic virtue to break the unstoppable perfection of a Sue/Stu. You don't do this to make characters weak; you do it so they can get better, stronger, and develop as characters.

Sure, characters can be absolutely amazing sword fighters, but also, why not have them suck at leadership? Think about it: during the midpoint conflict,

## The 27 Plot Point Outline: When Plot Meets Story

as they realize they can't lead, it challenges them. And at the end of the third act, they find a strength within to be the leader everyone needs. I'd even argue that this growth doesn't mean they're now a great leader, but that they can now lead.

Thirdly, I've seen it before; authors want interesting characters for the sole purpose of having readers like them. This leads to those perfect, strong, and unstoppable female protagonists.

Additionally, to elevate their female characters, authors write their male characters as weak, unintelligent buffoons. I've seen the opposite too, where male protagonists are strong and powerful characters opposite a completely weak and helpless female character.

Both are poor writing. Both are boring and lazy. Writing characters like that does a disservice to a narrative. There's nothing interesting about those kinds of characters, and it doesn't add anything to the narrative's movement either.

But, Thomas, isn't James Bond a Gary Stu?

Maybe. I'd argue that Daniel Craig's Bond is far from perfect. In all five of his Bond films, James failed often and got reprimanded by superiors, bled, and got outplayed by characters. Even more tragic, the people he loves end up dying around him, causing change, building walls, and leading him to his final moment in No Time to Die (2021).

In the novels?

James Bond's a functioning alcoholic, struggling with most, if not all, of his relationships, and might have a few traits that cause him to risk his life. Bond, James Bond, in the novels also has a scar on his face. Sure, he possesses an array of incredible skills, effortlessly excelling in various dangerous situations, but at the end of the day… It's the character development that makes him relatable.

It's like saying a master carpenter is a Mary Sue because she's great at her job, cutting wood and building cabinets. That's the thing; your characters can be great at the thing they do. A detective can be perfect at finding the clues. A singer can be amazing at singing. A lover can be a living ocean controlling the motion.

All those things can be true and fun to watch. But being great at those things and everything else in life, including somehow instantly knowing how to heal creatures using the Force on their first try, will create disdain from audiences for the characters and lead them to be a Sue/Stu in your narratives.

*Start With Character*

It's the same reason the debate goes on about Luke Skywalker versus Rey Sky—um, I mean Rey Palpatine. But I'm not going to debate that here, though I could write a thesis about characters who are and who are not Sues/Stus.

Which leads me to my final point: mix things up. Great narratives don't need perfect characters, and they for sure don't need a hundred flaws. Find a nice balance that fits who you want a character to be and who they end up being as you work your narrative. Plus, embrace the benefit of showing their growth, since the engagement comes from watching a character's failures lead them to success.

And before you ask, flat characters need flaws, tragic virtues, and a way to move a narrative forward too. Conflict, tension, stakes, or mishaps aren't just external and shouldn't be. You're not writing an 80s action flick starring Arnold Schwarzenegger. You're writing characters in a novel that you want to stand out, that feel real, and that ultimately resonate with your readers.

# CHAPTER 21

# Outlining A Character Arc

## OUTLINING A CHARACTER ARC

This book defines a narrative as both plot and story. Plot is what needs to happen, no matter what, and story is how plot unfolds through the emotional experiences and choices of characters.

As this is a book on outlining, which focuses on what needs to happen no matter what, let me show you ways to strengthen plot. At its core, outlining sets up plot events. It's through these events that characters have a chance to develop their character arcs, growing in every choice they make and their experiences.

Character arcs can be as simple as overcoming fear or literally the main driving force of a central conflict that fuels a narrative to its conclusion. However, there are two kinds of arcs: central character arcs and subarcs (subplots).

Each main character has one central character arc that drives the plot for their character's growth. However, I use the main protagonist's central character arc as the driving force for the narrative itself.

And I know that traditionally a character arc is an internal journey for a character, and a plot arc is an external journey of events propelling the narrative forward. With that said...

## The 27 Plot Point Outline: When Plot Meets Story

I look at character arcs as the driving force behind a plot for two reasons: one, plot is what needs to happen no matter what, and two, story is how we see the plot unfold through the character's emotional experiences and choices. Since the central conflict of a narrative is usually directly connected to a character and their choices (which is story), their character arcs drive the plot forward.

Let me explain. See, every character can have one or more character arcs. However, one of those character arcs will be directly tied to the central conflict of a narrative. This is usually, and often, the protagonist of the narrative. And yes, more than one protagonist can exist, though I'd argue a main protagonist should still drive a narrative. A secondary or even a tertiary one won't drive it forward.

Though other protagonists and characters could help push a narrative.

With that said, all character arcs have growth (except flat arcs); thus, by attaching a central conflict to a protagonist, you'll see growth in them (story) and in the narrative's plot.

My point is this: if you start with character arcs, you gain so much more room for growth based on what they'll end up doing. Besides, their starting point sets the context, a conflict in that arc challenges their positions on it, and finally in the resolution they change completely, somewhat, or not at all.

But, Thomas, what if I want to figure out all the traits and little details?

Then do it. I'm suggesting that you leave room for development of that character by working out a narrative's plot first and then let the movement of the plot develop in the story of a narrative second.

Of course, do what you're comfortable doing, but allow yourself room to adjust, change, add, or subtract from your methods. Besides, you never know what you'll find in characters as you develop a narrative in the outline and prose.

Remember, you don't know who these characters are. You can't know until you play with them in the sandbox for a bit, challenging them and pushing back on them to watch how they behave.

Quentin Tarantino has said in interviews that he'll write about 40-50% of a script. It's at that point he realizes that he's finally learned who his characters are. Afterward, he goes back to the beginning and reworks what he had written, adding the newly discovered voices and behaviors to his characters.

But, Thomas, how does that help me find out who the characters are?

*Outlining A Character Arc*

Character arcs leave room for discovery. Having traits and solidified ideas could lead to walls, or maybe you'll write that the character is Italian, so now he always eats pizza and does hand gestures. Sure, I'm Sicilian, and I both eat pizza and can't shut up unless I sit on my hands, but starting with that is what leads to stereotypes, leads to false behavior, and leads to unoriginal positions (beliefs).

For example, if the character arc is a simple, general, and broad summary:

Geno Esposito is stuck at a dead-end firm as an accountant, working with his best friend, and sits across from a woman he's been quietly in love with for ten years. All this as he deals with a terrible boss too.

This gives room to develop several things, just from that summary. I can develop his emotional experiences for his dead-end job, the relationship between him and his best friend, him and his boss, and, as you probably guessed by now, the relationship between him and the woman he secretly loves.

The character arc summary gives you room to play in the narrative. Sure, his name is Geno Esposito, making him most likely of Italian descent, but maybe his mother is Haitian, born in Alabama. Still, it doesn't matter or determine who he is… unless… you want it to. Unless the narrative calls for it.

But, if it does call for it, let it be something you can lean into when the narrative calls for it, not something that drives you to write a generic thing that states he loves pizza, and only because he's Italian. Besides, anyone can love pizza. It's pizza. Only heathens hate pizza.

Time to talk about the two kinds of character arcs. First, let's look at the central character arcs and how they're broken into two categories, then we'll look at subarcs (subplots).

## THE PROTAGONIST'S CENTRAL CHARACTER ARC

The majority of narratives are driven by a protagonist's central character arc, full stop. Sure, character arcs can grow (positive arc), decline (negative arc), or end up as a flat arc. However, the truth still remains: even in an ensemble, there's still one protagonist that leads the bunch, telling the narrative through their POV.

## The 27 Plot Point Outline: When Plot Meets Story

And yes, before you ask, even a plot-driven narrative must still be pulled or pushed by a protagonist's character arc, flat or otherwise. I say this because the plot of what must happen needs to be tethered to an emotional journey. The plot is going to be the external things that need to happen, but without the narrative's story, well, we've talked about that—it feels flat and unearned.

Whether you're writing about Ned Stark being the central driving force in A Game of Thrones to uncover the murder of the previous Hand to cover up a conspiracy, or if it's about Mark from The Martian trying to get back home, it's all driven by their emotional choices and experience. In other words: story.

This is why outlining starts with a protagonist's central character arc. I'll add that the good news is, you can build around this central character arc, adding subarcs, secondary protagonist character arcs, and even writing parallel character arcs that are absolutely not directly connected to the central one, etc.

For example, Ned Stark goes to King's Landing, bringing his young girls along with him. They have their character arcs. Arya Stark learns to fight with a sword, and Sansa develops relationships and begins her journey to understand the inner workings of royal life.

Beyond that, you still have Bran, Jon, Cersei, Tyrion, Jaime, and Rob. I didn't forget Daenerys, but like I said above, her character arc happens far off and away from the central narrative, running parallel with it.

Jaime and Cersei's character arcs are subarcs directly connected to Ned and his central character arc. Tyrion is affected by Jaime's actions, linking back to Bran's character arc, linking back to the central character arc of Ned Stark—the conspiracy. In fact, even Robert Baratheon is directly connected to asking Ned to be his new Hand.

So yes, subplots and secondary character arcs can have their own fun and development, but at the end of the day, there are thick and thin narrative threads reaching out and connecting to the protagonist's central narrative.

In this case, Eddard Stark's central character arc is of him becoming the new Hand of the King and his investigation into the conspiracy. After all, he did reluctantly choose to become the Hand (PP2: The Inciting Incident).

But, Thomas, if it all connects back, how does a parallel arc do that?

Daenerys is spied on, and it connects back to Ned at King's Landing.

*Outlining A Character Arc*

# SECONDARY CHARACTER ARCS

Secondary character arcs are just as valid to a narrative as the protagonist's central character arc is. I'd even argue that without them, a protagonist can't be explored in greater depth. Not to go into it, but character foils pull out dimension in other characters and the protagonist.

My suggestion when writing secondary characters is to only worry about them for their arcs. You don't have to force them into the protagonist's central conflict, at least at first. Characters, whether it's a lead or a supporting role, must stand on their own. They must earn their spot on the page. Once their secondary arc is worked out, tie it to the protagonist's central character arc when possible.

> A quick aside: Remember, words have a cost, taking away from your word budget, and every character costs words to explore them.

But, Thomas, do one-off characters need a full character arc?

No. For the love of gods, no. A waiter doesn't need a full character arc. As the bellhop running luggage up to your hotel room doesn't need one either.

These are not secondary characters; these are day players. In the industry of film and television, we call them "under fives" (five lines or less). I'd go on, but the rule should be, unless they influence narrative movement, don't put that kind of weight into one-offs.

However, that doesn't mean you don't have to put depth into them. I'm all for an eye-patched bellhop carrying luggage up for a character in a romance. Or hell, even a personality can go a long way in a waiter.

Technically these characters are given flat arcs, but don't get confused; a full arc needs to be laid out through the complete 27 Plot Point Outline. Day players don't get any if they're lucky.

All I'm saying is that you should allow your secondary character arcs to have their own depth and journey—even for flat arcs. This attention to detail will elevate the characters beyond simple supporting roles instead of easily becoming lost in the fray as another forgotten character. Otherwise... are they really worth the page time and word count?

*The 27 Plot Point Outline: When Plot Meets Story*

## CHARACTER ARC SUMMARIES

But, Thomas, how do I know what my character's arcs will be?

Great question, and my answer: character arc summaries. I'll go into this deeper, but first let me explain what it is.

> Character arc summary: A two- to five-sentence passage that explains a character's central arc, setting it up, exploring it, and resolving it.

Remember that every character arc and subarc has a beginning, middle, and end. The beginning sets up their character arc's status quo. It gets challenged in the middle and resolves by the end.

In a flat arc, they begin the narrative, live through it, and end it all as the same person. The world around them might change (and does), but they do not. Alright, now for an example.

> Bored at a job he hates, Geno Esposito is an accountant working at a firm he wishes would fire him so he could live off unemployment.
>
> He hates his boss but gets to work beside his best friend and sit across from the woman he's been quietly in love with for ten years.
>
> Geno's world quickly changes when aliens come down, changing his life as he goes from a mundane employee to a hero that saves Earth.

This summary allows for lots of movement. If you've got a keen eye, you know I'm using the alien invasion narrative from this book. I hinted at it in the chapter introduction, but now you're seeing it in its full glory. So let me break it down for you and show you how I can play with it as I please.

Summaries give you lots of wiggle room if you simply write them out in broad, general sentences. In our example, Geno hates his job. This gives us room to show why he hates his job, establish a status quo, setting up the beginning, and his motivations that'll heavily change once the aliens come down from space.

## Outlining A Character Arc

Another aspect of the summary that gives us some room to play with is his relationships with his best friend and love interest. And these relationships are automatically primed to build on Geno's inner depth.

A quick aside: Each relationship will have its own subarc. Basically, the best friend, the love interest, and the boss he hates become their own subarcs, and Geno Esposito's central character arc from a basic mundane life to a hero is the narrative's driving force.

That's right, the alien invasion is the central conflict to the narrative and is told through the POV of the protagonist and their journey to save Earth. Since it's told through Geno's POV, it also makes it his central character arc. This sets the skeleton foundation of the whole narrative.

Now, as an exercise, take characters from your narrative and think of at least one character arc for each. You'll learn quickly that characters have one character arc but many subarcs.

As mentioned above, Geno's relationship with his best friend is a subarc because it's connected to and influences Geno himself.

If something narratively influences a character emotionally, physically, spiritually, morally, psychologically, etc., it becomes a character arc or subarc.

I'll add that even in a flat arc, like with Sherlock Holmes, his relationship with Watson is still connected to Sherlock because he, as in Sherlock, bounces ideas off of Watson. Their relationship is a subarc.

Now, with that said, each character should have at least one character arc summary, but they can have multiple subarcs. However, as a process, work out the central character arc first, then add on the subarcs later. Though, as always, I know, and you know, you're going to discover more character arcs and subarcs in the drafts.

That's right, new characters will come up in a draft, behavior shows you how they deal with things internally, or you blow their leg off.

Anything can happen when you're writing the drafts. And like with all aspects of what I'm teaching you, this writing process is one step at a time, adding a little each time. Which brings us to the next section...

*The 27 Plot Point Outline: When Plot Meets Story*

## BUILD AS YOU GO, BUILD AS YOU NEED

This method is helpful because as a writer, you don't know who these characters really are at the beginning. Yep, that's right, you'll learn more about characters on the page than you'll get from sitting at a desk writing every trait they have.

As plot plays out in a narrative, you'll figure out who characters are and, believe it or not, their appearances, behaviors, etc. I mean, things need to happen no matter what, so, as things happen, characters will respond by making choices. Those choices tell you who they are. This is also where a writer can go deeper into their positions (beliefs).

The build-as-you-go part of this method gives you the freedom to pants a little while you develop the outline. Even more so when you're writing out your prose. If you know everything up front, you'll write within restraints. Maybe not always, but if a character has half a brain before you write one word in a chapter, you might realize that they needed the other half.

And character arc summaries are written in broad, general strokes so you can add to their truths as needed: learning their positions, appearance, abilities, skills, etc. No, really. Think about it. A character summary might give you an idea of who they are, but maybe the narrative needs a group of characters to get out of a tight spot. To do this, one character needs to know XYZ. So... one of them now knows XYZ to get out of there.

But, Thomas, isn't that a deus ex machina?

Yes. This is why you're creating an outline and/or still working on a zero, first, or second draft. See, the purpose of this tool is to give you a way to build on your narrative, develop characters, and give yourself the freedom to make sense of everything to best serve the narrative.

Again, a character walks into a tavern. Fantastic, here's a great moment for a potential description. The secret is to best serve the narrative. It can be done by saying they have a limp, a scar, or a specific eye color. And descriptions should tell a deeper truth than "they look like this." It should add to the narrative's story.

So whether you're figuring out what a character looks like or what they are capable of, the build-as-you-go method gives you room to do so. Now once you do learn a little about the characters, it's now time to do the work.

*Outlining A Character Arc*

Whatever you come up with, go back and seed information, foreshadow it, and drop little nudges that'll end up paying off any and all newly added ideas. Yes, it's okay to add information to chapters as you go. It's not against the law to go back to earlier chapters and change things. I promise, you're not beholden to what you write. It's not like you're writing it in stone... are you?

A narrative is a living, breathing entity if you allow it. Giving it a chance to breathe lets you see things play out, form, and come to life. As you're writing a narrative out, those broad general ideas give you room to develop narratives and characters. Remember, those elements should come from the emotional choices and experiences of your characters (story).

Besides, no reader has ever truly cared that a character fought ten people and won. They cared about how they fought ten people and won. It's that how that shows who characters are by the choices they make. That's why John Wick is so awesome to watch: we loved seeing how he killed all those people... the choices he made to kill them and, even more so, the reason why he did it. R.I.P., dog.

My point is this: when writing a narrative, it's not about right now; it's about what benefits a narrative as a whole. I've seen far too many clients get in the trap of "My idea is what it is and must be in the narrative no matter what." After all, it's been an idea for months, even years. What happens is that this trap creates unearned, contrived cause-and-effect results, making narratives bland as if they're missing something special.

Give yourself the freedom to build as you go, and build as you need. The narrative will be stronger for it, whether a narrative and characters need to change to best serve the narrative itself.

## USE THE 27 PPO FOR ALL ARCS

The best approach: do each character arc separately. Because secondary character arcs, by their very nature, don't line up with the central narrative. They begin and end as needed (and should serve the narrative) and should be added later to fit in and around the protagonist's central character arc.

Honestly, once you have the protagonist's central character arc mapped out, secondary character arcs and subarcs can easily slip in and fit within an outline.

*The 27 Plot Point Outline: When Plot Meets Story*

As you learn how to use the 27 PPO, it becomes easier to figure out what works best for you. In fact, for myself, I went all in, mapping out everything all at once (I'm still tired from it). It took me a while to figure out what I liked best, what helped me develop my narrative, and my happy place. If you're wondering what my method ended up being, you're currently reading it.

## ADDING SUBARCS (SUBPLOTS)

You're going to be able to watch a narrative grow and develop in each step of the outlining process, including any zero or first draft work you do. What you should notice are additional subarcs that pop up from time to time. They'll come out of nowhere but are just as important to characters as their central plot.

A good rule of thumb is that subarcs should complement and intersect with the central narrative; otherwise, they risk drawing too much attention away, becoming more important. The goal should be to add layers of complexity to the narrative without taking over the central narrative itself. In most cases, subarcs end up helping to develop characters, reinforce themes, and/or raise stakes.

Here's a list of some subarcs, but I assure you, the list is far larger.

1. Romantic, familiar, or friend relationships
2. Mysteries or developing historical clues
3. The best friend begins gambling to cover debts
4. Their rival coworker secretly trains at night to outshine them
5. Forbidden romance risks the family's reputation
6. A mentor loses their confidence as a student progresses beyond them
7. Witnessing a brutal battle, a soldier deserts, struggling with cowardice
8. Having fallen ill, the parent hides it from their family
9. A squire dreams of knighthood but compromises honor to get noticed
10. Love is challenged when a new person comes into their life
11. After overhearing a secret, a servant must decide silence and honor
12. Red is a man who's known to locate certain things from time to time
13. Mary Jane's relationship with Peter Parker in Spider-Man 2
14. Aragorn is the heir of Elendil and Isildur

*Outlining A Character Arc*

I'd use this list to get your brain thinking and less of a point and choose. But it is a nice guide for you to use until you start to notice similar things pop up in and around your own narrative outlines and drafts.

But, Thomas, these feel like central conflicts too.

Ah yes, of course they do. It's a plot to tell. Aragorn is the heir and could, I dare say, be its own novel. What makes it a subarc is that it's within the central character arc of Frodo's narrative.

Could Frodo and the One Ring be in Aragorn's book? Yes. But the One Ring would yank the wind right out of Aragorn being an heir narrative. Why? The ring narrative is much bigger than taking his place on the throne.

I'd argue that even if Frodo didn't exist, Aragorn's heir subarc is still going to be a subarc in his own narrative—if the One Ring is the central conflict.

My point still remains true: look for moments from the list of narrative subarcs, mark them, and play with them. Even if a small, sole crumb appears deep in the dust of an idea, I'd say it's worth paying attention to.

For example, a character mentions a talent or skill: "I'm known to locate certain things from time to time." This is a subarc and a chance to go deeper, seeing if there's anything there to explore for that character.

Maybe a character experiences something, like the brutal battle. How do they respond to it mentally, emotionally, physically, or spiritually?

Things will sneak up on you, they will, and it's your job as the writer to ask questions, find answers, and have confidence in the choices you make. This is what makes you a writer.

Now, you don't have to follow every breadcrumb, but in the beginning stages it's good to at least think about them. You never know where it'll take you, and besides, that's part of the fun of being a writer.

# CHAPTER 22

## Short-Form Outline

### SHORT-FORM OUTLINE

A short-form outline is a loose, flexible layout for a narrative, mapping plot beats out in broad, general statements. It's here where the 27 Plot Point Outline comes into play, so use it as a guide to fill in all associated plot points connected to the protagonist's central character arc. Essentially, it's the narrative's skeleton—the bones before the meat.

An initial short-form outline is a general look at a narrative, not the final, fully detailed version. This gives a narrative space to breathe, so listen to it as you develop it, and change it as needed. I'll add that the short-form outline is a chance to see when and where stronger ideas feel weaker in narratives. If so, adjust things, or take it out completely.

Another outline reality is that plot beats need to move occasionally. If a specific plot beat felt like it originally belonged in PP4, but then you realized it should move to PP3 or PP5, then do it. It's absolutely okay to do this, as it's part of the outlining process. It'll happen from time to time.

Remember, it takes time to get used to and learn the flow of a narrative and how to structure it within the 27 PPO. Solution: practice, and practice often.

## The 27 Plot Point Outline: When Plot Meets Story

Yeah, sure, I can pop an idea out in about an hour using the 27 PPO, but as I suggested, practice got me there. I've been practicing it in my downtime... for fun... for years. Because, well, I'm crazy. That, and I want to improve my craft.

But, Thomas, where do I begin?

Well, the first step is always to lay out the protagonist's central character arc into the 27 Plot Point Outline. Next, slip any other character arcs and subarcs in place in and around the protagonist's central character arc.

> A quick aside: Character arcs and subarcs have leeway to be placed at different times in and around the protagonist's central character arc.

Secondary character arcs and subarc plot beats don't have to be placed in the same moment as the protagonist's central character arc's PP1 (they could be). Ultimately, that secondary character could be introduced in Chapter 23, where their arc's PP1 would begin. This becomes the start of "their" ordinary world.

I'll add this much: you can place other character arcs into corresponding plot points associated with the protagonist's central character arc, but you don't have to. There's room for subarcs, secondary character arcs, etc. to play. You'll get a few examples of that in the next couple of chapters.

Speaking of the example, I'll be using the full alien invasion narrative as I organize it into a short-form outline, showing what a short-form outline could look like. Keep in mind, as you learn how it works and what works for you, take what you like and use the method in a way that works best for you, even if it looks different to you when you're done as you adjust things like I once did.

In the next chapter, Chapter 23, The Extended Outline, I'll add more of the subarcs and go into deeper exploration for each character arc. For this part of the process, the short-form outline is pretty clean and straightforward.

That doesn't mean short-form outlines don't have deeper elements. For example, the fact that Geno has unrequited love for the woman he's worked with for ten years is a subarc, one that'll need work later on when I write the extended outline out. That doesn't mean I can't mention it in the short-form outline.

With that said, let's get into the alien invasion narrative. And to make it easier for you, I marked character arcs with placeholder names (you should too).

*Short-Form Outline*

# ACT 1, SECTION 1
# SETTING UP THE ORDINARY WORLD (SETUP)

PP1: The Ordinary World Before the Disruption (Introductions)

Geno Esposito: He works at a mundane job as an accountant beside his best friend, James, and Lisa, the woman of his dreams (she works at a desk next to Geno). Geno hates his boring life, job, and boss. Geno's boss always pushes him to do other people's tasks. Working a crappy job, he just wishes his life was more.

PP2: The Disruption of the Ordinary World (Inciting Incident)

Geno Esposito: At work, Geno deals with another normal day until aliens arrive out of nowhere, taking over the office building as they smash through the windows and walls. Some employees transform near him from humans to aliens (having been in disguise).

PP3: The Protagonist Reacts to the Inciting Incident (Fallout)

Geno Esposito: Geno leads James and Lisa as they sneak around the building. Employees freak out on different floors, doing what they can to hide from aliens. A few employees blow Geno and his friend's cover, causing the aliens to chase them. Geno runs with his friends, eventually finding a place to hide, far away from others.

*The 27 Plot Point Outline: When Plot Meets Story*

# ACT 1, SECTION 2
# A PROBLEM DISRUPTS THE PROTAGONIST'S LIFE (CONFLICT)

> PP4: The Protagonist Reacts to and Reflects on The Long Term Impacts of the Inciting Incident (Reflection/Choice)

Geno Esposito: He and his friends try to make sense of what had just happened. The aliens have calmed down after the initial attack and are rounding people up—having taken over the building. Hidden, Geno tells James and Lisa that they won't die but need to get out of the building and figure out a long-term solution to stay protected.

> PP5: The Protagonist Takes Action (Action)

Geno Esposito: He tries leading James and Lisa to safety. They move through the building, hiding from aliens as the aliens collect people. He eventually leads them to the exit of the building.

> PP6: The Immediate Consequences of the Action Taken By The Protagonist (Consequences)

Geno Esposito: He and his friends exit the building and realize the city is consumed with aliens too. They agree that it's safer to hide in the building they know than out in the city. They go back inside.

*Short-Form Outline*

# ACT 1, SECTION 3
# THE PROTAGONIST'S LIFE CHANGES DIRECTION (RESOLUTION)

> PP7: The Protagonist's Life Changes as a Result of the Action They Took, Creating Pressure and Stress (Pressure)

Geno Esposito: Aliens continue gathering citizens and employees, both inside the building and outside. Geno and his friends return inside, sneaking around to find a hiding spot. Reaching the third floor, it's filled with lots of aliens. More employees are held captive here. There's nowhere to hide. The aliens spot Geno with his group, and they run to survive, jumping into an elevator to avoid the aliens.

> PP8: The First Major Plot Twist, or Pinch, Happens (Plot Twist/Pinch)

Geno Esposito: Moving through the building, Geno spots his boss, Derrick. Derrick hides, shaking, holding his side—he's badly hurt, bleeding down his back and legs. His blood is a mixture of deep red and a light blue, exposing the truth: he's an alien who's been living on Earth for a while and grew to love and appreciate humankind. He reveals his true appearance and begs them to help him. He tells them to grab his bag that was away from him.

> PP9: Because of The Plot Twist or Pinch, The Protagonist Is Pushed into a New World (Pushed)

Geno Esposito: He and his friends carry Derrick into a room, doing what they can to help Derrick. They grab a first aid kit, and Geno cleans up Derrick's wound. Lisa helps, threading the wound. James watches the door for aliens. Geno knows they'll die if they don't leave the room. He and Derrick get into an argument: he wants to help.

*The 27 Plot Point Outline: When Plot Meets Story*

## ACT 2, SECTION 4
## THE PROTAGONIST EXPLORES THE NEW WORLD (SETUP)

PP10: The Protagonist is Introduced
To the New World (New World)

Geno Esposito: He accepts his new reality, that Derrick is an alien, James is hesitant about their chance for survival, and Lisa's worried too, let alone doing anything to stop the aliens. Together, Geno and Derrick make a choice to keep his friends alive. They're not giving up. Derrick might have insight into what's to come from the aliens.

PP11: The Protagonist Can Take A Break
And Have A Little Fun (Fun & Games)

Geno Esposito: Derrick presents a device that enhances individuals. He had it in his backpack. It's during this moment that Geno gains abilities and must learn how to best use them. However, there's a learning curve, and the enhancement itself doesn't last long. The group makes too much noise, and aliens arrive.

PP12: The Protagonist Compares Their Current World
To How Things Were At The Beginning (Juxtaposition)

Geno Esposito: The group runs from aliens and uses the device to power up. This helps them survive a major explosion caused by the aliens. They're hurt but survive because of their abilities. They must now learn to use their new powers if they're going to fight back or survive. However, it's revealed that the machine could also kill them if they use it and their abilities too much.

*Short-Form Outline*

# ACT 2, SECTION 5
# THE CRISIS OF THE NEW WORLD (CONFLICT)

### PP13: The Buildup To The Midpoint Conflict (Buildup)

Geno Esposito: Derrick says there's a communication device that'll help them contact other sympathetic aliens to the cause. They need to contact them to fight back. The device is at Derrick's apartment. However, the other device that gave them powers also activated a beacon of their whereabouts. They head to the apartment, unaware of the tracker.

### PP14: The Midpoint Conflict (Midpoint)

Geno Esposito: They're ambushed at Derrick's apartment and are now surrounded. The alien commander orders his men to execute Derrick for his betrayal, triggering a battle. The humans are forced to overuse their abilities and, in turn, are weakened and overwhelmed by the aliens. Derrick tells the group to find Suena, his life partner; she believes in the cause and will help. He gives them information to find her before sacrificing himself so they can escape.

### PP15: The Immediate Reaction or Consequence Of the Midpoint Conflict (Reversal)

Geno Esposito: Geno, James, and Lisa are forced to retreat, only to be crushed by the building as it collapses from battle damage. Geno and his friends appear to be dead to the aliens. The aliens fall back. Geno and his friends push their way out of the rubble and learn the power-replenishing device was destroyed in the collapse.

*The 27 Plot Point Outline: When Plot Meets Story*

# ACT 2, SECTION 6
# FINDING A SOLUTION (RESOLUTION)

PP16: The Protagonist Reflects on the Long Term Impacts
Of the midpoint Conflict (Consequence)

Geno Esposito: They find people underground in a massive sewer area underneath the building that collapsed. Geno and the others are hurt and wounded but are taken in and cared for. They meet those in charge of the human resistance. They're not alone, but they are dealing with the fact that they don't have superpowers anymore and the loss of Derrick to help them.

PP17: The Protagonist Takes Action to Resolve the Problem
Created by the Midpoint Conflict (Trials/Tested)

Geno Esposito: He stands with reinforcements, other humans who plan to fight back against the aliens. Lisa stays behind as Geno and James go with the resistance to find Suena. During the attempt they find Suena, but it leads to James being captured and most of their human allies being killed in the debacle.

PP18: Despite the Setbacks, The Protagonist Decides
They Will Succeed No Matter What (Dedication)

Geno Esposito: He emotionally deals with James being captured. He wants to go back in alone, but the remaining humans create a distraction as he infiltrates the alien headquarters to save his friend.

James: Meanwhile, James gets processed by Suena and surrounded by aliens. James tries to convince her that they knew Derrick. Suena doesn't trust humans but is curious and decides to search for Geno for answers.

*Short-Form Outline*

# ACT 3, SECTION 7
# VICTORY SEEMS IMPOSSIBLE (SETUP)

PP19: The Protagonist Faces Difficult and Significant Trials,
Something They Have Never Experienced Before
(Calm Before the Storm)

Geno Esposito: He sneaks around the headquarters as human allies distract the aliens. After surviving several near-death situations, he fights a powerful alien working in the control room. Winning that battle, Geno uses an alien computer to reveal James' cell location.

PP20: A Second Major Plot Twist or Pinch
Where The Protagonist Experiences A Completely
Unexpected Event, Making It All Worse (Plot Twist/Pinch)

Geno Esposito: He searches for James' cell, fighting aliens to get to him. He locates his friend, arriving to save James, but it's a trap—an alien in disguise as his friend. Zapped, the alien commander orders Geno to be brought to him.

PP21: The Final Major Plot Twist, or Pinch,
Leads to the Darkest Moment, and Success Feels
Incomprehensible (Darkest Moment)

Geno Esposito: Brought to the alien commander, Suena reveals that they used James as bait. The commander monologues, mentioning how Derrick failed him for having fallen in love with Earthlings. Suena realizes James told the truth. She does right by her love and causes a distraction, saving Geno. Suena knows where James is. They run and rescue him. The commander demands his people kill Suena, Geno, and Earth. The commander activates a launch for a nuclear weapon after other alien ships begin departing the planet.

*The 27 Plot Point Outline: When Plot Meets Story*

# ACT 3, SECTION 8
# THE PROTAGONIST FINDS THE POWER (CONFLICT)

>PP22: Having Hit Rock Bottom, The Protagonist
>Finds A Power Within To Succeed (Power Within)

Geno Esposito: He still has abilities; however, if he uses his powers, he could die—a life-or-death option. He's going for the weapon.

Suena: She focuses on the ship's destruction.

James: He is urged to warn the other humans about the launch and for them to all get underground to safety.

>PP23: The Protagonist Takes Action (Action To Rally)

Geno Esposito: Geno tries to stop the bomb.

Suena: She tries to stop the ship from leaving (to stop the weapon).

James: He finds the other humans, getting them underground.

>PP24: The Convergence of Storylines
>And Building up to the Final Battle (Converge)

Geno Esposito: He fights a few alien scientists. The commander has a remote to stop the bomb. Two guards and the commander arrive. He feels his powers draining; to save everyone, it'll cost him his life.

Suena: She destroys the ship's ability to leave the planet.

James: He gets people underground. Believing they're going to die in the explosion, they attack aliens fleeing to reach the remaining ships.

*Short-Form Outline*

# ACT 3, SECTION 9
# THE PROTAGONIST FIGHTS AND WINS (RESOLUTION)

```
PP25: The Protagonist Begins Their Final Battle
              (Final Battle)
```

Geno Esposito: He defeats the guards but struggles with the alien commander. Facing defeat, the nuclear weapon is about to launch. He uses his alien abilities, regardless of the cost.

Suena: She activates the ship's self-destruction sequence.

James: The resistance kills aliens—James nearly dies but is saved.

```
PP26: The Protagonist Will Succeed or Fail (Climax)
```

Geno Esposito: He uses the last of his abilities, knowing he'll die. The commander goes to use his own enhancing device. Geno takes it from him—overcharging it and enhancing his power tenfold. He easily kills the commander and collapses.

Suena: She escapes as the ship explodes. Knowing Geno died in the blast. Everyone watches the ship blowing up.

```
PP27: The Resolution Or Immediate Reaction
    To the Results of the Climax (Resolution)
```

Geno Esposito: Suena points up to Geno floating in air. The device and explosion gave him unlimited power. All the characters reunite, having won, and Earth is safe.

Suena: She watches the ships all explode as she stands beside humans, knowing she'll never see her home again.

# CHAPTER 23

## Extended Outline

**EXTENDED OUTLINE**

It's time for the extended outline. What we'll do here is start making chapters out of the notes, breaking up the plot beats within each plot point. I'll map out who is who with their names, like I did with the short-form outline. And from there, I will fill in more details, going from the broad, general ideas to more refined ones.

However, I'm constantly going to keep things broad and general, even when I add new information. The reason for this is simple: I want to leave room for discovery as I write the zero draft chapter outlines, and even more so for when I write the first, second, and third drafts of the narrative.

To be clear, the extended outline isn't where I outline my chapters. As its name suggests, the zero draft chapter outline is designed for that.

The process is simple for me: I map out a protagonist's central character arc with the short-form outline, break plot beats into smaller, more isolated beats with the extended outline, and organize it all into my zero draft chapter outlines.

Remember, each main character needs to have at least one full character arc; otherwise, they're just kind of there, doing nothing. And I assure you—don't have characters just kind of being there. Especially to only advance a narrative.

## The 27 Plot Point Outline: When Plot Meets Story

With that said, I'll lay out the short-form outline notes into the extended outline, using the alien invasion narrative. I'm only going to show Act 1, Section 1, and its three plot points, PP1-PP3.

Thus, I won't reach Suena's plot beats (Derrick's love interest).

But, Thomas, if Suena doesn't even get mentioned until the midpoint conflict of the narrative, how's she going to get a full character arc?

That's a great question. First, as I said in earlier chapters, you shouldn't introduce new narrative plot beats beyond the midpoint conflict, unless they're connected to earlier plot beats and move the narrative forward.

In the case of Suena, she's introduced in the midpoint conflict. That hits the red line, but it counts. Additionally, she's directly connected to the alien boss, Derrick. She's what I'd consider passing the narrative relay baton. Derrick took us to the midpoint conflict, and Suena will take us to the end.

Which brings me to my second point: you can do this with characters as well. For example, if you have a character die, but narratively their character arc is tied to another character, you're in the green zone. To add to this point, as I have stated before, the short-form outline is a broad, general representation of what must happen (plot). It's in the extended draft where you seed even more.

But, Thomas, do I have to seed everything, or can I write and discover?

Write and discover, always. Seed what you can now, what you know, and what makes sense for the current narrative. Also, whatever you can seed now can be changed and adjusted, just like everything else. As you write drafts out, you'll add more information that'll need to be seeded earlier.

For our alien invasion, this means I must reference Suena in the narrative before the midpoint conflict happens.

Third, character arcs for secondary, tertiary, or quaternary characters and beyond have more leeway with how you insert their arcs. For example, with a protagonist, try to get, at minimum, one full chapter in per plot point of the 27 PPO. You can add more than one chapter, but one per is a great start.

For other characters, slip in one, two, or three, and sometimes a fourth, plot point in a chapter. A good rule of thumb is to slip at least one plot point per scene per character. But for clarity, and to allow any of their character arc beats to breathe, one per scene is smart.

*Extended Outline*

This means a chapter with three scenes could potentially have multiple secondary characters all move three of their plot points forward.

Now, what about a protagonist (or any other character) with more than one subarc? You can do the same thing with those subarcs.

Again, the only character arc that should absolutely get one full chapter per plot point is a protagonist's central character arc. However, like all rules, I'd say you can break it once you understand it and if it all makes sense in the context of what you're doing. After all, Ned Stark only has 15 POV chapters.

Now it's time to venture back into the world of the alien invasion.

# ACT 1, SECTION 1
# SETTING UP THE ORDINARY WORLD (SETUP)

PP1: The Ordinary World Before the Disruption (Introductions)

SFO Note: He works at a mundane job as an accountant beside his best friend, James, and Lisa, the woman of his dreams (she works at a desk next to Geno). Geno hates his boring life, job, and boss. Geno's boss always pushes him to do other people's tasks. Working a crappy job, he just wishes his life was more.

CHAPTER 1

Geno Esposito: He arrives at work, immediately beset by the daily grind. Dealing with a difficult boss and general chaos, he's reminded why he hates being an accountant. He's left with a brief moment of calm, saying hello to Lisa, a woman near his desk.

James: He's upset that Geno left the bar earlier last night because Rebecca from the 2nd floor showed up. She sang a soulful rendition of "I Will Always Love You," and you, sir, missed it. Geno says he had to get up for work. James laughs—you were thirty minutes late. Geno smiles. "I should have left earlier from the bar."

## *The 27 Plot Point Outline: When Plot Meets Story*

Geno Esposito: His frustration boils over, and he tells James he's at his breaking point and needs to quit the job. James points to the cleaners outside the window, giving him a harsh dose of reality and a sharp, visual metaphor for what life could be.

Lisa: Overhearing them, Lisa turns to them at her desk, "It was great. You missed a good time." Geno said he didn't see her there. Lisa says that she showed up after he left, I suppose. You would have loved it. Geno is sorry he missed her; Lisa says, "I'm sorry I was missed."

Derrick: Geno is approached by his boss, Derrick, asking for Geno to handle a new task. As always, he can wallow in his frustration or do something meaningful and help. Geno agrees to it.

### CHAPTER 2

Geno Esposito: He works on a server, helping technicians. They're a bit bothered that he's even down here. The men have been working on the servers for two days. The servers get hot. Geno takes off his dress shirt, revealing his Marine arm tattoo. When asked about it, he tells them he's not a soldier. He was a computer scientist. He looks up at them. Don't worry, I'm not here to take your jobs.

James: He texts Geno about getting lunch at a new place he heard of. Geno is sweating and annoyed he's even doing the servers; he was hired as an accountant for the company. He texts James back that he'll try whatever but must get back to these damn servers.

Geno Esposito: He catches corruption in the files. Geno checked the storage devices, searching for failed components or poor ventilation. He runs a virus scan on his computer. While waiting, he checks the hardware, has the two men clean the ventilation system, clean the dust buildup, and adjust the cooling system.

## Extended Outline

Geno Esposito: His computer found a potential threat—something about government contracts showed on his screen. He goes to check it, and the system cuts out. Geno looks for the cause, realizing one of the men pulled out a wire. The guy apologizes, plugging it back in. It reboots, but Geno's computer no longer shows the virus, and he can't find the information in the system about the contracts.

## CHAPTER 3

Geno Esposito: He orders lunch with James. Geno tells James that two tech guys think he's going to take their jobs. Complaining that Derrick only has him do jobs to make everyone hate Geno. It's like Derrick doesn't want Geno to make friends.

James: He brings up Rebecca again, telling Geno that he's going to ask her out and maybe they can all double date. Geno has nobody to bring. James mentions Lisa, and Geno laughs. She's out of his league, and besides, after years of working alongside one another, you'd think she'd make a move. James drinks his soda, laughing, and tells him that Lisa is into him. He needs to make a move. She's old-fashioned and wants Geno to make the first move.

Geno Esposito: Food shows up; he had ordered a greasy lunch that was all heavy foods. James tells him that'll come back and bite him in the ass. Geno says that he can handle it.

Lisa: Geno asks James how he knows Lisa likes him. He tells Geno that if he has to tell him, he'll never understand women. Just ask her on a date for this Friday. You, me, her, and Rebecca. Double dates are safer. Genos nods along to the idea of the double date—not agreeing or disagreeing with it.

## The 27 Plot Point Outline: When Plot Meets Story

Derrick: As Genos eats, food falls down his shirt. Derrick calls Geno on his cell, asking him to see him after lunch. Genos shakes his head at James. "He probably wants me to fix the plumbing next." James laughs at Geno. "Stop worrying; the only plumbing you'll be doing later is when you stuff the toilets."

### CHAPTER 4

Geno Esposito: Derrick asks him if he got specific reports done from yesterday. Geno says, "I couldn't because I was helping Vincent in receiving, at your request. The day before, I was doing even more nonaccounting things, again, at your request, and today I've been working on the server all day... fixing it... again, at your request.

Derrick: Geno is the only one he can trust to get the job done. Geno says it's okay if he asks other people to get them to step up and show what they can do. I won't be mad if you do. Derrick says Geno thinks he probably hates him or is picking on him, but really, it's furthest from the truth; you can say no. "Only if I want to get fired."

### CHAPTER 5

Lisa: Geno sits at his desk; Lisa's frustration can be heard as she tries to get her computer to do something. He slowly turns to Lisa as she turns to him and asks if he can help her. Before she can finish her sentence, Geno nods, coming to help her with the computer.

Geno Esposito: He says it's not her, it's the server, but don't worry, I've been working on it all morning. He resets her computer and reconnects it to the servers. The computer works. Lisa asks if he had a good lunch. When he asks why, she points to a stain on his shirt. He pulls his suit coat closed, embarrassed. She pours ginger ale onto a few napkins, telling him to hold still as she cleans it.

## Extended Outline

Geno Esposito: He thanks Lisa, telling her he has another shirt in his employee locker. Lisa thanks him for the help. As he walks back to his desk, he stops, turning to her. "Lisa." She turns to him, he says... "Are you free this..." His stomach hurts, running to the bathroom.

**PP2: The Disruption of the Ordinary World (Inciting Incident)**

SFO Note: At work, Geno deals with another normal day until aliens arrive out of nowhere, taking over the office building as they smash through the windows and walls. Some employees transform near him from humans to aliens (having been in disguise).

## CHAPTER 6

Geno Esposito: In the bathroom, Geno listens to an audiobook. He has headphones in, listening to a book about being more confident, taking steps to be a better leader, and learning how to stand up for yourself. The audiobook says something he agrees with while he's looking at pictures of Lisa on her social media account.

Geno Esposito: He hears banging; he lowers the audiobook to hear. He wipes his ass, and the banging is louder, and it sounds like a low hum of noise.

James: Geno washes his hands, getting a text from James asking him where he is. He laughs, saying he had to shit—too much grease. He writes another text that he almost asked Lisa out, but Montezuma's Revenge attacked him.

Geno Esposito: He waits for a text message back. He doesn't get a response. The noise gets much louder. Opening the bathroom door, laser guns shoot past him, people are running and screaming, and aliens are busting through the windows.

*The 27 Plot Point Outline: When Plot Meets Story*

## CHAPTER 7

Geno Esposito: He runs around, trying to avoid the chaos. He runs into an employee from earlier, and the man turns into an alien.

James: Geno screams, backing up as James hits the alien over the head with a fire extinguisher. It does nothing, and the alien turns around to attack James. Geno attacks the alien from behind, and the two of them are able to knock the alien down enough to run off.

Lisa: As both Geno and James run around, they see Lisa under a desk; they grab her, telling her to run with them.

Geno Esposito: They take off down the hall, and lasers shoot around them. Three employees are shot with the laser, evaporating.

Derrick: Freaking out, they try opening a door, only to see Derrick coming out of nowhere and attacking the aliens. This gives Geno and his friends a chance to break through the door and out of danger.

**PP3: The Protagonist Reacts to the Inciting Incident (Fallout)**

SFO Note: Geno Esposito leads James and Lisa as they sneak around the building. Employees freak out on different floors, doing what they can to hide from aliens. A few employees blow Geno and his friend's cover, causing the aliens to chase them. Geno runs with his friends, eventually finding a place to hide, far away from others.

## CHAPTER 8

Geno Esposito: He moves them around the lower levels, trying to get to the stairs, but they're forced to hide in a utility closet, hearing people get shot and screaming as they cuddle in safety.

*Extended Outline*

James: What's going on? Is this really happening? Are aliens out there? What in the hell would they want with this company? James gets quiet, then looks up at Geno. "Do you think they got Rebecca?" Lisa says she saw her heading out for a late lunch.

Lisa: She is freaking out. Geno holds her arms and looks her in the eyes, telling her to breathe, to look at him, and that they're going to be alright. If we stay close to one another, we're going to be fine.

Derrick: Geno saw something on the computer—it vanished as he worked on the servers. He saw government contracts associated with the company. James asks if he saw what they were. The system cut out; they were gone when it came back on. Geno figured it was a glitch or something that was above his pay grade.

Geno Esposito: Twenty feet from the stairwell, he peeks out the door.

CHAPTER 9

Geno Esposito: They get to the stairwell and head to the lower area. Dust outlines of people are on the walls and floors. Geno says, "If we get to floor X, we can use the window cleaning elevator."

Geno Esposito: They get to a room at the end of the hall; it leads to the Building Maintenance Unit. Four employees run out from a hallway, screaming; two are shot, and the other two run into them. They all fall, and aliens arrive around the corner, shooting at them.

Geno Esposito: He tells them to follow him and run into a room. Aliens shoot at them, destroying the walls and floors, opening up a chance for Geno to jump down to the next level. He pushes Lisa and James, and Geno follows as the aliens shoot at them. Two employees get down but are shot and evaporated.

*The 27 Plot Point Outline: When Plot Meets Story*

Geno Esposito: The aliens shoot at them, destroying another floor. As it collapses under them, they fall and hit the next floor. That floor falls, hitting the next one. The ceiling tiles and debris fall atop them.

Geno Esposito: He sees a doorway to the server room, grabs Lisa's hand, and tells them to follow him. They reach the door, and Geno looks around, seeing no one, and enters, locking the door.

## ANALYSIS

As you can see, the extended outline uses the broad, general statements of a short-form outline and extends the information. From there, I'm able to break it into potential chapters (chapters I can break up even more as they develop).

Within the potential chapter, I'll continue writing summaries of broad, general statements. This gives me room to expand on those ideas in the next step: the zero draft chapter outlines.

Basically, I'm searching for a flow of cause-and-effect, what characters do in each chapter, and how it drives the protagonist's central character arc forward. Keep in mind I can absolutely add other central character arcs into the extended outline, and I should (as well as subarcs).

The goal is to get the protagonist's central character arc in there first.

Now, I'm sure you noticed that PP1 has five chapters, but PP2 and PP3 only have two chapters. That's because PP1 set up the ordinary world and needed a bit more time to explain who these characters are before the chaos came.

Too much happened in PP2 and PP3 to sit and learn more about each of the characters—well beyond showing who they are through action and behavior. These plot points moved faster than PP1 and didn't need as much information. Thus, they got fewer chapters. Could they have gotten more? Yes. If needed.

The lesson to take from this is, plot points need as many chapters as they need to fulfill their purpose. At minimum, they need at least one chapter—at most, well, that comes down to a lot of factors, factors I'll discuss in Chapter 26: How Long Should a Chapter Be?

With that, let's move onto Chapter 24: Outlining a Chapter.

# CHAPTER 24

## Outlining A Chapter

**OUTLINING A CHAPTER**

We're finally getting to the magic of zero draft chapter outlines. I love using zero draft chapter outlines for structure, pacing, and rhythm. I'll explain how I do this in greater detail in the next chapter, where I'll show an actual example.

The method you use doesn't matter much, since there are many ways to outline chapters—so find what works for you.

For me, I use the zero draft chapter outlines. ZDC outlines are a specific method that I've used for a while. But even experienced authors are prone to use bullet points (or similar) for plot beats and vague summaries of chapter events. A minimalist might list out any basic details of what needs to happen.

And yes, there are many ways to outline a chapter. For the purpose of this book, I'll show how I use zero draft chapter outlines to map out chapters and go deeper into my writing process.

Whatever you choose, you must still write complete chapters out. There are general rules and guidelines for what to include in a chapter (or scene) to get the most out of a chapter, making it a complete chapter. Once you know the rule of law, you can start trimming, breaking, and playing with them.

*The 27 Plot Point Outline: When Plot Meets Story*

Speaking of rules, everything we discuss about chapters applies to scenes too. That's because every chapter/scene has a beginning, middle, and end.

All chapter beginnings must set up any needed context. Middles must challenge that context, adding one or more conflicts/problems to the chapter. And by the end, resolve its conflict or problem, keeping the narrative moving forward.

In this chapter, I'll explore a chapter's purpose, showing you what needs to go in the chapters before getting into your prose, passages, subtext, immersion, and author voice. Honestly, these extra things aren't important at this stage. The focus at this point should be on writing out the plot and making sense of it all.

To ease your mind, remember, outlines don't need every detail, but they do need context to make sense of the narrative's purpose, what'll push back on it and the characters, and how it'll all resolve.

An outline is an opportunity to write the bare minimum of what must go in a chapter (narrative). Yep, bare minimum (broad and general). There's no pressure for you to add the entire history of the Kingdom of Blur den Dontales.

With that said, let's talk about what every chapter needs to be considered a full and complete chapter when outlining and developing them and scenes.

## THE BEGINNING: START WHERE?

No chapter will be complete without this method: see what I did there? I hooked you, the reader. Okay, this isn't about adding compelling questions or mysterious terror in chapter beginnings. It's about where to start. That, and I wanted to get the generic advice on making a great chapter out of the way.

And before I go into that, I know there's always nuance to the rules, and, of course, you can break every rule if you really wanted to. Who'll stop you from writing avant-garde, experimental narratives about people acting weird, only to reveal they were chickens the entire time? Chickens! Genius, I tell you. Genius.

Don't get me wrong, you might get drunk on power and break a chapter up into a series of short, unconnected vignettes, ending with questions that you won't answer until the next chapter, or try to mess with stylistic voicings. By the way, you're not Andy Warhol, but even he filmed an eight-hour movie of a silent, single-shot stationary view of the Empire State Building, called "Empire."

*Outlining A Chapter*

Me? I'm teaching you how to outline, using the widely accepted writing principles meant to keep a narrative structured and controlled. Obviously, once you understand this information, I implore you to go off and try things and do as you can and wish to do, having fun with this thing called creative writing.

Now, with that said, chapter beginnings.

Start in the middle. Oh, I did it again, another hook. That's right, when working on your outline, think about where the movement is in the chapter.

But, Thomas, how can you start in the middle?

I'm glad you asked. Starting in the middle of a movement means getting to the good stuff, the context that feels like something is happening. In Laymen's Terms—get to the emotional truth of the scene, chapter, and characters.

No one cares if a character pulls up their driveway, parks the car, gets out of that car, walks to the house, gets in the house, puts their jacket away, and then tells their partner that they got fired. It's slow, slow, slow.

However, if you want to earn the plot beats, set up the emotional truth of the character while they pull up the car. How they feel walking up to the door. The pain of having lost their job, standing at the door in their fear and pain of having to tell their partner they went from one income to no income.

When people say, "Start in the middle," it's there, right there where you set up the emotional context of characters entering a scene or already a part of it. Get to the movement. As stated earlier in this book, movement is the narrative's story, showing the emotional experiences and choices of your characters. Which in turn is where things are actually happening.

## THE BEGINNING: CONTEXT

Context is king. Let me repeat that. Context is king. Chapter beginnings need context. For example, this chapter's introduction set up the context for what'll be explored in the chapter itself. It gave you enough to know it's about outlining a chapter but kept it vague enough for you to still need answers. Ultimately, you know what the chapter's about, but you have to keep reading to learn about it.

Imagine the introduction set up the chapter as it did: that it will explore the needed elements all chapters must have to be complete. Then the first section

## The 27 Plot Point Outline: When Plot Meets Story

explains worldbuilding, character development, or a recipe to make the world's greatest red velvet cake? Okay, who wouldn't love a yummy red velvet cake?

My point is, you'd be confused.

But, Thomas, that's an extreme example.

Okay, how about this one? The introduction is about a man pulling up in his car; his heart is heavy, having just lost his job. He walks up to his house, and when he knocks on the door, it's an alien standing there, and without skipping a beat, the man says nothing. He just walks in sad. But the location he walks into is really a spaceship.

That's pretty extreme too. Let's simplify it. The man pulls up to a house; he says nothing and doesn't explore any emotions. He simply pulls up to a house. He gets out of the car; still no information, just walking to the door. Still nada.

Alright, pretty straightforward. You know what he's doing, but you still don't know the why of what he is doing. The emotional truth.

Narratives need context for emotional truths, or it's just a series of things happening: thus, "something is happening, but nothing is happening." To make things happen, characters must move through emotions. And context sets up the emotional states of characters. If you don't, the beginning will lack engagement.

Let's go a bit further: setting up the context of what's going on, why it's going on, where they are, etc. Remember, you don't have to explain everything in great detail. Vague but informative is the golden rule of writing.

The information should be enough for readers to think they're figuring out what's going on, but not enough to give it all away. Sure, in the example with the man coming home, the reader is kept in the dark about who the man is. It doesn't even have to explain that he lost his job (yet). But they did lose their job. Which means their behavior is influenced by this emotional truth.

So yes, that part needs to be explored. Not the fine detail of why they are sad, but that they are emotionally influenced by a deeper truth (a movement).

> A man pulls his car into his driveway and parks. He sits there, unable to look up at his house, his heat blasting, and the engine rumbling over his thoughts (the man lost his job). He finally looks up at his house, letting a heavy sigh out, and shuts his car off and its lights.

## *Outlining A Chapter*

This information sets context for the who, what, where, when, and why. The context establishes the man we'll be following, the chapter's POV. What's he doing? Arriving at a house, feeling something heavy that weighs on him, but we don't yet know. It sets up the where: his car and potentially his house. We know when this takes place. His car lights went off, which means it's dark out. It could be really early morning or nighttime.

Ah, and the why. The why is nicely hidden in the note (the man lost his job). It's in this note the emotional truth presents itself and thus should be in the entirety of the opening scene of the chapter.

As you see, it's all presented using the vague but informative method to keep readers aware of what's happening while leaving some unanswered questions.

> A quick aside: Don't dumb down your prose for readers, but if you don't give readers enough context, readers can't nor won't be able to understand what's going on—none of it matters at that point.

If this was a written scene with prose, you'd still keep what information was needed and hint at what's left unanswered. Yep, that's right. The truth of any unanswered emotional, physical, and honest subtext must still be on the page too.

To recap: chapters need to answer the following questions when setting up their beginning: the who, what, where, when, and why (context).

First, write out the ZDC outline. Once finished, go back and check to see if those questions are answered. You don't have to answer the questions fully, just enough for context to be present while being vague but informative.

Second, keep the information flowing in the narrative movement. Make the outline follow the movement of the narrative itself by hitting each step of the chapter as plot beats play out. Even in the broad, general sense, make sure things are playing out as you design them (even if they'll change later).

Once a chapter's opening has enough context, it's time to challenge that context by adding a conflict/problem. Conflicts and problems create tension, and tension is needed to help with reader engagement.

Remember, characters need to make emotional choices and experience things. To do this, they must be challenged or given problems to solve.

*The 27 Plot Point Outline: When Plot Meets Story*

## THE MIDDLE: CONFLICT AND CHALLENGE

Narratives need to challenge established context. Challenges are conflicts that can be good or bad, positive or negative. Conflicts create tension, raise the stakes, and move character arcs forward.

Challenging context creates conflict, driving reader engagement.

> For example: You're stuck in traffic, sitting in your car angry on a hot summer day, and nothing: movement has stopped. You have places to go. "The light's green, go!"

This happens because of the "what's going on here, and what's going to happen next" curiosity of people. People are rubbernecking, trying to get a good look at what's going on. Tension builds as you get closer and gain more and more information until your brain is satisfied and the tension is released. Go!

The same happens in narratives. Readers want to know what's going on and what's going to happen next. Conflict keeps readers rubbernecking, turning the pages, and wanting to know what'll happen next.

Can you have a scene or chapter without conflict? Yes. Do I recommend you avoid making that decision? Yes. I'm not saying do it my way or trying to give you that one-size-fits-all writing advice.

But to elevate your narrative, you have to add conflicts and/or problems to chapters. Otherwise things won't be earned on the pages, and you'll end up with "things happening, but nothing is happening." Conflict gives characters a very specific thing to do: make choices and reveal themselves through behavior.

Readers don't care that characters argue about being lost in an unknown area. They care about the why behind their argument, behind their conflicts. It's about the reasons behind why it's all happening and how characters feel about it. The closer readers are to characters, the more empathy they'll have for them.

That's right, we care about the characters we intimately know. By the way, that's another reason for the writing advice of not putting characters in any deadly situation on page one of Chapter 1. Readers know nothing about them, so they don't care about them or have any idea of what's happening with them.

## *Outlining A Chapter*

Again, I'd emphasize that chapter beginnings set up enough context to start building an emotional connection between readers and characters. Readers care about characters as they invest in them, giving that emotional connection weight when the characters do get challenged. Readers are engaged by this.

With that said, middles need problems or conflicts. To be fair, you don't need them to pop up in the direct middle of a scene or chapter. You can build up to conflicts and/or problems. My point still stands: chapters and scenes benefit by having a problem to be solved or a conflict driving characters to make choices.

But, Thomas, what if I don't want my characters always fighting?

Conflicts and problems aren't always characters going all fisticuffs. And a conflict/problem isn't always negative. The good news is that there are plenty of conflicts to choose from. Off the top of my head, I can name four; in fact, here's a list for you. Though, I recommend using this list as a way to get your brain to think when you're unable to naturally figure out a narrative conflict/problem for your characters.

Basically, don't just close your eyes, point to one of the four choices, and use the choice. Have conflicts and problems come from narrative internal logic, driving the plot, story, and character arcs forward.

1. Internal Conflicts (Character vs. Self)
2. Interpersonal Conflicts (Character vs. Character)
3. External Conflicts (Character vs. Outside Force)
4. Plot-Driven Conflicts (Plot is going to plot)

Negative conflicts, problems, or consequences might have a character in a moral dilemma of having to choose between two difficult options: does Mother A get the full baby back, or does she cut the baby in half so Mothers A and B can each have one side? Ah, that Solomon, always making insane judgments.

A positive conflict, problem, or consequence could be a moral dilemma that places a character in the middle of having to choose between their partner of ten years and their parent. That dilemma could be as small as them agreeing with a parent over their partner (sleeping on the couch tonight) or keeping a secret so everyone can throw a surprise party for the partner.

## The 27 Plot Point Outline: When Plot Meets Story

Internal conflicts can be doubt, depression, or a debate of goals they're fighting over within, like wanting to develop their career or go on a much-needed vacation, but if they go, it'll cost them a promotion.

Don't get me wrong, you could try the old character misunderstandings, rivalries, betrayal, etc. But not all chapters and scenes need to be major fallouts or big events. Minor conflicts can be just as interesting if they form a problem that'll eventually lead to a future consequence. Yep, a conflict now can lead to issues in a later chapter. Act 1 issues can come out later in Act 2 or near the end of Act 3.

My point is this: chapters/scenes need a problem or conflict to drive the narrative's plot, story, and character arcs forward. Nothing says "this is absolutely boring" like making a character wake up right on time for work, get to work, do their job, and then go home for the day to a fresh meal already made for them before they go to bed.

Don't believe me? Imagine Braveheart just being a guy living his Scottish life, no issues, just his wife and friends tossing rocks at each other's heads for fun, and then randomly he's taken at the end of a three hundred page narrative and is executed, screaming "Freedom!"

Who would watch that a second time?

What if you watched all 134 minutes of Bridges of Madison County and not one scene had conflict, and the movie ended with Francesca having to choose between her husband and Robert out of nowhere?

Marty McFly doesn't have to worry about anything when he goes back in time. He gets there, realizes he's in the wrong time, and hits the gas. Before he knows it, he's in 1985 again, but a few minutes earlier, and saves Doc Brown.

Conflict not only gives characters a chance to develop, but it also helps a narrative move, bringing it together in a dance of potential and possibility. All of this keeps readers engaged and interested in what's going on and what's going to happen next. Yes, fuel their curiosity.

## THE MIDDLE: CHALLENGE CHARACTERS TO MAKE CHOICES

Choices make interesting narratives. Within these choices, characters come alive, moving around scenes in emotional truths. Beyond their behavior, choices show readers who a character is. Oh, and show as much as you can. Honestly, showing is better than telling readers who a character is—it earns you and readers a bigger return on your investment of words.

But, Thomas, telling gives readers insight into who a character is, yes?

Something I've learned over the years is that telling is the opinion of you, the writer. At best, it's hopefully the truth. At worst, telling is a lie. After all, have you ever heard the phrase, "Actions speak louder than words"?

That's one of my favorite lessons. You can tell a reader all day who one of your characters is, but at the end of the day, if their behavior isn't matching it, it's all lies. And the less a character behaves based on what you've told the reader, the less readers will believe what you tell them. An unreliable narrator doesn't make for a fun reading experience (unless your goal is to be unreliable).

Of course, Writing 101 says, "show, don't tell." I believe on the surface that's bad advice. It should be "show, sometimes tell." You know, because you'll need to add context for things to make sense. So yes, you can tell the reader who a character is, but their actions need to give weight to the words. And the secret to that is this: show first, tell later.

Showing characters behaving as truthfully as you can tells the reader one thing, but then afterward having other characters or even the narrator confirm it makes it become evidence of their truth.

But, Thomas, how can I show a character's truth and behavior?

Challenge characters to show who they are by the choices they make. I'll say this much: choices give characters a chance to show their truth, even if they lie in their choice. So when you present a problem or conflict in chapters, this'll give characters a moment to react to it, making choices based on who they are within, and moving the narrative forward for the plot and story (character arcs).

> A quick aside: this is a book on outlining, not a prose writing book. These ideas should help you outline a narrative properly, giving you the tools and advice to do so. And to do that, you'll need to know who your characters are.

But, Thomas, who are my characters beyond what I say they are?

## The 27 Plot Point Outline: When Plot Meets Story

Characters are made up of morals, missions, positions, goals, wants, and motivations. And I'm sure you're wondering where these come from. If you're unaware, know that you could make it all up, since it's a creative medium. Or you can go crazy with it like I do, thinking about the psychology of it all.

If you're willing to go there, you have to understand that these concepts naturally get developed by many factors. If you don't want to study psychology, these three elements are a good starting point: nature, nurture, and circumstance.

Nature is who characters are inherently: personalities, positions, ideas, morals, and other aspects from their internal reasoning they formulated based on external factors. Which brings me to nurture.

Nurture is their upbringing and background: what is their faith (if they have one), where are they from, who raised them, any heritage, etc. These aspects don't guarantee they'll become XYZ but can influence it. Their inherent nature will guide how their nurture influences them.

There's a saying, and I'm paraphrasing, from Dr. Gabor Maté, that "No siblings grow up in the same house, and no siblings will have the same parents."

This idea implies that each child's experience within the same home is going to be unique to them due to factors like birth order, changing parental circumstances, and individual temperament.

Not to get into the psychology of it all, but parents are not static people; they'll change as they develop (or devolve) as parents with the birth of a child, the next kid, and the third, fourth, and maybe fifth. These elements, and a lot more, influence the relationships between the siblings and the parents, etc.

Which finally brings us to circumstance: any given situation characters find themselves in. And, of course, whether they come from New York, Ohio, or the southernmost peninsula of Florida, characters can adapt, change, and make choices based on their new environment and circumstances.

Here's a wrap-up.

All chapter/scene middles must challenge characters to make a choice or choices, exposing their emotional truths. I'd add that you should challenge them as much as possible within a chapter/scene. And by "as much as possible," I mean if they get through the chapter/scene with no resistance, something is missing.

But, Thomas, can you challenge characters too much?

*Outlining A Chapter*

Yes. The rule of thumb is to pay attention to how muddled things get on a page. Challenge characters to create movement for them, but not at the expense of clarity, plot, or other character arcs. In other words, let traffic flow.

## THE END: RESOLUTION

As with the endings of all acts, sections, and plot points, scenes and chapters need a resolution to be complete. The purpose of a resolution is to move character arcs and the plot forward, giving momentum to the overall narrative.

Of course, there are different forms of resolutions, but ultimately, scenes and chapters resolve the conflict or problem created in the middle of it. A conflict or problem doesn't have to resolve completely at a chapter or scene's conclusion but at least ends with an earned narrative closure that keeps the plot going.

Oh sure, scenes/chapters have different purposes in how and why they'll resolve, but they must still resolve conflicts or problems created within them.

For example, a scene's resolution creates a change that happens as a result of a character's actions and choices. Every scene starts in one narrative place and ends in another, creating changes to the plot, relationships with other characters, or a character's emotional state.

Even multiple scenes that make up a single chapter need a full narrative thread with a beginning, middle, and end. Not every scene in a chapter needs to connect to the previous one either, but the narrative throughline should. If the first scene is in one POV, switches to another in the second, and finally, switches to a third in the last scene of a chapter, the best course of action is to link them with their themes, tones, and purposes of the overall chapter itself.

But, Thomas, how would that play out if a chapter has multiple scenes?

Like all things, a plan helps, but if you're writing from the seat of your pants, think about what each of the scenes have in common. However, since this is an outlining book, let's use the extended outline chapter summary, shall we?

These three example scenes are from a single chapter idea. While reading them, look for specific details that connect to one another. You might not be able to catch things on your first read (which is fine), but you should be able to see it clearly once you go back after giving it a read-through.

## The 27 Plot Point Outline: When Plot Meets Story

Scene 1: David worked in a local tavern, cleaning a table. He had just begun his work shift but couldn't stop paying attention to the sun's location. His mind focused on seeing the love of his life that night. He should have called in sick.

Scene 2: Edward entered a local tavern and sat at a table in the far corner. This gave him a perfect view of the entrance. He called over a waiter. A young man stepped to him.
  "Hi, I'm David. What would you like?"
  "Please, your finest ale," Edward asked. "And stay close. A friend is meeting me here tonight."

Scene 3: Lord Adam slammed down a large bible, telling his young daughter, Eve, that he must meet with a potential suitor he chose for her. She's forbidden to see this poor barboy, who could never give her what she needs. Their argument ends as Lord Adam closes the door, leaving, complaining that he's already late for a meeting.

These scenes follow three POVs and still have a narrative thread between them. David is in love with Lord Adam's daughter, and Edward waits at the same tavern to meet Lord Adam to discuss the next step in marrying his daughter, Eve.

Now chapters, on the other hand, act as a much larger unit of the overall narrative and can often contain several smaller scenes (the example above). Still, chapters must have resolutions that provide a sense of closure for that section of the narrative while also setting up the forward momentum for the next chapter.

To add, when outlining chapters, remember chapters don't have to be a continuation of the previous chapter (though they can be).

Narratives must continue, but for example, one chapter can follow David on a date with Eve, but the following chapter doesn't have to be David dropping Eve off. It can jump to another character traveling to the city or another city far away. Nonetheless, chapters must link in narrative tone, themes, and purpose.

To conclude, there are many resolutions: character growth, a new piece of information is revealed, a character succeeds or fails, the relationship of two or more people changes, etc. But the truth remains: endings should feel like chapters or scenes have accomplished what they set out to do.

My point is this: a chapter/scene must take the context established in the beginning, challenge it in its middle, causing a conflict and/or problem that must be resolved by its end, pushing character arcs and the plot forward.

## THE END: NARRATIVE DRIVE

"I couldn't put the book down." Ah yes, a quote authors want to hear from all of their readers. The pull that keeps them turning. Oh sure, a cliffhanger can do this every single time... Maybe, okay, sometimes, but too many in a row loses effect.

Alright, that meandered a bit near the end, losing narrative drive. Which brings me to my point: every chapter/scene needs narrative drive, pushing your readers forward. Narrative drive keeps momentum going, compelling readers to continue reading through the beginning, middle, and end.

Engagement is a mixture of tension, curiosity, and emotional investment that keeps pages turning even when nothing explosive is happening. That's right, not every engaging thing must be a full-fledged explosion, literally or figuratively. True engagement is something deeper, something profoundly interesting in how your characters exist on the page.

Remember, plot is what needs to happen, no matter what, and story is how plot unfolds through the emotional experiences and choices of characters. This means when the bomb goes off, its plot, how characters react to it and make choices because of it, and how it all plays together is story.

While narrative drive boils down to a sense of pure anticipation from an unfolding plot, the characters making choices, leaving readers with unanswered questions, showing the emotional stakes of a narrative in general, etc., it all means nothing if it's not compelling the reader to continue.

And before you ask about the how, narrative drive isn't tied to one single technique but rather revealed within the direct purpose of a chapter's end. Don't get me wrong, a mystery's breadcrumbs leading to solving it can be as engaging as a character readers can't look away from. Even prose creating mood with rhythm can carry readers forward.

## The 27 Plot Point Outline: When Plot Meets Story

At the end of the day, it's all about anticipation: the readers should feel like something important is coming, and they don't want to miss it. FOMO: The Fear of Missing Out. And who really wants to miss out on all the fun?

As a writer, read the room, or rather, the chapter. Strong chapters follow the rhythm of what's happening in the actual chapter or scene and let it tell you what the narrative drive is, or what's needed, to keep readers going.

And, honestly, it's less about "what would keep readers interested" and more about "what is interesting about this chapter."

Oh sure, there's always placing readers ahead of the protagonist, letting them know more than the characters. This taps into a reader's curiosity, both intellectually and emotionally: the whole "When will the character figure it out?" thing. You'll usually see this in mysteries—you can create mystery in any genre.

Known as dramatic irony, a reader knows more than the characters. The ole five minutes remaining before the bomb under the table blows gag. Sounds like a mystery creating tension. You can thank Alfred Hitchcock for that.

What about when both a protagonist and a reader know the same thing? Everyone knows a bomb will go off in five minutes. Will they save everyone? Find out next week, for only the Shadow knows what evil lurks in the hearts of men.

Honestly, it never has to be that insane or big. A deeply intimate scene or chapter can do the same thing. An ending where the reader knows the man lost his job but doesn't tell his wife until the end of the chapter will create conflict, tension, and narrative movement.

No matter what you choose to do, this only works if readers are invested in both the plot and the story of your narrative. They must know what's going on, who a character is, and the deeper emotional truth affecting it all. No one cares if they don't know what's happening or if they don't know who the characters are.

When it comes down to it, narrative drive should create anticipation for what could potentially happen and what'll happen next, leaving room for some questions to be answered as others go unanswered, making readers care about the protagonist and their potential outcomes.

I'll say this much: yes, you can control narrative drive by only having a great plot or fantastic characters who have strong personalities or motivations, even giving readers enough information to know what's going on. But really, the

*Outlining A Chapter*

true secret is to mix and match these things into the overall book you're writing. Never just focus on great plot points, a fantastic character, etc. I assure you, when done right, a little of this, a little of that, will go a long way.

Like with prose, vary sentences to create rhythm, and give readers enough information to know what's going on while leading them forward, giving them a chance to see what else they might learn along the way.

Basically, lower the stick so the carrot dangles, but occasionally change out that carrot for steak or werechicken.

# CHAPTER 25

## Outlining A Chapter: Zero Draft Chapter Outline

**OUTLINING A CHAPTER: ZERO DRAFT CHAPTER OUTLINE**

It's time for the zero draft chapter outlines and how I outline with them. I'll use the alien invasion narrative's extended outline of the first chapter for the example.

Before I start, let me explain how my approach to a zero draft is different from what you may know or have been taught. First, I'll define what a traditional zero draft is, then go into how I use a zero draft chapter outline.

A zero draft is your first, uninhibited pass at getting a narrative out. It's a throw-up draft, where you respectfully ignore spelling, grammar, any tense being used, structure, and standard formatting. Teachers might tell writers to use it as a raw, free-flowing exploration of ideas, characters, and plot. Or just get your ideas on the page and worry about it later.

Whether you're putting an artistic spin on it or writing what happens to come to your mind, the sole purpose of zero drafts is either finding the narrative from nothing or trying to get an entire narrative out of you and on the page. This draft is more about getting words out and less about being perfect.

Now that you know what a zero draft is, you can attack it with the above approach, or you can try my personal approach below.

## The 27 Plot Point Outline: When Plot Meets Story

My approach expands on this known method and adds bullet points for rhythm, pace, some dialogue, and broad general statements. If I feel like it, prose. My goal: map out a chapter using extended outlines and play out those plot beats through character and movement.

Things to pay attention to: my first bullet point sets the main plot beat. From there, I go deeper into the main plot beat, using indented bullet points for the subbeats. Finally, another indented bullet point explores the subbeat of the main plot beat. If I go any deeper than that, the same rules would apply.

After I finish a zero draft chapter outline, I step back, using bullet points as a visual guide of what's working and not working. I can check the pace by how main plot beats cluster or not, how far indents go, and if I'm lingering for far too long or not long enough in any main plot beat.

If anything stands out, I adjust as needed. I'm checking to see if any of the bullet points are moving the narrative's plot forward or lingering too long. I then take notes and adjust the zero draft chapter outline from there.

I do this to make sure the plot beats are flowing smoothly and organized. After all, this isn't a first draft with pretty prose and immersion. It's simply plot getting laid out into a chapter as I watch chapters/scenes take shape.

Besides, main plot beats and subbeats (even random dialogue) give me a general rhythm of the zero draft chapter outline and its pace, letting me know the movement before I add pretty prose, detailed character development, or complex worldbuilding.

Oh, and not that this book is focused on the writing part of prose, but if you're wondering, once I finish all the zero draft chapter outlines, I go back, take each bullet point, and write prose out to that bullet point. Basically, I write to the plot beat, play in it to see where it goes, and move away from it: repeat.

## CHAPTER 1: ALIEN INVASION NARRATIVE EXAMPLE

I'm going to use the original expanded outline notes for Chapter 1 to show how I lay out zero draft chapter outlines. On the next page there are five character arc summaries in the first chapter. I must get all five of their summary points into the first chapter before I can move onto Chapter 2.

## *Outlining A Chapter: Zero Draft Chapter Outline*

Since you have the below cheat sheet for the character arc summaries, I recommend reading them first to take note of the beats and where they occur in the first chapter to see how and where the beats fit in the chapter.

`Act 1, Section 1, Plot Point 1: Setting up the Ordinary World`

Geno Esposito: He arrives at work, immediately beset by the daily grind. Dealing with a difficult boss and general chaos, he's reminded why he hates being an accountant. He's left with a brief moment of calm, saying hello to Lisa, a woman near his desk.

James: He's upset that Geno left the bar earlier last night because Rebecca from the 2nd floor showed up. She sang a soulful rendition of "I Will Always Love You," and you, sir, missed it. Geno says he had to get up for work. James laughs—you were thirty minutes late. Geno smiles. "I should have left earlier from the bar."

Geno Esposito: His frustration boils over, and he tells James he's at his breaking point and needs to quit the job. James points to the cleaners outside the window, giving him a harsh dose of reality and a sharp, visual metaphor for what life could be.

Lisa: Overhearing them, Lisa turns to them at her desk, "It was great. You missed a good time." Geno said he didn't see her there. Lisa says that she showed up after he left, I suppose. You would have loved it. Geno is sorry he missed her; Lisa says, "I'm sorry I was missed."

Derrick: Geno is approached by his boss, Derrick, asking for Geno to handle a new task. As always, he can wallow in his frustration or do something meaningful and help. Geno agrees to it.

*The 27 Plot Point Outline: When Plot Meets Story*

# CHAPTER 1

- Geno arrives at his office, grabbing paperwork from Carl as he steps off the elevator.
  - Geno continues down the open floor layout, nodding at people asking him for help when he has a chance, and heads to the break room without even looking at his desk.
- Geno lays his briefcase and paperwork on the break room table.
  - Geno takes a sip of nothing from his empty coffee thermos and hangs his head in defeat.
  - Turning around, he grabs the coffee pot, smirking at the sign that says 'coffee for mugs only,' and pours most of it into his thermos.
- Nancy enters the break room, scaring Geno for a moment, with some coffee splashing up and out of the thermos.
  - "Great, you're finally here," Nancy said. "Derrick said you'll be able to help me with some numbers later."
    - Geno nodded, ignoring her but nodding.
    - "You know how upper management feels. The wrong decimal here, dollar amount there."
  - Geno takes a slow sip from his thermos.
    - "What's a few hundred dollars to a major corporation?" she said, turning to him. "Right?"
      - "Right."
  - "You bring that from home?" Nancy asked.
    - Geno looked at the empty coffee pot, then back to her. "Yes."
  - Nancy huffed, grabbing the pot and filling it. "Someone keeps using it all without filling it back up."
    - "I just got here myself. If I see anything…" Geno said, grabbing his briefcase and paperwork, "I'll let you know," he finished, stepping out of the break room.
- Geno heads to his desk, his body deflated and his eyes darting around for anyone else who'll try and disrupt him before he can sit at his desk.

## Outlining A Chapter: Zero Draft Chapter Outline

- His shoulders lift at the sight of a woman, a desk away from his own. Lisa, unaware he's approaching, is hard at work.
- Geno reached his desk, and before he could put anything down, a kind and welcoming voice stopped him.
  - "Morning, Geno," Lisa said.
  - "Morning... Did..."
  - "Nope. Yes. Well, sort of. I told Derrick you were helping Matt on the third floor."
  - "Who's Matt?"
  - "I don't know," she said, smiling. "There's always a Matt."
- Geno laughed. "Thanks for covering," he said as he moved his chair to sit.
- "You left way too early last night," James said, stopping Geno from sitting.
  - "What?" Geno stood there. "I left at the right time."
    - "You left at an old man's time."
    - "I'm old, James."
    - "If you're old, then I'm old."
  - "You are old," Lisa said, keeping herself working.
  - James gave her a playful look, turning back to Geno as he sat down.
    - Geno let out a sigh, resting back in his office chair.
    - "Am I really that old?"
    - Geno nodded, closing his eyes, leaning back further.
  - "Thirty-seven is not old."
    - Geno opened one eye. "It's not young."
- James waved him off, sitting on the edge of his desk. "Rebecca from the second floor showed up."
  - "And?" Geno put his feet up, resting them on James' legs.
  - "She sang a soulful rendition of 'I Will Always Love You,'" he said, pushing Geno's feet off him and standing. "And you, sir, missed it."
- "I needed to get up for work." He cleaned up his desk a little.

## The 27 Plot Point Outline: When Plot Meets Story

- ☐ James laughed. "You're thirty minutes late."
- ☐ Geno smiles. "Huh, I should've left the bar earlier then."
- ☐ Geno searched for paper, finding a large pile of new folders. "These aren't mine," he said, grabbing a yellow sticky off the top of the pile. "Christ."
  - ☐ "What?" James asked.
  - ☐ "I need to quit this job," Geno said, looking through the files. "None of this is even accounting."
    - ■ Geno tossed the folders to the side, shaking his head. "I'm quitting."
  - ☐ James pointed at cleaners outside the window. "You could be those guys out there."
    - ■ Geno turned and looked at men cleaning the windows on the outside. Their faces had less of a smile on them than Geno currently did. "Eh, maybe."
- ☐ "It was great, you know," Lisa interrupted. "You missed a good time."
  - ☐ "When? Oh, last night?" Geno glared at James. "You got her in on this now too?"
    - ■ "She's right," James said, smiling.
  - ☐ "Okay." Geno hit a few keys on his computer. Nothing happened. He turned it on.
    - ■ "Really," she said, turning to face them. "It was a lot of fun."
    - ■ "I didn't even see you there." Geno sat up. "I would've stayed if I did."
  - ☐ "You stay for her, but not your best friend?"
    - ■ "I have nicer legs than you," Lisa said.
    - ■ "She's right, she does."
      - ☐ Lisa stretched her leg out. "I do, don't I?"
    - ■ James stares. "Mmhmm."
      - ☐ Geno poked James with a closed pen.
      - ☐ "What? Hey, she was advertising them."
  - ☐ Lisa laughed. "It's okay; they distract me too."
    - ■ Geno smirked, turning to his computer after it beeped.

*Outlining A Chapter: Zero Draft Chapter Outline*

- ☐ "I probably showed up after you left," Lisa said.
    - ■ "I'm sorry I missed you."
    - ■ "You missed me?"
    - ■ "I mean... No, like, we missed each... Yes, I missed you too... I'm..." He corrected his posture. "I'm saying that I'm sorry I missed you."
  - ☐ Her face held in the warmth of a smile trying to hide a deeper truth. "I'm sorry I was missed," she said, turning back to her computer. "You'd have loved it."
- ☐ "Mr. Esposito," a voice from across the office floor called out.
  - ☐ Geno hung his head.
    - ■ "Good luck," James said, patting him on his shoulder as he ran off.
    - ■ "Thanks."
  - ☐ Geno sat up in his chair. "Derrick."
    - ■ "Mr. Esposito, did you get a chance to speak with Nancy?"
    - ■ "Yes."
  - ☐ "Great. Oh, and is that thing with Matt taken care of?"
    - ■ "What?" Geno asked, looking up at him. "Matt?"
      - ☐ Lisa coughed.
      - ☐ "Matt, yes, yes I did."
- ☐ "Great. Since you're free, I need you to do a special task for me."
  - ☐ "I'm swamped. I really can't."
    - ■ "You're the only one I can trust with this."
    - ■ Geno pointed to the pile of folders. "I have a whole day's worth of crap—stuff here to do."
  - ☐ "You'll get to it. Leave that for tomorrow," Derrick said, taking a sip of his coffee.
- ☐ Geno sat back. "What is it you need me to do?"
  - ☐ "The server is acting up, and with your background and the thing you did last week for me," Derrick said, chuckling. He turned to Lisa. "A wiz with computers. Are they still saying 'wiz' nowadays?"

- ▪ "Only when taking the piss out of someone," Geno said.
- ▪ "Piss out of someone?" Derrick asked.
  - ◻ "British for making fun of."
  - ◻ "Interesting. They use that here in New York?"
- ◻ "No. So you need me to work on the server?"
  - ▪ "Give it a once-over. The two guys on it now seem to be having trouble. I'm sure it's nothing. But the computers are acting slow today."
- ◻ Geno looked at the window cleaners. "Fine. You need me to do it now?"
  - ◻ "Yes, please. Thanks, Mr. Esposito."
  - ◻ Derrick started to walk away. "Lisa, get that cough checked out. Colds are killers, and we can't afford for half our employees to go home sick."
    - ▪ Lisa took a sip of coffee. "Will do, boss."
- ◻ Derrick left, and Geno grabbed a laptop from a desk drawer. "Suck up."
  - ◻ Lisa laughed. "Good luck, Mr. Esposito."

## ZERO DRAFT CHAPTER OUTLINE ANALYSIS

Now that Chapter 1's zero draft chapter outline is complete, let's look at how the notes from the expanded outline were built upon. What originally began as brief, plot-focused summaries had a chance to breathe in the zero draft chapter outline, exploring a detailed scene, some dialogue, action, and plot beats mapped out.

What I'm sure you noticed is that the "prose" and passages connected to the bullet points aren't lyrical, pretty, or immersive. This draft's main purpose is to get the plot out and down in the chapter, showing how each extended outline note expands into movement.

For reference, the extended outline notes were a total of 240 words. And once I wrote out the zero draft, the word count reached 1,172. Again, I'd say that you shouldn't worry about the word count. I zoomed in on the word count so I could show you how it increases to gauge the count in your own work.

Meaning, an extended draft will be way lower in word count than your zero draft chapter outline, and so you know, zero draft chapter outlines will most

*Outlining A Chapter: Zero Draft Chapter Outline*

likely be a third the size of first drafts. I say this because prose eat up word count. That's not a bad thing, but it's nice to know this beforehand—so you're not shocked or thrown off by the jumps in count.

Looking at the structure of the chapter, we see that there are a few scenes in the chapter itself. The first scene: Geno gets to work, stepping off the elevator and heading to the break room. The middle brings us to the third set piece when Geno gets to his desk, starting the second scene.

## CHAPTER 1'S OPENING SETUP

The opening scene sets context for the chapter, giving insight into the who, what, where, when, and why information. This information prepares readers for what's to come, the deeper emotional and external conflicts and problems.

Without this the chapter will lack a foundational strength for the challenges in the middle of the chapter. This opening establishes who Geno is, seeding what he does, where he works, and the people around him, and we learn that he's tired. It's seeded that he's potentially late too.

## CHAPTER 1'S MIDDLE CONFLICT

The middle dives into the chapter's conflict and problem, showing Geno dealing with the emotional effect his work life has on him. We learn that he's asked to do everything at his job, usually for and from other employees. This leaves him with no time to get his work finished. Geno tries to have a social life, but he's too tired, cutting out early, and he really wants to quit his job and move on.

## CHAPTER 1'S RESOLUTION

In the resolution readers now understand the frustration Geno feels for his job, the chemistry of his friendships, and his unrequited love for Lisa, as well as her flirting with him. The chapter ends with narrative momentum toward the next plot beat: Geno must work on the server.

*The 27 Plot Point Outline: When Plot Meets Story*

## SCENE BREAKDOWNS

You saw how the full chapter had a beginning, middle, and end. Now look closer at how both scenes of the chapter have their own beginnings, middles, and ends. There's a setup for each scene, conflict, and resolution pushing them forward.

## SCENE 1: BREAK ROOM | BEGINNING

The scene opens with Geno getting off the elevator and being handed paperwork from Carl. He ignores his desk, heading directly to get coffee in the break room. He's already overwhelmed by the day before it starts. His first defeat of the day is his empty thermos as he takes a sip, realizing there's no coffee.

## SCENE 1: BREAK ROOM | MIDDLE

The conflict/problem begins as Geno pours the whole pot of coffee, ignoring the sign 'mugs only.' Nancy arrives, creating tension (did she catch him?). She asks Geno for help, mentioning Derrick (his boss) said Geno would help her. Nancy doesn't know who's taking the coffee. Geno leaves.

## SCENE 1: BREAK ROOM | ENDING

Geno grabs his belongings and skedaddles out of there, avoiding the conversation to continue with Nancy. The ending doesn't resolve the need to help everyone or that Geno still has to deal with his tiredness and coworkers. The end of the scene is only a temporary reprieve and not a solution.

The opening is 98 words, the middle 99, and the end concludes with 45 words. The count will increase when I write out the first draft, but as you can see, every word, line, and movement did what it had to for the scene, making it tight and keeping it moving.

And sure, a first, second, and even third draft would explore more of the immersion and go in on the emotional elements, but even then, every word, line, and passage must do one thing: keep the narrative drive moving.

*Outlining A Chapter: Zero Draft Chapter Outline*

## SCENE 2: DESK | BEGINNING

Geno arrives at his desk, drained and keeping an eye out for more interruptions. This sets up his emotional truth as he gets to his desk.

## SCENE 2: DESK | MIDDLE

A massive pile of irrelevant folders causes Geno to break down, wanting to quit his job. In the middle of that conflict/problem, James and Lisa talk with Geno about missing out on the night's fun at the bar (conflict). James brings up his problem, trying to get with Rebecca, and seeds of Lisa and Geno are hinted at.

## SCENE 2: DESK | ENDING

The scene resolves by pushing the narrative forward when Derrick interrupts the friends. He asks Geno to work on the servers. This moment pushes Geno to grab his laptop and head off to do another job that's not his. The end gives a really nice playful nudge to Geno and Lisa's potential romance with a supportive, albeit slightly teasing, "Good luck, Mr. Esposito."

The second scene's opener is 117 words, the middle 493, and the end lands on 320. This full scene is much thicker, as it has the bulk of the chapter's main conflict and character development. It does some heavy lifting with setting up Geno's ordinary world, his relationships, job life, etc.

But, as you can see, every word, line, and passage in the second scene still keeps the narrative drive moving. Get the plot down and avoid the fluff.

# CHAPTER 26

## How Long Should A Chapter Be?

**HOW LONG SHOULD A CHAPTER BE?**

Chapter lengths are a big part of the conversation in all writing communities. I'd even argue that there's no definitive answer unless you ask writers. I know; that's contradictory. But let me explain: because who's right? Is it one thousand words, fifteen hundred words, or three thousand words? My least favorite advice is a firm stance on never ever writing more than five thousand words a chapter.

Whatever is said, each answer is never clear, whether read online or heard from a professional source or writer groups; the chapter length and word count end up being an endless debate. So what's anything I have to say about it going to add to the conversation?

How about perspective?

Honestly, each stage of writing has a different purpose. An outline could have as many words as it needs. A majority of them are notes that'll never see the pages of a book. And that's because you need to know the deeper ideas of where characters are going emotionally, maybe some backstory and worldbuilding, and, of course, the details of the plot laid out with broad, general statements. But the point still stands; those general statements could still take up a few pages.

## The 27 Plot Point Outline: When Plot Meets Story

None of it matters; they're notes and guidelines to help you write your zero draft chapter outlines. Which brings me to my next point. Who cares how many words you have in your zero draft chapter outlines? It's all going to change once you get to the first draft. And in a zero draft chapter outline, you'll quickly find out if you need to break a chapter up or not, how much you're lingering or not sitting in a moment long enough, and even the fun stuff of still leaving notes.

Now, the first draft? This is probably going to be the first indication of how many words a chapter will truly have. And, of course, this won't answer the age-old question: how long should a chapter be? But a first draft will balloon up with each new sentence, the prose you write, and the developing scene.

Remember, the first draft, at least in my process, doesn't add immersion. That's what I do in my second draft, when I add sensory elements, give characters internal processing, build on the world, etc.

Basically, the first draft takes the zero draft chapter outline plot beats and writes to them, plays in them, and writes out of them. This is why I suggest not worrying about the word count of a first draft but still keeping an eye on it.

I say that because the second draft is going to approach the first draft in a way that should and will explore more changes. Look, you should have taken a break and come back to the first draft, read through it, and taken notes. Those notes will be applied to your second draft. Which means more or less immersion, cleaning up the plot where and when it's not working, adding and subtracting to your scenes, etc. It truly is a process and will pay off with doing the work.

So worrying about the word count right now still doesn't matter. It's all going to change anyway, even more so with beta reader feedback. They're reading the second draft with their experience in mind. After they read it, you're going to get notes from them, lots of notes, notes that'll influence the word count of the chapters... again.

But, Thomas, when does the chapter's length matter? Draft eight?

Ready? Here's the perspective I'm offering you. Think of chapter needs, and not chapter word count. Chapters need beginnings, middles, and ends. At the end of the day, chapters need immersion, sensory, and character experiences. Chapters need both plot and story clearly written out. And every single time you write a chapter, it needs narrative drive, whether for character arcs or the plot.

## How Long Should A Chapter Be?

We already know that beginnings need context. So read the chapter and make sure there's enough information to set up things. It needs to be clean, clear, and make sense to the readers. After all, readers must know what's going on, even if a chapter has lots of vague but informative information.

Second, a middle needs a conflict or problem, pulling characters in and out of moments, giving them choices to make and opportunities to experience it all in emotional ways—creating engagement for readers and narrative drive.

> A quick aside: every chapter or scene needs a conflict or problem, but I'm not saying a problem or conflict must start in a chapter's actual middle, but conflicts and problems do need to start sometime after a chapter's context informs readers of what's going on. Follow the circular rhythm of context → conflict → resolution.

And of course, chapters need a resolution, bringing the problems and/or conflicts to a close. Though closure doesn't have to be a complete one right then and there at the very end, it should at minimum move the narrative forward for either the protagonist's central character arc (CC) or character arcs (or both).

Which brings me to the question: how long should a chapter be?

Chapter word count and length isn't about a specific number. It's about a chapter doing what it needs to accomplish. It's about more than one thing. Ask yourself, does it have...

1. A beginning (context), middle (conflict/problem), and end (resolution)?
2. Immersion and characters' emotional experiences and choices?
3. Plot forward, character development, or worldbuilding beats?

If you answered no to one or more of those questions, it's time to do the real work. The work that makes you a writer. Writers writing isn't the real work. Writing is easy; being a writer is hard. Being a writer and doing the work is asking questions and pulling things apart, analyzing the chapters, prose, characters, etc.

My point stands: a complete chapter is more than its length. A complete chapter comes together when it satisfies all of its needs.

# CHAPTER 27

## Revising Your Outline

**REVISING YOUR OUTLINE**

Revising an outline is part of the process, as is going back and adjusting each of your drafts: zero, first, second, third, etc. With each revision, you have the control to add here and there until you fatten it up to be something it was always meant to be: a complete narrative.

This step goes back through finished outlines and drafts to see where, what, and when you should seed, foreshadow, and add details to earn payoffs or qualify things that came up in later chapters during the outlining and writing process. Readers feel cheated when something happens that wasn't earned.

You can't just have Billy Bob shoot a fireball out of his butt to save his friends and then have them all run off in the third act. How did he learn how that works? Did someone teach him that off the page? Wait a minute, this book is not a fantasy novel; it's a romance.

Okay, sure, who wouldn't want a fireball in a romance novel?

The revision is less about cleaning things up and more about going back and adjusting things to make sure every element of your narrative is connecting. I mean every element. Character choices, behavior, and truths must come logically.

*The 27 Plot Point Outline: When Plot Meets Story*

Plot beats must be earned. Information, worldbuilding, and the unfolding of the plot must connect to earlier scenes or established truths.

And to do this, here's my One Forward, One Back Method.

# ONE FORWARD, ONE BACK METHOD

Plot takes time and a lot of patience to shape it, mold it. Character arcs take time too, watching characters form as they develop, evolve, and start making realistic choices. And worldbuilding itself will take you on a long, revealing path.

Nothing in a narrative just happens. If it does, it's unearned. This is why you must seed, foreshadow, and connect the dots of your plot and character arcs. Without these elements, narratives can feel abrupt or disjointed, collapsing under their own weight of inaccuracies. The One Forward, One Back Method gives you the space to develop narrative elements a step at a time, while keeping the creative method moving.

Instead of plotting every single detail upfront, you're able to develop the narrative with broad, general statements, starting with character summaries, then the three outlines, and eventually expanding deeper into each written draft.

I love how this method lets a narrative evolve organically, maintaining a strong cohesion between what you already know and what you'll discover as you develop and refine the truths of your narrative.

But, Thomas, I already know what and where I want my narrative to go.

You do. Most writers intimately understand the narrative and characters. But the reality is, how can you truly know the characters or where the unfolding narrative will take you if it's still being worked on?

Hear me out.

Where we begin a narrative isn't going to be where we end it. This is the thing: characters form on the page through their lived experiences, in scenes when they make choices to do or not do, say or not say. We have ideas of who they are, sure, but that can change on the page and does (and should).

Same with your narrative. You might know what it is, and you know what? It might just start and end the same way you had always wanted it to. But the other stuff, within scenes, chapters, and plot points: it won't.

*Revising Your Outline*

Your characters won't let it. They won't let you go right if they'd go left. And you need to listen to them... Well, you need to listen to the movement of the narrative. You do this because you must write for a narrative's ever-beating heart. And your northern star, the rule of rules, stands: always serve the narrative.

Which brings us to the One Forward, One Back Method. A method that balances structure and creative spontaneity, giving you the freedom to explore a living, breathing narrative. Yes, narratives breathe. And when you're able, adjust things, react to cause and effect, and listen to your characters make choices. This is an opportunity to add value to the writing.

After all, you're not beholden to the law of the outline or the ideas that'll break the will of your characters. You. Can. Change. Things. Period.

But, Thomas, my characters are not real.

Correct. But they will make real choices on the page. Yes, you're going to make choices for them, but writing characters, truly authentic ones, comes from something deeper, something purer: behavior, positions, and choices. I'm saying this because if you take away the natural movement of characters, they'll fall flat, feel like a game piece, or just come off like a thing moving around on the page.

## HOW TO USE THE METHOD

Whether you're outlining, writing the zero draft chapter outlines, or in your first, second, or third draft, the process below is the same. It's a process that will help you take an ever-growing narrative and reel it back and help maintain cohesion.

Keep in mind, take what you learn, adjust it as needed to better suit your strengths and weaknesses, and have fun. Besides, you might end up developing an even better method for yourself. With that said, these are the steps for my One Forward, One Back Method, starting with writing the short-form outline.

1. One Plot Point Forward, One Plot Point Back

Not that every plot point needs an overhaul, but it's wise to start with PP1 and take it from there, writing broad, general statements of what must happen in that plot point. Once you've moved to PP2, write out its plot points as needed.

## The 27 Plot Point Outline: When Plot Meets Story

Now here's where the method takes shape.

Once you've completed writing out PP2, take a few small notes on what happens in the second plot point, and figure out if any new information needs to be added to PP1.

Now at this point in the process, you might notice PP1 has information in it that'll need to be moved and adjusted into PP2. Feel free to do that, and then move onto PP3.

The process begins again. Write PP3 out, take notes, and go back to PP1, checking if any notes must be added to PP1 and PP2. Of course, you're looking to see if any notes and new information now need to be placed into PP3.

Repeat this process for each of the plot points until you reach PP27.

The good news is that you won't need to add information to plot points every time, but this method gives you a heads-up before getting too deep into the outline itself. The method also helps to get all the different elements in, like plot beats, character arcs, seeding, foreshadowing, etc. You know, all of the stuff that makes a chapter "complete" by ensuring new information gets filtered backwards into earlier plot points.

2. One Extended Outline Chapter Forward,
One Extended Outline Chapter Back

Welcome to the extended outline. As you know, this is where you're going to take some time and build on the short-form outline plot beats. The hope is that you'll figure out the chapters within each plot point and create a rhythm with how you want things to unfold for the narrative.

With that said, begin with Chapter 1 and go through it, add information as needed, write out what goes in the chapter, and see if what should happen in that did happen. Remember, extended plot beats continue to be broad, general statements. But now, you're expanding the short-form outline and giving depth to each potential chapter.

If you're already catching on, you know that Chapter 2 would get a nice layout of its extended outline beats. Once completed, you'll take notes and return back to Chapter 1, adjusting and adding anything that's needed.

## Revising Your Outline

Again, not all chapters will need new information added. However, it's still good to give each chapter a once-over. Some chapters could feel complete, and others might have more narrative information than needed. If this happens, the solution is usually to break a chapter up into two, three, or four chapters.

Now, just as you did with plot points in short-form outlines, do the same with extended outline chapters. Every time you move to the next extended outline chapter, go back to the first one and work your way through the extended outline chapters till you reach the next one. Rinse and repeat.

The process continues as with the plot points in the short-form outline. Do this until all extended outline chapters in the 27 PPO are completed.

### 3. One Chapter Forward, One Chapter Back

Now moving onto the zero, first, second, third, and one hundredth drafts of the writing process. Um, I know it's a joke, but a hundredth draft means you've gone too far. In reality, I've seen some real monsterpieces (terrible) that needed a lot of work, and I promise you, even those didn't need more than twenty.

> A quick aside: A draft is considered finalized when everything they need is in them to make complete chapters—full character arcs, full CCs, and other subarcs, etc., all completed and tight.

> A quick aside: Each draft has a specific purpose—first drafts are the first rounds of prose. Then move onto the second draft: immersion. If that's not completed, you're not ready for draft three, etc.

Okay, "One Chapter Forward, One Chapter Back" works the same as the above two steps. Start with Chapter 1 and write it out—move to the next chapter and write it out, take notes, and go back to the first chapter, adjust it, and add or subtract what's needed. Now of course, once you do go back to the first chapter, take any new notes and adjust Chapter 2.

Which brings you to the repeating pattern: write out the third chapter, take notes, and head back to the first chapter to adjust it. Take notes from the first

## The 27 Plot Point Outline: When Plot Meets Story

chapter if needed, and move to Chapter 2. Repeat. And finally, getting back to Chapter 3, adjust it if needed. You'll keep doing this until you reach the last and final chapter of the narrative.

Let me end with this: again, you don't have to adjust every single aspect of everything you write as you go back and forth through the method's process. Some plot points and chapters won't need adjusting. However, Chapter 5 might get skipped eight times in a row, and then Chapter 25's events need to be seeded in Chapter 5. It happens. And that's okay. Serve the narrative.

Also, just because you go back to a chapter doesn't mean that you have to find something to adjust because you fear the wrath of the writing gods. The writing gods don't care. Don't search for reasons to adjust. Search for what needs adjusting. Give it all a look-see, keep building, and when and where you find stuff to adjust, do it.

Something you'll notice as you outline is how plot points can turn into one, two, three, or even four chapters as you continue to add information. Those chapters will expand and potentially be split into more chapters as you add prose.

Let the method do its thing as you develop the three levels of outlines and drafts. The real test of what's working or not working comes from the alpha and beta readers.

Their feedback will point out any and all major issues with pacing, plot, character, or general issues in a narrative. Use this information to give you insight into what chapters or scenes should be removed or moved, or what must be added or subtracted to make it all flow better. Serve the narrative first.

With that said, have fun with the method. Know that nothing is final in writing because it's all made up. It's fake. It's fantasy. It's fiction. It's something you thought of while taking a shower, or you were unable to sleep at night, or you experienced something so profound in your life that you had to write about it.

Whatever inspired you to write the narrative, the fact remains: do what you have to to serve the narrative, to give it weight, to give it purpose. To do that, you have to listen to the almighty narrative... It'll tell you what it needs.

At the end of the day, you're the writer writing the written word, so make choices, ask questions, and do the work to mold your idea.

It's creative writing for a reason. Be creative.

# CHAPTER 28

## My Writing Process

## MY WRITING PROCESS

Here we finally are, a look into my writing process. I've been working on this one for years, and at the time I wrote this book, the below list is what I was using. The process guides me to write each of my fiction books and scripts, getting me from a concept to completion.

To be clear, my method is constantly in flux. I'm not afraid to do what I must, adjust as needed, and still use my chapter forward, chapter back, and repeat method for every step of my writing process.

As a reminder, I'm by no means telling you this process is the right one, or the only one. It's merely one of a million other approaches to writing. To write a book takes time beyond just getting words down. You have to find what works, and this process is something I established over the years.

Therefore, I implore you, as always, to take what works, adjust what you want, and if my process helps you as is, great. If it influences you, even better. The hope for all writers is that in the end we get a narrative written for others to read! I mean, after all, it's so satisfying to finish a book and have it read?

P.S. If I change anything up, I'll always stick to these four rules.

*The 27 Plot Point Outline: When Plot Meets Story*

1. Start with broad general ideas.
2. Build on those ideas a little at a time.
3. Challenge those ideas, the characters, and the plot, then adjust.
4. Return to the beginning and go through it all again.

Now that we're here, let's get to the list below and then explain each one.

## THE WRITING PROCESS CHECKLIST

1. Brainstorming and Brain Dumps
2. Character Arcs and Summaries
3. Short Form Outline
4. Extended Outline
5. Zero Draft Chapter Outlines
6. Take Notes On the Zero Draft Chapter Outlines
7. Adjust the Zero Draft Chapter Outlines
8. Alpha Readers (Foundational Feedback)
9. Revise the Zero Draft Chapter Outlines
10. First Draft (Prose, Dialogue, & Immersion)
11. Take A Break (2 to 8 Weeks)
12. Take Notes On the First Draft Chapters
13. Second Draft (Deeper Immersion & Note Adjustments)
14. Beta Readers (Reader Experience)
15. Third Draft (Beta Reader Note Adjustments)
16. The Big Read
17. Fourth Draft (If Needed: Minor Adjustments)
18. Line Editor (Prose & Flow)
19. Copy Editor & Proofreader (Grammar & Typos)
20. Format the Manuscript
21. Finalize Artwork (Covers & Promotional)

*My Writing Process*

## 1. BRAINSTORMING AND BRAIN DUMPS

Freedom!!!

William Wallace screamed it best. Freedom is how I discover what I'll write about in the first place. Sure, the randomness might not make sense at first, but by the end, it's enough to understand what I'll outline and write.

During this stage I have no real rules; I go where the brainstorming takes me. I might write scenes, interactions, or create loose character ideas. During this time, I'm not thinking about what must go in the narrative. I'm thinking about things I want to write about. Usually emotional opportunities. Character A deals with the loss of a parent, a sibling is estranged and trying to reconnect after being gone for ten years at war, etc.

At times I reach into my illustrating roots and draw a few designs, maps, weapons, or maybe character concepts—anything to induce random, or not so random, narrative ideas. When they hit me, I explore them, asking questions, going deeper, and writing something as straightforward as "X must happen to Y."

The point is that I have nothing to stop me, nor do I say no to anything. I like to pull on threads and see where they take me.

Will I use everything I brainstorm, just because I brainstormed it? Nope. In fact, the original brainstormed ideas might start on the page as is but slowly change, adjusting as I outline, and vanishing by the time I reach the end of my third or fourth written drafts. What does stay in the narrative is the essence of it all.

It's like an actor who does all that research on their character only to toss it aside and take their emotional work and let it move them.

Brainstorming, like with actors, is about discovering a deeper truth, that core emotional truth within the characters. And still, none of it holds firm until I do the real work: outline, draft, edit, and rewrite.

## 2. CHARACTER ARCS AND SUMMARIES

Fresh off of brainstorming, I don't outline character arcs just yet. I want to figure out what their journey is and summarize it. Besides, I'm still trying to make sense of my notes. Rather, I'm trying to create opportunities for movement.

## The 27 Plot Point Outline: When Plot Meets Story

Remember, audiences don't care that *things* are happening on the page. Sure, it might keep them interested for a little while, but how many buildings can they watch get destroyed in an Avenger's movie before they're bored? Audiences are engaged by character arcs and pulled along the narrative by their growth.

Which means the protagonist's central character arc is a vital aspect of a narrative's emotional drive. However, I only need to figure out some, not all, but some of their central character arc. My goal: to see how it'll move in and around a narrative. It's not about figuring out every aspect of their arc, but enough to see the dots clearly to make sense of any narrative nodes.

And, as you know, a protagonist's central character arc is my narrative's central conflict—the driving force I wrap a narrative around. Once I know it, it's fairly straightforward from there. I move to the protagonist's subarcs.

Once I know the protagonist's central character arc, I work on the other character arcs (supporting, antagonist, etc.) and subarcs. I do this by working out character arc ideas for them and their journey specifically: are they afraid of XYZ, do they love Jane, are they the youngest sibling, do they have demons, all the way to mundane ideas, like wanting a job?

When I write out character arcs and summaries, I try to stay away from connecting their arcs to a protagonist's central character arc only. Instead, I try to give characters their own lives, goals, motivations, and positions. I want them to be part of the narrative, not just serving the protagonist. Just like in real life, we're not the main characters in everyone else's lives.

And even if a secondary character's arc doesn't work in a narrative, I'll still explore the arcs I create. You never know where they'll lead the narrative. Besides, it's still early; any and all things should be on the table.

Keep in mind, each character might have more than one subarc, a lot more than one, but that doesn't mean all of them end up in a narrative. In fact, as I outline, write, and edit, newer arcs appear, older ones fall away and get removed, and even still, there's a chance that newer and older ones mix together.

Don't be scared of the narrative when you start noticing more arcs pop up. Characters can and should have as many arcs as you can think of at this stage of the game. You can remove, add, adjust, merge, etc., and still, you never know where it'll take you. But the truth is, don't take the option away by ignoring it.

## 3. SHORT-FORM OUTLINE

This whole book explores how to use both the short-form and extended outlines, but, to save you time reading and searching, let me give a quick summary.

First, I organize the narrative beats of the protagonist's central character arc into the 27 PPO. Remember, I use broad general statements, connecting each plot point until all twenty-seven plot points are filled out. Once finished, I do this for each character arc separately.

Second, I filter all character arcs, including subarcs, into the short-form outline of the protagonist's central character arc. I try to figure out where they'll be best utilized and how they add to or serve the narrative. Keep in mind, this can change and should change as you find the voice of the narrative you're writing.

At this stage of the game, I occasionally understand a narrative so well that, for me, I'll outline the protagonist's central character arc, then add the other character arcs and subarcs to their 27 PPO, slipping things in and trying to figure out the natural rhythm between all of the arcs. Basically I've learned to slip other character arcs and subarcs in as I go.

## 4. EXTENDED OUTLINE

I take the short-form outline's plot points and organize and expand them into as many potential chapters as I can. Still using broad, general statements. I break chapters up in a way that serves a narrative's movement. Of course, these are not full-on chapter outlines (that's what zero draft chapter outlines are for). These are ideas and summaries written out.

My end results should be a clear understanding of what the beginnings, middles, and ends of each plot point will be and to make sure chapters are doing their job within the plot points.

If a plot point needs to establish how boring a character's life is, working as a clerk at a convenience store, I'll have to establish this as their ordinary world. The ordinary world could end up being a single chapter or even more.

Even more so, at times a single chapter could be broken up into two, three, or four chapters depending on how much I want to explore the ideas within it.

*The 27 Plot Point Outline: When Plot Meets Story*

In my first novel from The Maven Wars epic fantasy saga, Chapter 1 had a lot happen, making the pace rush along. I knew I had to break it up, and I did. I split it up into multiple chapters, moving them around within the opening plot point and slipping the secondary protagonist's POV chapters in for rhythm.

The point is, use the extended outline to figure out what chapters might look like, and make sure there's a beginning, middle, and end for each plot point, whether that is accomplished in one chapter or more.

## 5. ZERO DRAFT CHAPTER OUTLINES

My zero draft chapter outlines are when I outline chapters, adding greater detail to the extended outline ideas. I'll add dialogue and some prose if I feel like it, but mostly it's still broad general ideas using bullet points.

In this book I've dedicated chapters to short-form and extended outlines and even zero draft chapter outlines with examples. With that said, here's a quick summary of the step and what I try to get out of the zero draft chapter outlines.

I build on each plot beat, working on pacing and foundational elements, adding character behavior and dialogue to discover my characters, and I see when and where I can challenge things within chapters.

Zero draft chapter outlines aren't perfect and shouldn't be, but they are a playground to see what does and doesn't work. I love this draft for helping me find insight into the character's voices, motivations, and positions.

Ultimately, if I'm not trying things, I'm not really utilizing the value of a zero draft chapter outline. Therefore, I challenge myself, the chapters and scenes, and all of the characters on the page; otherwise, what's the point?

Give yourself the freedom and time to fail during drafts. If a character is going to head down a hallway, see where the narrative goes; open a door, throw a monster in the corner of the room—it's all on the table.

You're not writing prose or deep immersion yet. But you're writing with bullet points and using broad, general ideas to show a chapter's movement. Sure, you'll write some prose, a lot of dialogue, etc., but they're quick ideas and can easily be adjusted compared to reading a five thousand-word chapter versus a few hundred or even a simple thousand words in a ZDC outline.

*My Writing Process*

I love the bullet points because they help pace a chapter out, telling me if I'm spending too much or too little time in a plot beat. It gives me a better chance to organize a chapter's plot beats for quick edits, adding or subtracting beats, etc.

## 6. TAKE NOTES ON THE ZERO DRAFT CHAPTER OUTLINES

It's time to read each of my ZDC outlines from their beginnings, take notes, and cross-reference them with my brainstorming notes to make sure the narrative's plot is all in there. It helps to see what is or isn't working. Whatever I find, I mark down what I might want to adjust, add, or subtract in the next step.

This step takes time, but it's important to go back to my brainstorming notes and think about what I left out from my original idea, and if it still matters.

Remember, in this step, a narrative is still at a point where things can be added or subtracted with the least amount of resistance. After all, these drafts are written with broad general statements, notes, and simple prose and dialogue.

In fact, any prose or dialogue should be limited in how it represents any subtext. What I mean is, just write stuff straightforwardly. If a character is angry, you don't have to write long, pretty prose. Write that they are angry.

A zero draft chapter outline guides you when you write the first draft. You won't be able to do this if you're trying to analyze or figure out everything you wrote in the ZDC outline. You should be able to look at the ZDC outline and know what you need to write out in the first draft.

With that said, during this process, it helps if you keep track of your plot beats as well as your character arcs, behavior, and dialogue.

> A quick aside: Use this time to take additional notes on your ZDC outlines, brainstorm, or make sure what you have is what you want.

The goal of this step is to ensure that the ZDC outlines are looking like the idea in your head. Is the narrative making sense on the page? Is the concept you've been dreaming about showing itself on the page, in the chapters, through the plot points? Give yourself the room to think about what is and isn't in these drafted outlines, because the following steps will start getting thicker and solidify.

*The 27 Plot Point Outline: When Plot Meets Story*

## 7. ADJUST THE ZERO DRAFT CHAPTER OUTLINES

I now take all the notes and go back to the zero draft chapter outlines, adjusting, adding, and subtracting what is needed. This process pays off once I know all my narrative elements are in place, plot points are naturally connected, and I can see if characters are living on pages. Additionally, now's a great time to clean up and make sure any potential plot holes are taken care of.

The previous notes from steps 1-6 will help you find any plot holes that are inconsistent character arcs, worldbuilding that's missing, and the general pace of chapters. Basically, are things being earned? Do you see a clear cause and effect? Are characters being challenged enough and making choices? I would add: are the chapters complete?

Keep in mind that this step is prepping your chapters for alpha readers. I would make sure that the zero draft chapter outlines are everything you feel they should be at this point. Not immersion or pretty prose, but that a narrative has a foundational base for the alphas to connect the dots.

## 8. ALPHA READERS (FOUNDATIONAL FEEDBACK)

Alpha readers pay attention to foundational elements of a narrative. After all, I'm giving them a narrative's skeleton without its skin. But that's okay; they're not interested in how beautifully I write.

The bare bones of my chapters give them the best chance to see big-picture issues that need to be addressed. Since alpha readers are there to look for major issues related to a narrative's structure and core elements: character arcs and plot point holes, pacing issues, weak scenes or chapters, worldbuilding that feels lived in or like exposition, and the overall coherence.

As a heads-up, they're going to find issues, and that's okay. Expect issues, potentially lots of them, so listen to your alpha readers, and try to fix what they bring up (especially when it's based on the majority's concern).

But, Thomas, how do I even know what they'll be looking for?

It's time to create some questions and hand off the chapters to the alpha readers with intent. It's not about having all the questions, but the right ones.

1. What expectations did the opening create for you?
2. Did the narrative follow through on those expectations?
3. What questions were you naturally asking as you read?
4. Did anything feel unearned, rushed, or too convenient?
5. Did the resolution wrap up all character threads?
6. Which characters felt real vs. underdeveloped?
7. Did anything feel like it came out of nowhere?
8. Which character did you feel the most connected to, and why?
9. Where did you feel engaged, and where did your attention wander?
10. Where did you feel confused, disoriented, or unsure of moments?
11. Was the climax satisfying?

Sometimes you'll find great readers, who might be fantastic beta readers, but alpha readers—that's a specific kind of person. If your alpha reader gives you back a list of typos and grammar corrections, they're not giving you alpha notes, nor are they being helpful (at least at this stage).

Their advice shouldn't suggest things that have nothing to do with the plot or narrative drive. For example, a zero draft chapter outline isn't here to tell us about a character's background. If an alpha reader gives you notes suggesting that you need to explain what a character's favorite color is, their work schedule, or anything that doesn't influence the narrative—it's not helpful at this point.

You'll run into alpha and beta readers who'll give you notes based on the narrative they want to read, when in reality their feedback should be about the narrative they are reading: yours.

## 9. REVISE THE ZERO DRAFT CHAPTER OUTLINES

Now I go back, just as I did with my own notes, and use the alpha reader's notes to revise the ZDC outlines, adding, subtracting, cleaning it up, etc. The process is the same as it was in step seven.

Keep in mind, I'm still not writing prose or pretty writing yet. I'm only working on the ZDC outlines. It's about prepping my zero draft chapter outlines for the official first draft so I can write out prose and add my author's voice.

## 10. FIRST DRAFT (PROSE, DIALOGUE, & IMMERSION)

With a strong foundational starting point, it all begins—the writing of the prose. The first draft is where my author's voice takes shape, kind of, but I do have some fun and let it shine. I'm coming out to play and see where the passages take me.

I might write the occasional immersive prose, going as all in as I can with the first draft, but really I'm here to expand on each plot beat from my zero draft chapter outlines, writing the narrative's story out. Yep, that's right, the plot of the narrative has nine steps of work. It's time for the characters to come alive.

So here I am, letting the plot unfold through the emotional experiences and choices of the characters (story). Basically, these are my three steps for writing my first draft. Take each plot beat from a zero draft chapter outline, write to that plot beat, write within the plot beat, and write away from that plot beat (repeat).

Since a zero draft chapter outline is written with the use of bullet points, as per the example in a previous chapter, I delete each bullet point as I write out prose leading to it. I already know there's still lots of work to be had beyond this first draft, which includes adjustments for clarity, dialogue, and any immersion in my second draft. I try not to get worked up over every passage, single line, or page.

I don't worry about perfection. I repeat, I don't worry about perfection. I'm focused on getting prose out, keeping the writing straightforward, and sure, I might use a lyrical, cinematic style from time to time, let that subtextual dialogue sneak out, and/or go deeper on passages, but I'm not trying to. It happens when I'm in the groove, and I can't stop my fingers from typing.

## 11. TAKE A BREAK (2 TO 8 WEEKS)

Take a break. It's that simple. I don't know about you, but I must step away from my narrative for at least two to eight weeks. This helps me kind of forget the little details before I dive back in with Step 12. After all, I just spent a lot of time going all in, one step at a time with brainstorming, outlining, and writing.

My point is that I'm too involved and know the narrative inside and out. I now have the horrid bias of knowing all the details so closely, I can't see between the lines. Therefore, I must take a break, relax, come back, and get to work.

*My Writing Process*

But, Thomas, does that mean you can't write during this time?

No. To help me forget what I can from the book, I use this time to focus on other books, diving into a new narrative or narratives. Traditionally, I have a collection of three to five books I'm working on at any given time. Hopefully the other books make me forget as much as I can—which is a good thing.

The idea is to come back with fresh eyes, so... take a break.

## 12. TAKE NOTES ON THE FIRST DRAFT CHAPTERS

As with my own personal notes and the zero draft chapter outline, it's time to do the same for my first draft with more personal notes. After that wonderful break, I'm back, sitting down, and ready to read every chapter and take notes. I don't try to adjust anything. I don't clean things up. I just read and take notes.

These notes are for plot point adjustments, making sure they're working or not. I'll note where I believe more immersion is needed, emotional character beats would add something to the narrative, etc. I know a majority of notes will be to expand on scenes, add openings, and add those emotional character scenes.

I'm acting as a developmental editor. So if I'm going to do right by my narrative, I must ask the hard questions, as if I'm getting paid. I need to look back from a distance and read the first draft as if I don't know what's coming or who these characters are.

When things come up, like background information, a specific character makes a choice, etc., I ask if it's earning or feeling consistent with their established positions and behavior. I also take a lot of organizing notes: what details did I add about the plot, characters and backgrounds, and the world (spreadsheets), etc.

## 13. SECOND DRAFT (DEEPER IMMERSION & NOTE ADJUSTMENTS)

If you've gotten this far, the pattern should be clear: it's time to write the second draft using my first draft notes. I go through the narrative and clean chapters up, add, subtract, and/or move scenes, chapters, or beats around.

I use the notes to show me where and what I need to add and subtract, if any scenes need more immersion or emotional truth.

*The 27 Plot Point Outline: When Plot Meets Story*

During the second drafts, I often find myself adding stronger opening chapter introductions and endings, filling in a bit more character behavior, etc. After all, I did just spend a few outlining stages and a full first draft with all of my characters. It's here that I'm seeing the characters clearer and clearer now.

For me, this is a chance to purposefully search for things on the page to play with, not only from my notes but also from how I'm feeling things are or are not unfolding in the characters' choices.

In fact, in my first epic fantasy novel, I added scenes to chapter openings and gave secondary characters a bit more page time. Not to fluff chapters up, but to add value to the narrative and the characters within it.

At the end of the day, you should be looking for areas to elevate, escalate, and innovate scenes, chapters, characters, worldbuilding, and the plot.

## 14. BETA READERS (READER EXPERIENCE)

Beta readers are as important as alpha readers in my process. Where alpha readers give me feedback on the foundational elements, beta readers give me feedback on their emotional experience reading the narrative. A simple way to approach this: alphas pay attention to a narrative's plot, and betas read a narrative's story.

While you're asking alpha readers about the foundational elements, you must ask beta readers questions that give you guidance on the story.

Remember, these readers should align with your prospective audience. Alphas can be writers, editors, or readers who understand narrative structure. But beta readers should always be people who like the genre you're writing.

Basically, if you're a romance author writing a romance novel, don't get beta readers who've specifically stated A) they don't read romance and B) they can't stand how fake those happily ever afters are.

I assure you it'll lead to reviews starting off, "I don't read romance. One star. Plus, it had too much kissing."

Since beta readers are often just fans of reading, they don't always know or understand writing terms. Instead of asking them about pace, character arcs, or whether the arc of so-and-so hit all the right beats, stick with questions that won't confuse or, worse, mislead them, skewing the result into poor responses.

To get a more audience-based response from beta readers, it's important to ask them questions about their emotional reading experience:

1. What are your general thoughts on character X?
2. What are your general thoughts on what you read this week?
3. Did the chapter(s) drag or move along?
4. Where did you get excited, engaged, or bored?
5. Tell me what you liked or didn't like about XYZ.
6. What character were you waiting to read again?

You can also have fun questions.

1. Which character would you love to watch being interviewed, and why?
2. Which character would you want to survive within the narrative world?
3. Which character would you like to be friends with in real life, and why?

## 15. THIRD DRAFT (BETA READER NOTE ADJUSTMENTS)

More notes means more adjusting. This is when I take the beta reader feedback I got and organize their notes to make changes, adjust, and improve any flow issues for specific scenes and chapters in the book.

This'll probably be my last time writing a new chapter or scene, though I'm okay if I have to take stuff out or put stuff in if needed. It just means I have to do a bit of work. However, I'll only add stuff if I really have to. At this point I'm trying to clean up the reader's experience without going overboard.

Which brings me back to an important rule: majority rules. If I have five readers and three or more of them say something specific isn't working, I'll fix and adjust it. If I have ten readers and five say something is not working, I'll look closer, but it would take six to make me listen and take action from hearing it.

Basically, if half or more of my readers point something out to me, it gets my attention right away and puts me to work. However, every note gets me to sit with it—you never know where a note could lead you; it might end up being the key to it all as it breaks your narrative in an amazing way.

## 16. THE BIG READ

This is my final hurrah. So I gather my closest friends (authors or readers), people I trust, people who understand narrative structure and love to read the genre I'm writing, and ask them to do a big read for me.

> A quick aside: Create a book club or writing group. It helps build a relationship in a community and is a resource for those involved.

The big read is for general feedback and thoughts only. A conversational approach to hear their thoughts. I'm not looking for big-picture insight or their beta reader experience. No questions beyond, "What are your thoughts on it?"

I'll take mental and physical notes, depending on how many people are involved. But really, their answers are a big part of my process to determine if I need a fourth draft or to move onto the last few steps.

Now don't get me wrong, if I get to this point and all the notes are vast and filled with extreme negative thoughts or major suggestions, I definitely didn't do the work beforehand to adjust and clean up the narrative.

I say that because, at this point, I've done a lot of work leading up to this. My third drafts are more like a worked tenth draft if you use this process.

Between the character arcs, character summaries, the short-form outline, extended outlines, zero draft chapter outlines, adjusted ZDC outlines, my alpha reader notes, more adjustments to my ZDC outlines, the first, second, and third drafts, and beta reader notes—it's fifteen steps of foundational work and writing.

So basically this big read and conversation should result in some of the best feedback I could be hoping for. However...

## 17. FOURTH DRAFT (IF NEEDED: MINOR ADJUSTMENTS)

If it turns out that I need to do another draft—well, here it is. I shouldn't have to do more than minor adjustments or clean up at this point (not a full edit at least). I'm trying to only do revision if the feedback merits it, but no major overhauls at this point... Otherwise I'll basically start over (because it means it's trash).

*My Writing Process*

## 18. LINE EDITOR (PROSE & FLOW)

If there are no revisions, I skip Step 17 and go directly to Step 18. Depending on where I'm at, I might do a line edit myself or hire someone. As a developmental editor, script doctor, and known to line edit from time to time... I'd say this...

If you're not an editor or even know what line editing is at its core, then please hire one. It's not worth the cost of poor feedback or brand destruction to save a few bucks. Again, if you do it professionally for others, you have leeway, but if you don't do it at all—really, hire someone. It's worth it.

If you're wondering what a line editor is, let me tell you. Line editors will focus specifically on sentences and the prose in your draft. They are looking to improve overall clarity, flow, style, and the impact of the writing. It's more about the presentation of things and if it all makes sense.

Line editors should come in before copy editors, because they check to see if your sentences are concise, varied, and clear to understand. So there's no reason to have copy editors fix stuff and then hire them again because the line editor came in and adjusted your sentences and prose.

If you're worried about your author voice, style, or tone, don't be. Line editors do keep that stuff in mind when editing.

One of the most important aspects of line editing is keeping track of how well the logical narrative movement is in the sentences and prose, basically watching for smooth transitions and connecting ideas.

A big part of line editing is checking and adjusting awkward phrasing or convoluted sentence constructions. As a simple example:

She tossed her legs up on the desk, sitting down in a chair.

The order is convoluted and not smooth. This second example fixes the order of the physical truth and logical narrative movement.

She sat down, tossing her legs up on the desk.

Here's a quick list of other areas a line editor would check.

## The 27 Plot Point Outline: When Plot Meets Story

1. Word choices
2. Redundancies
3. Author voice consistency
4. Pacing issues
5. If descriptions and actions show emotional truth or not
6. Is information naturally revealed or just outright "telling"
7. Consistent POV and tense.

## 19. COPY EDITOR & PROOFREADER (GRAMMAR & TYPOS)

Time to make sure all the spelling errors are fixed. This is something I'll look into. I have dyslexia. Copy editing is a completely different brain function. You can be great at line work in comics but have no idea how to color the panels. Trust me. That's okay. No one will judge you for being good at one thing but not another. We don't have to be great at everything. Besides, great writers have great editors.

I recommend getting a copy editor. If you can't afford a developmental, line, or copy editor, find people who can, and trade services, read for them, etc.

Not to get into the insanity of what a copy editor does, and it's a lot, but ultimately, they'll check grammar, punctuation, and spelling as a standard part of the edit.

The big job is making sure you have consistency in spelling (American vs British English—yes, that's a thing) and capitalization, verifying names and dates, checking for factual information and accuracy, more sentence clarity, pointing to the ambiguous statements or ideas that can be misinterpreted, and, the most fun part of being a copy editor, ensuring internal consistency with your world's logic, details, plot points, descriptions, and how characters look...

Yes, that's true. You have no idea, but a sure giveaway that an author did not hire a copy editor is the moment you read a sentence that says Jacob has blue eyes in Chapter 3 but brown eyes in Chapter 8.

Even George R.R. Martin has a team, a whole TEAM of people who got hired to handle this. People he has on call to contact and ask if a horse is male or female (a real thing), eye colors, relationships, etc.

My point is this: hire a copy editor.

## 20. FORMAT THE MANUSCRIPT

Time to organize and format the manuscript's layout. I format novels myself. I've been doing this and other design work for years as a graphic artist. That, and I enjoy doing it (at times). It's relaxing, watching a book come together as I make headers, chapter titles, etc. I know, I'm weird. It's the artist in me.

For yourself, I'd highly recommend hiring someone if you don't have the knowledge, skill, programs, or know-how to use InDesign or another program.

## 21. FINALIZE ARTWORK (COVERS & PROMOTIONAL)

Book cover time, though honestly, if I'm super excited about a book, I'll make a cover whenever. Even a simple design just to motivate me. And you know what? It might change at a later time (and does/could), but having that cover for a book I'm passionate about is a great elevator and motivator!

Once I have a cover, I need promotional artwork. That's right, I want all my marketing items in place before I launch my book. You should too. You don't want to say a book is available and then run around trying to get all the ads, posts, and other marketing and advertisement materials together. It's a headache.

Also, hire someone if you can't do the artwork or marketing. Covers are as important as writing the book itself. It says your book is professional, just as a poor design yells to potential readers that you don't care about your covers... So to them, if you don't care about the cover, why would you care about the writing?

They must be... dun dun dun: self-published.

By the way, and this is very important for the community, self-published really shouldn't be a bad word. At least not in this day, as the system has changed over the years. But readers aren't aware of the change in the industry like authors are. A good chunk of readers believe traditionally published books automatically mean they're high quality, and self-published means they need a lot of work.

I don't agree with this mentality, and the industry is changing in a strong way for indie authors. Once authors couldn't get an agent, let alone get published by a major publisher, if the author didn't write to market. But now they have a chance to publish their own books (and should).

# CHAPTER 29

## Final Thoughts

## FINAL THOUGHTS

You've made it this far, so let us part with my final words of wisdom. For parting is such sweet sorrow; however, you'll always have these pages to journey back into whenever you need help outlining or writing in general.

With that said, this book was never really about me having a stance on plotting or pantsing. You don't have to outline if you don't want to. I know, a book about outlining telling you, a writer, that you don't have to outline if you don't want to! It's true, but do I believe outlines help? Yes. 1,000% (that's a lot).

The truth is, writers all have different approaches because every writer is different. Our brains process creativity in different ways, and if some writers want to write a narrative from the seat of their pants, start to finish, go back to the start and read three thousand words a chapter, and take notes, all to reverse engineer everything anyway, creating an after-draft outline, so be it.

Their method doesn't stop another person's process.

Outlining, on the other hand, does a lot of the heavy lifting near the very beginning. So either way, there's still heavy lifting. It depends on when it happens.

Does that change the narrative outcome?

## The 27 Plot Point Outline: When Plot Meets Story

Maybe. Who knows for sure? Maybe the narrative was always meant to be what it was meant to be—outlined or not.

Whatever it is, I'll say this: it comes down to preference. Do you like to dissect before or after the prose is written? Either answer is correct for you.

For me, my brain works faster when I use the writing process shown in the previous chapter. Outlining a little at a time, then building on it with broad general ideas, adding to that, and so on, helps me really find my rhythm.

For you? Do what works. But know that this book in your hand can still guide you on your narrative's journey. Besides, a narrative still needs an ordinary world to set up its status quo, an inciting incident to kick it into gear, challenging characters to create engagement, tension, and conflict, and so on. All of that will still be relevant for both a plotter and a pantser.

As for the 27 Plot Point Outline, if you want to use it but feel it might have genre restrictions like other outlining methods, you should know that this is a flexible outline. It's presented to help guide you, showing narrative emotional beats, action for agency, moments to slow down to let characters and readers get a chance to process what happened, and how to give a rhythm with the Rule of Threes. The 27 PPO is designed to give you guidance, not hold you back.

A romance still has a meet-cute for its inciting incident as much as you have to set up an ordinary world before it happens: who are these characters and what do they do, where do they live, and what's the context before bringing two lovers together, or three, or five lovers? Love triangle? Try a harem triangle.

Mystery? Fantasy? Thrillers? Plot beats are the same. They all end up in the plot points designated to the rhythm of a narrative itself. The big thing you'll need to look out for is genre conventions.

Yep, romances must have happily ever afters; otherwise, it's not romance. A mystery must have—well, a mystery, with clues, twists, and turns at a certain point. Fantasy has worldbuilding (a lot), a soft or hard magic system, potentially a dragon or two, and maybe Bob running around with the Sword of Bloop Bloop!

Genres have specific needs. But all narrative skeletons are essentially the same. For example, you're in the kitchen making pizza. Mmm, pizza—where was I? Oh yes, pizza. The skeleton of making a pizza is easy: you'll need dough, sauce, and cheese. That's the foundation for making a pizza. Just like a narrative, there

## Final Thoughts

are skeleton rules. A leads to B, which leads to C. But how you get from A to B to C is you, the writer, adding your special ingredient to the story of the narrative.

Genres add additional ingredients above the skeleton of it all. Is it a pizza romance? Add onions to peel the layers away and get to know the characters. Are you an epic fantasy? Add anchovies. Are you a horror narrative? Add pineapple. Maybe it's a crime novel? Add extra pineapple.

You can frame genres inside the 27 Plot Point Outline, molding it into what you need it to be as long as you maintain genre conventions. Because genre itself doesn't change the underlying rhythm of setup, conflict, and resolution. It doesn't change the need for context, disruption, and characters making choices to develop. The 27 PPO is a narrative's skeleton waiting for you to hang the flesh of specific genres over it. The kiss, clue, sword fight, or spaceships.

Now in closing, from the deepest parts of my heart, thank you truly for all of the love and support you're giving me by purchasing this book and trusting me with your time as you gave me a chance to show you one of a million ways to approach outlining.

Besides, I know you know that you're a writer. Writing is a place for your soul to be free, writing with unlimited potential, words to be sought and found, ideas of plenty, and a passion to explore the minds of characters all trying to live through these fictional worlds... through you.

Never let another person tell you to stop, change your mind, or convince you that it's not worth it in a saturated industry, that you should have a Plan B in case this whole "writing thing" doesn't work. Raise your Sword of Bloop Bloop and remind yourself to do what you love to do: write, write, write, but also to promise that you'll do the work, work, work.

For great writing is rewriting, and the first draft isn't your last.

So I say to you, my fellow writers, may the ink of your pen never dry and the well of your imagination keep you going... peace in harmony, truth in action.

~ Thomas J. Bellezza

# AUTHOR FRIENDS

## Elevate and Celebrate

**Dawn Aurora Hunt**
www.CucinaAurora.com

**Dr. Sheena Howard**
www.SheenacHoward.com

**Ellen Karis**
www.EllenKaris.com

**Eloise Bahr**
www.EloiseBahr.com

**Emma Bennet**
www.Emma-Bennet.co.uk

**Gene Edwardson**
https://amzn.to/4aaKyf9

### J. Carson Rose
www.TheGreyWoods.com

### J.K. Lambo
Linktr.ee/j.k.lambo

### Jim Avelli
www.JimAvelli.com

### JM Celi
www.JMCeli.com

### Jody J. Sperling
www.JodyJSperling.com

### Leni Flowers
amzn.to/429sCNz

### Lilla Glass
www.LillaGlass.com

### Lori Hayes
www.LoriHayesAuthor.com

### M.M. Ward
www.YouTube.com/@PenumbraMineMMWard

### Mark London Williams
amzn.to/3DSq2SP

### Nicole Pierman | Nicole Brona
www.NicolePierman.com

**Rhayne Coleman**
www.YouTube.com/@ReadingWritingRhayne

**Thomas J. Bellezza**
www.MakeARightLeftHere.com
www.BBRProductions.com
www.Altayon.com

**Thomas R Clark**
www.ThomasRClark.com

> WORK, GROW, AND RISE TOGETHER

www.ingramcontent.com/pod-product-compliance
Lightning Source LLC
Chambersburg PA
CBHW050523100526
44581CB00002B/89